He Just Needs To Be Loved

Patricia Zimmerman

ISBN-10: 150052042x
ISBN-13: 978-1500520427

DEDICATION

To Rosemary, the sister I always wanted, thank-you for your
commitment to help me finish this project.
And to my husband and my sons who bring me joy everyday.

FOREWORD

Eighteen years ago, my son, Tyler, was diagnosed with RAD, Reactive Attachment Disorder, by a psychologist and a few months later, another psychologist diagnosed him with PDD-NOS, an autism spectrum disorder. Over the past eighteen years, mental health professionals have changed the criteria and symptoms that lead to those two diagnoses. I understand that the DSM-V states that the two diagnoses are not compatible. However, this book is based on my experiences in 1994. In the end, Tyler's diagnosis of PDD-NOS was the diagnosis that carried with him throughout his childhood and qualified him for the services that he needed, although as a mom, not a professional, I always felt that the majority of Tyler's difficulties stemmed from his inability to attach to the family rather than from PDD-NOS.

CHAPTER 1
DECEMBER 24, 1992

My two young sons waited in the foyer of our home for the limousine to take us to JFK Airport on Christmas Eve to pick up my husband, Roger, who was bringing our newly adopted son home from Ukraine. Standing by the door, Trevor, our biological six-year old child, wore a red sweatshirt with a vintage picture of St. Nick on it that said, "I believe," although I doubted he still did believe. Worrying that the limo was going to be late, he only occasionally gave a subtle glance towards the sky in search of Santa. A shy child, Trevor had his father's sturdy build, a good sense of humor and my mother's laughing Irish eyes. Unable to conceive another child after Trevor was born, Roger and I adopted a child from overseas. Eighteen months prior, Roger had brought five-month old Jonathan home from war torn El Salvador. Now twenty-three months old, Jonathan stood with his face pressed against the storm door window, clouding the glass with his breath. His dark, Hispanic eyes sparkled with excitement as he searched the sky for Santa's sleigh. Pressed against his tan skin, spikes of black hair poked out from beneath an elf's stocking cap. Mischief lay behind his ever present smile. Jonathan had brought so much joy to our lives, Roger and I naturally wanted to adopt again.

The limo arrived as scheduled which was not a moment too soon. Asking two little boys to wait for anything other than presents on Christmas Eve was out of the question. With the help of friends and relatives, Santa would arrive at our house while we were at the airport. I grabbed a bag with the necessary snacks and games for traveling with children as we hustled out the door and piled into the limo. Inside, we found a television, a refrigerator, a VCR, velvet seats and chrome trim. The boys could not conceal their excitement as they chose a movie. As we drove along, my thoughts drifted back to the flurry of events that had brought us to this evening.

After the heartbreak of other failed adoptions, we heard about Peter Ciascu, an adoption facilitator from Romania who lived on Long Island and had helped several other American families adopt from the former Soviet Union. We made an appointment to meet with him at his home in early November. Often parents wait for more than a year to bring home a child from another country, but things happened quickly with this adoption.

On a cool November evening, we drove up the winding driveway lined by oak trees to Peter Ciascu's house in upscale Roslyn Heights. I saw the silhouette of a man standing in the doorway to the kitchen which had probably once been a servant's entrance. As we pulled the car up to the three car garage, the man stepped from the doorway and approached us.

"You must be the Havliceks," he said extending his hand. "I'm Peter Ciascu. Welcome to my home."

"I'm Roger and this is my wife, Patty," said Roger.

"I'm happy to meet you. Please come in," said Peter leading the way into the enchanting Victorian home. We entered a spacious living room with eight foot windows, high ceilings and a blazing fireplace. Although the twelve bedroom house was old, Peter and his wife had decorated it warmly and maintained it well.

"What a great house you have," I said. "It's so romantic!"

"Thank-you," said Peter as Roger's eyes feasted on the elaborate architectural features, taking in details my untrained eyes would miss.

"Roger has been a policeman for years, but he is an architect by profession," I told Peter.

"He must be very handy to have around the house," said Peter.

"You have no idea," I said. "Roger and I married about seven years ago and both had careers. Older than typical newlyweds, we shopped for a house right away. I envisioned raising my family in a cozy home with a country garden in the backyard and grassy spaces for children to play. Roger had a similar vision of a home for us, but a different plan for getting there."

Roger laughed at the memory of the home we had purchased. "I found Patty's dream house, a four bedroom colonial on a nice sized property in a cul-de-sac in an up and coming neighborhood. It just needed a little work."

"A little work!" I exclaimed. "This house needed everything! The cedar shakes on the front of the house were blackened and had been attacked by woodpeckers leaving large holes. Someone had dropped a can of beige paint on the black roof over the garage and there was no landscaping except for some weeds dotting the yard. Every room needed painting, and the floors and carpeting throughout had to be replaced. The bathrooms and all the appliances were damaged and outdated. Oh yeah, it was my dream house."

"And you are still with this man?" asked Peter grinning.

"Whoa, give me a chance to defend myself," Roger said. "You see, Patty worked at a retail store managing the home goods department. I knew no matter what house we purchased, we would both want to go room by room and use our skills to decorate and remodel. So why not buy the house that offered the most for the money?"

"Don't you mean the worst house in town?" I laughed. "Don't worry, Peter. If you help us to adopt a child, he'll be living in a very nice home. The house no longer looks like it did when we purchased it and now it really is my dream home. Roger has worked miracles."

"I wasn't worried," said Peter, a man about fifty years old with thick, dark, wavy hair and black eyes. Although this meeting was taking place in his home, he wore a suit and looked professional. He led us up an oak staircase to the second floor where we were met by a beautiful little girl.

"Mr. and Mrs. Havlicek, I would like you to meet my daughter, Elisa," Peter said. "My wife and I adopted her from a Romanian orphanage last year when we learned of the plight of so many children suffering in orphanages there. Today, the Romanian government has closed its doors to foreign adoptions because of the embarrassing revelations of the ABC News 20/20 investigative report. I'm sure you've seen the videos of naked children warehoused in deplorable conditions. I'm now working in the former Soviet Union because I know I can help the children there as well. Elisa, say hello to the Havliceks."

"Hello," she said. Knowing Peter himself had adopted a child gave me a feeling of confidence about working with him. He would have insight into the wide range of emotions evoked by the adoption of a child.

"Elisa, go find mommy," said Peter. "It's time for you to go to bed."

"Okay, Daddy. Can I have a kiss first?" She stood on her tiptoes as Peter bent and kissed her goodnight. Then she scampered down the hall, soft curls bouncing on her shoulders.

"She's beautiful," I said.

"Thank-you," said Peter. "Please come into my office." He motioned to a nearby door. Books lined the office walls and a huge wooden desk stood in the center of the room. Roger and I sat on the two leather chairs in front of the desk.

"I have some photos for you. These children are living in a Ukrainian orphanage and are available to be adopted immediately," said Peter as he spread three photos on the desk.

Roger and I moved our chairs closer to the desk. The first photo showed a little boy the same age as Jonathan. Roger and I didn't spend much time on that one because we had already decided we did not want Jonathan or Trevor to have to compete with a child who was the same age as them. In the second picture, a seven-year old boy smiled confidently. He would be older than Trevor and we knew we didn't want Trevor to lose his spot as the oldest child in the family.

We moved on to the third photo which showed a boy smiling through blue gray eyes. He had short, blond hair with cowlicks sticking out everywhere. Standing next to a chair, he appeared to be healthy with a husky build. He wore a printed, blue, flannel shirt, gray tights and his small feet were clad in soft-soled, brown shoes buckled across the top with a strap. He had a shy expression and his chin was tucked into his chest as if he were not sure what to make of the camera. I looked over at Roger as he stared at the photo of the little boy.

"How old is he?" Roger asked picking up the photo for a closer look.

"He is three years and eight months," said Peter. "He is the third of four children and his mother is unable to support him. I understand she receives the equivalent of two and a half cents a month from the government for him."

"How can she raise a child on that?" Roger asked returning the picture to the desk and sliding it towards me.

"Has he been with his mother until now?" I asked wanting to learn as much as I could about this little boy.

"I don't know for sure, but I think he's been in the orphanage for a while," said Peter. "I will try to find out for you."

Roger looked at me and then at Peter. "Is he healthy?"

"I'm told he just needs the love of a family," Peter responded.

I moved to the edge of my seat to study the picture more closely. "He's very cute. How soon could you make this happen?"

"It can happen quickly," said Peter. "It depends on how

soon you can get the paperwork completed."

"Getting the paperwork done will be easy for us because we were recently caught in a Romanian adoption scam," said Roger. "We had all the paperwork done for that adoption and we can transfer everything to fit this one. It's just such a big decision to make."

"I understand," said Peter. "You should know this adoption will require both of you to travel overseas for about two weeks. Why don't you take the picture home and think about it. You can let me know your decision in a few days."

"That's a good idea," said Roger.

We left the house and as soon as we got to the car, Roger turned to me. "So what do you think?"

"I think I'm excited!" I said. "This little boy might fit perfectly between our two sons. Neither of them would have to give up his position in the family. And look at this little face!" I held the picture between us.

"I agree," said Roger.

"Yeah, but there's one thing troubling me," I said. "Did you hear Peter say we would *both* have to travel to Ukraine? Russia requires *both* parents to appear in court. Who will care for Jonathan and Trevor if we are both out of the country?"

We had never left our children for more than an overnight. They were everything to us and it frightened me to think that Roger and I would be out of the country for weeks. I knew we had friends and relatives to help us, but still...

"I know it's hard to think of leaving the kids, but we'll work something out," said Roger.

"What do you think of Peter?" I asked. "Do you think he can be trusted?"

We knew better than most people that nefarious individuals preyed on the emotions of people who wanted to adopt children and illegal activities existed throughout the system. We had been caught in a large Romanian adoption scam perpetrated by a couple in our own town.

"Why don't we sleep on it and in the morning we can check out Peter's references," said Roger.

To reassure us, Peter had given us a list of names of families that had successfully adopted children through him. Over the next few days, we called the names on the list. Those parents assured us that Peter was reliable and honest. They gave us the confidence to tell him to start the paperwork.

When adoptive parents receive a name and picture of a child, or a referral, as it is called, they often have the same feelings as a birth parent has when they see a sonogram of their child growing in the womb. Suddenly, it is not just a vague dream, but rather a reality, in the form of a living, breathing child. As soon as we gave Peter the go ahead, we thought of the little, blond, Ukrainian boy as a member of our family and we named him Tyler. When we talked about him, we used his name. "This will be Tyler's room," "I wonder if Tyler would like this toy." "This jacket might fit Tyler."

A few days later, we sat down with Jonathan and Trevor to tell them the news. Excited about the prospect of getting a new brother, they grinned at each other.

"What does he look like?" asked Trevor. I showed him the picture. "He has blond hair and blue eyes. He doesn't look like any of us."

"That's true," Roger said, "but you and Jonathan don't look like each other."

"I think that's cool," said Trevor. "Where will he sleep?"

"He'll get the extra bedroom," I explained.

The boys leaned into each other to study the picture.

"I think it will be fun to have another brother to play with like I do with Jonathan," said Trevor.

"Me too," Jonathan chimed in although he was too young to really understand what it meant to adopt a child.

CHAPTER 2
NOVEMBER 1992

By late November, Roger and I had completed the paperwork and made plane reservations for the trip to Russia. At 5:30 a.m. on November 28th, the limo arrived at our house to take us to the airport. My sister-in-law, Rosemary, and a dear friend, Karen, agreed to take turns staying at our house to watch over the boys. Roger and I tiptoed into Trevor's room. I gently kissed him and he woke up.

"I'll miss you," he said through sleepy eyes.

"We'll be back before you know it, buddy," said Roger.

"Take care of Jonathan," I said. I put my arms around him and hugged him, not wanting to let go.

"We'll be okay," said Trevor.

"Go back to sleep," I said. "You have school today."

I went to Jonathan's room and kissed him, but he never stirred. I stood in the hallway between their rooms watching them sleep.

"We really have to go," said Roger. "The airport limo is here."

"I know. It's just so hard to leave them," I said taking a deep breath and a final picture of them in my memory.

The limo took us to Roslyn Heights to pick up Peter. We

were dressed casually, wearing sneakers and jeans. Peter got into the limo wearing a suit, a long wool coat and dress shoes. He looked ready for a business meeting, while we appeared ready for vacation, but his attire made me relax. He would give a professional and confident appearance to the foreign officials we would have to deal with to complete the adoption.

The long flight to Moscow gave Roger and me a chance to get to know Peter. He told us about his life as a young man in Romania. He had studied and become a lawyer, but was not happy living in a communist country. He met his wife and they married when he was thirty. In the late seventies, they fled communism to begin a new life in America. Unable to practice law in America, he found many other ways to earn a living. As I had initially suspected, he had a great sense of humor. While he took his work seriously, he did not take himself too seriously. Roger and I filled Peter in on our backgrounds and by the end of the trip, Peter had become our friend.

Stepping off the plane in Moscow and entering customs, we passed a number of austere looking soldiers. They all stood over six feet tall and wore stern expressions. Having grown up in America during the Cold War, I found it disconcerting to be entering a country that had only recently opened its doors to the world. I wondered if Russian children had been taught to hide under their desks in fear of American nuclear attacks.

We cleared customs, gathered our bags and stepped out of the airport. A scruffy looking man jumped in front of us. "Taxi?" he asked, pointing to a long row of dirty little cars, each with a hopeful driver standing nearby.

Peter spoke to the man in Russian and then shook his head. He walked towards the rows of cars, explaining to us, "Taxi rides are negotiable as is everything in Russia. I'll talk to the drivers to get the best price, but there's no guarantee we'll make it to our destination. Taxis in Russia are unreliable. They often break down or run out of gas."

I found it hard to believe that the world power Americans had feared for years was unable to ensure its cab drivers would have enough gas to make local stops. Peter haggled with the cab drivers and soon we were on our way to our hotel. Driving through Moscow, I saw what must have once been a grand country, but communism and time had left many of the buildings in need of major repairs. Everywhere I looked, walls needed paint, brickwork needed resurfacing and metal surfaces needed polishing.

We checked into a four star hotel across the street from Red Square. I entered the room, snapped on the light and saw several insects with long feelers climbing the wall.

"Bugs," Peter said pausing in our doorway. "They are simply a part of life in Russia. This is one of the best hotels in Moscow and has a four star rating. We'd be hard pressed to find a hotel here that did not have bugs."

"It's okay," I said, putting on a brave face, although the thought of sharing the room with bugs left me checking my arms and legs for crawly things. "I can live with a few bugs as long as we come home with Tyler."

"Good," said Peter. "I'm glad you're okay with that because I'm sure bugs won't be the worst inconvenience we'll encounter on this trip. It would be good to get some rest now because tomorrow we'll be running around Moscow trying to get the paperwork started."

Peter left the room and I looked past the bugs for the first time. I saw twin beds without sheets. Faded comforters lay on the beds like a pile of discarded rags. Two nightstands without lamps sat on either side of the beds, the only lighting coming from a small lamp hanging between the two beds. Two worn and discolored red armchairs were pushed against a wall covered with faded, dreary wall paper. I took a deep breath and headed for the bathroom. The once blue and white tiles covering the walls were now discolored, chipped and in many spots missing altogether. The sink and tub had a yellowish hue, but I suspected they had once been white. A single thin, damp towel lay over the tub. Age had cast a film of cloudiness over the mirror above the sink. The toilet matched the sink and tub with an extra ring of darkness inside. There was no toilet paper in the bathroom, but fortunately, Peter had warned us toilet paper was scarce in Russia and we had packed our own.

Although Roger and I craved a good night's rest, nothing about this room invited sleep. We forced ourselves to lie down on the bed with the hope nothing would crawl across us as we slept. Just as we dozed off, a loud noise came from the room above us. Apparently, construction was going on upstairs.

"A four star hotel," I groaned. "I wonder what an average hotel in Moscow looks like."

All night long, a jackhammer pounded overhead and when we met Peter in the lobby the next morning, fatigue overwhelmed us, but we knew our schedule left no room for delay. We headed for the American Embassy to check in and make our intentions to adopt a child known. Many Americans wanted to get a foot in the door to expand their businesses in a country newly opened to the west. The line wound around the embassy and we waited in the cold for over an hour, but at least we completed the first step in the adoption process.

After the long wait at the embassy, Peter wanted to visit the new Mc Donald's in Moscow, which looked exactly like the ones at home with one exception. All the signs were in Russian. We stepped up to the girl at the counter and Peter told her we were Americans. She smiled and called out to her coworkers who joined her at the counter giggling. They had obviously been through this before and knew what was coming. The girl pulled out a large colored board with pictures of the foods McDonald's offers. Roger and I pointed to indicate we wanted hamburgers.

"Hahmborgers," the girl called out. She sounded just like the "wild and crazy guys" from Saturday Night Live. We laughed and the employees laughed along with us delighted to be serving us.

As we walked back to the hotel, Peter suggested we go to Red Square. Three men in uniform guarded the entrance and when we approached, one of them told Peter that Red Square was closed for minor renovations.

Roger reached into his pocket and pulled out his wallet.

"What are you doing?" Peter asked, not wanting to cause any trouble.

"I'm going to show him my police ID," said Roger. "Do you speak English?" he asked the first man.

"Nyet," he answered.

Roger looked at the second man. "English?" he asked.

"Nyet," answered the second man.

Roger turned to the third man as Peter shifted his weight nervously, "Do you speak English?"

"Yes, I do," answered the third man.

"I'm a policeman in New York," Roger said handing him the wallet, feeling sure that the camaraderie of cops extended around the world.

To my surprise, the Russian cop said, "Ah, New York. You come in. See Red Square." He opened the gate and let us in. Amazed to have permission to enter, we took lots of photos of each other standing alone in Red Square because we didn't think anyone would believe us if we didn't have proof.

The next day we picked up our paperwork at the embassy and held our breath as we rode in a taxi to the airport. Finally, we would be flying to Ukraine to meet Tyler! We arrived on time, but the plane was grounded for lack of gas. Peter told us not to worry because we could catch a train from Moscow to Harkov in Ukraine, although it would be a twelve hour trip. We bought tickets for a sleeper cabin with four beds for the long train ride. The trip covered a lot of terrain and gave us a good look at the countryside. We passed peasant communities where we saw local people gathering sticks and twigs to burn for heat. In the frosty air, women used branches with pine needles as brooms and farmers herded sheep. Poverty reigned in this area. The trip to meet Tyler was taking longer than anticipated and Roger and I were becoming anxious. We passed the time reading, sleeping and chatting, but found it hard to concentrate on anything.

When we arrived at the train station in Ukraine, Peter haggled with another taxi driver for the hour long ride to the remote part of the country where the orphanage was located. After thirty minutes, the paved roads ended and were replaced by bumpy dirt lanes, eventually turning into a path that led to the orphanage.

As we pulled up to the orphanage, I turned to Roger, "Today our lives will change forever. We will soon be the parents of *three* boys."

The taxi pulled to a stop and the first thing we noticed was a playground outside the building. Swings and slides sat on a worn, grassy field where little feet had jumped and run. The weatherworn playground was old and needed paint and repairs, but after traveling the countryside, I expected this. We followed a rocky path to a tall brown stone building as my excitement grew. We were going to meet our son! One minute he would be a stranger and the next minute we would make a lifelong commitment to be there for him, accepting him into our family forever. I couldn't wait to see the robust little preschooler we had seen in the picture.

I glanced over at Roger, "This is unreal, isn't it?"

"It really is," he said. "I want to move in slow motion and remember everything about this day. You know what I mean?"

"Yeah, that's exactly how I feel," I said. "I want to be able to tell our son about the first time we met him and about his life before he came to America."

This was different than Jonathan's adoption had been. He

had come home at the age of five months, as a baby, with no memories of his life in El Salvador. We created his history. Tyler, on the other hand, might have attachments to friends and caretakers at the orphanage or favorite toys and preferred foods. Perhaps, his bedroom, his pillow and his blankets carried a scent we would not be able to recreate. I photographed the playground and the orphanage to have a tangible record of the day to share with Tyler when he was older.

Peter approached the entrance and rapped on the heavy, wooden door. A man looking like a nuclear scientist in a white lab coat and paper hat answered the door. Peter spoke to him in Russian and the man motioned for us to enter. He led us to an office with a large desk and three empty chairs, said something to Peter in Russian and left the room.

"The man we have come to see will be here in a minute," said Peter. "Don't be nervous. This is the easy part. We're among friends here."

Just then, an attractive, middle-aged man with blond hair, blue eyes and an average build entered the room. He wore a brown leather jacket with a fur collar, a plaid scarf, khaki slacks and a white shirt, making me wonder where he had found a store with stylish clothing in this area of the world. Peter hugged him and introduced him as Ivan, the director of the orphanage. He greeted us warmly and took a seat behind the desk. Peter and he exchanged a few words in Russian.

"Well, are you ready to meet your new son?" asked Peter.

"His name is Artiom," Ivan told us through his thick accent. "A happy, healthy, outgoing boy. He just needs to be loved. We go to playroom now to meet your son."

We followed Ivan out of the room. Halfway down the hall, he stopped in the doorway of a room and said, "Artiom's bedroom."

I saw a neat little room painted about three quarters of the way up in a soft, pale blue and then up to the ceiling in a pristine white. The room housed ten little beds with clean white headboards and footboards. Each bed had a powder blue bedspread and puffy, matching pillows trimmed with crisp, white lace. Two white chairs sat in the middle of the room and I assumed this was where the caregivers watched over the children at night. Burgundy carpeting covered the floor and a large window with airy, lace curtains made the room look bright and cheerful. On one wall a painting of two little ducks engaged in a conversation made me smile. The room seemed ideal for a group of orphaned children. I breathed a sigh of relief. Surely the children who slept in this pretty, little bedroom received great care. From down the hallway, I heard children laughing.

"Come," said Ivan. "We see Artiom."

As we followed Ivan down the hallway, I turned to Roger, grabbed his hand and said, "Here we go! This is it!"

We entered a large room and saw ten little children playing with an oversized ball. The first thing I noticed was how small these children were. I knew by the absence of diapers, that they were between three and four years old, but they looked more like two year olds.

I searched the room for the little boy from our picture, when Peter said, "Look, there's Tyler. He's the one with the yellow tights and gray shorts." My eyes scanned the room until they landed on the described child. I tried to reconcile the image from our photo with the boy I saw now. This boy appeared much smaller and thinner than the one pictured in our photo. As I looked around the room, I realized the child in the picture had been posed next to one of the tiny toddler sized chairs in this room and had been dressed in several layers of clothing giving him a larger appearance. I moved closer to him. Yes, this was Tyler. He glanced at me momentarily, then dashed across the room to play.

"That's him," I said to Roger, emotion running through me.

"I know. He looks like a mini version of the child from our photo."

I looked at the other children. "Are all of these children available for adoption?" I asked Peter.

"Some are, some are not," he explained. "Some of these children have conditions which make them impossible to place. Others have been placed here by parents who cannot afford to take care of them, but don't want to release them for adoption."

"So you're saying some of these children will grow up in an institution because their parents can't afford to keep them, but want to maintain their parental rights?" I asked.

"Yes," Peter said. "I suppose the parents hope some day life will get better and they will reclaim their kids."

"That's so sad," I said. "I can't imagine being unable to provide food and shelter for my children. Do you think things will improve since the Russian government is moving towards democracy?"

"Maybe," replied Peter. "But real change will take generations to occur."

An odd feeling came over me. I had experienced this same feeling when we adopted Jonathan. When people hear I have adopted a child from an impoverished country overseas, they inevitably say, "What a wonderful thing to do?" They react as if adopting a child is merely a charitable thing. In reality, I was there to prey upon another person's misfortune. In order for me to adopt a child, someone else had to suffer a great loss. I was not heroic. I wanted to take this child home and enjoy watching him grow up. I wanted to enlarge my family. I was there to dip into the country's most valuable asset, its youth. Yes, Roger and I would provide a good life for this child and love him with all of our hearts, but thinking about the loss his birth parents had to go through for us to achieve our happiness made me sad. I glanced over at Peter and Roger. They both stared at me.

"What's wrong?" asked Roger.

"Oh, it's nothing," I said. I pulled myself together to focus on meeting our new son and celebrating the new addition to the family.

I looked around the room again. I spotted Tyler transfixed on a metal top that looked like it had been left over from the forties, before toys were made of plastic. It had silver, red and blue stripes that caused a dizzying pattern when it picked up speed. I wondered what Tyler thought of us or if he understood we had come to take him away from this place. Roger and I watched from a distance not wanting to crowd him.

Several other children gathered around seeking our

attention. Each child wore a flannel shirt or a sweater with tights and shorts or skirts. All had short, easy to manage haircuts. The children looked well cared for, but I wondered why they were all so tiny. A little girl with big, dark eyes tugged on my sweater and raised her arms to me. I picked her up as she chattered in Russian. She didn't care that I didn't answer her. She just wanted the attention of an adult. I carried her across the room to a worn red couch where I sank down with her on my lap. Tyler continued to pump the top rhythmically, looking up occasionally, but never coming close enough for me to touch him. Roger joined me on the frayed couch and two children climbed into his lap. He smiled at me and I said, "Yeah, I know. It's too bad we can't take them all home."

Suddenly a scream pierced the air followed by inconsolable wailing. Tyler had sliced his finger on the sharp edge of the top and a trickle of blood emerged from the wound. Two women in nursing uniforms too sizes too small for them ran to him. Fashion was definitely an abstract concept for these women who had short bobbed hair and masculine faces. One of them scooped Tyler up in her huge arms and hustled out of the room. I wanted to go along, but I was still a guest in this environment and decided to wait for an invitation before moving around the building.

In a matter of minutes, Tyler returned, sporting a band aid. He came to me and proudly held up the bandaged finger. He looked me in the eye and smiled acknowledging me for the first time, but the interaction was short lived and he walked back to where he had dropped the toy. He resumed his steady pumping of the top until one of the large women said something in Russian.

The children ran to sit on a long, wooden bench about six inches off the floor. I looked around the room apparently a recreation area for the children. Gymnastic rings hung from the ceiling, although I doubted any of these children had the strength to use them. Colorful wooden ladders, hula hoops, balls and stuffed animals lay scattered around the room. I watched the women guide the children across another bench as if it were a balance beam. None of them looked very steady and I wondered how much time they actually spent in this room or engaged in any physical activities at all.

As Tyler walked along the board, he looked at Roger and me to see if we were watching him. Of course, we were. We couldn't take our eyes off him. He finished, jumped down and headed for a box of stuffed animals. He plopped down on the floor, sitting on his heels. Roger and I joined him. I picked up a stuffed bear and made it walk to Tyler. Delighted and giggling he rocked back on his heels. Roger took a turn making the bear walk and Tyler reeled with laughter. The three of us were lost in play when one of the caretakers gave another order in Russian. Tyler dropped the bear and ran to line up with the children at the door.

"It's lunchtime," explained Peter coming up behind us.

"Too bad," said Roger. "He was starting to warm up to us."

"I know," said Peter. "But he's your son and you have a lifetime to get to know him."

We followed the line of children down the hall to the lunchroom, knowing Peter was right, but wanting to make it all happen now. Two scarred, wooden tables sat in the middle of the lunchroom. The children knew where to sit and found their chairs. The caretakers from the recreation room moved from child to child tying one end of an oversized napkin around each little chin. They spread the other end of the napkin out on the table as a placemat and a bowl of soup was placed on top of it. If the children moved at all, they ran the risk of spilling the soup and losing their meals. None of the children dared move or even talk, but rather stayed focused on eating.

As Roger and I watched from the doorway, Peter said, "We have to go. We have a lot of running around to do if we're going to get the paperwork done before Christmas."

"Okay," said Roger, "but I hate to leave him now that we've met him."

"I understand," said Peter. "But we'll be back tomorrow." We took one last look at Tyler and went outside to a waiting cab. We left the dirt roads of the rural community and came upon the paved roads of the city heading back towards our next hotel in Harkov. I grew up in New York and know winter can be depressing, but winter in Ukraine seemed bleaker, ashier and grayer. I felt like I was moving in a black and white movie.

We neared the city and I saw the buildings on the horizon. Unlike American cities with tall skyscrapers, Harkov was a little city with two and three story buildings. Suddenly the taxi sputtered to a stop. The driver slammed his hands on the steering wheel, said something angrily in Russian, and jumped out of the car. Peter calmly followed him.

After a few minutes, Peter came back. "The cab has broken down. We'll have to walk the remaining few blocks to the hotel."

By the time we reached the hotel, my fingers and toes were numb and my lungs burned. We checked into a drearier room than the one we had encountered in Moscow. On a scuffed wooden floor sat twin beds without sheets or blankets. The curtains were too short and narrow, letting in light from all sides. The only other furniture was a framed mirror sitting on a wobbly credenza. The bathroom turned my stomach. The toilet seat was cracked and grimy as were the tiles on the floor. Leaky exposed pipes ran around the room and toilet paper and towels were nowhere to be seen. The tub was filthy and had no shower curtain.

I turned to Roger, "I wonder how long before the bugs appear."

"Don't get squeamish now," he said. "Just keep telling yourself we'll be out of here in a week. Peter's expecting us to meet him downstairs for dinner."

The dining room consisted of six-foot long tables covered with tacky paper tablecloths. A cook prepared food behind a luncheonette style counter. We ate grilled cheese sandwiches and I tried to buy a coke, but none was available. I had a caffeine addiction that I satisfied with coca-cola and I was anxious to find a coke somewhere.

After lunch, we walked towards the mayor's office to get his signature on the adoption papers because Tyler was a resident of his city. We passed a little food store selling coke in old fashioned bottles.

"Look Roger," I said. "Let's get a couple of bottles for

now and on the way back we can pick up a six-pack to bring back to the hotel."

We entered the market, grabbed two bottles, and approached the man at the counter who said something in Russian. I turned to Peter for an interpretation.

"We have a small problem. He won't sell us any soda unless we return an equal number of bottles," Peter explained. "Evidently there's a shortage of Coke bottles here."

"Oh, don't tell me that," I said.

"I'm sorry," said Peter. "There seems to be a law about this. I tried to offer him money, but he's not interested. We'll figure something out when we get back to the hotel."

As we left the market and walked down the street, we heard someone shouting. A man ran towards us and handed me two empty coke bottles. Peter reached into his pocket for his wallet, but the man waved his hand and walked away. The sleeves on the man's coat were worn thin and he had patches on the knees of his pants He did not look as if he could afford to give anything away, but he had heard us talking in the market and decided to help us. We returned to the market and bought two bottles of coke. We hung on to the precious little empties so we could buy coke throughout the rest of our trip.

A small building with an overcrowded waiting room housed the mayor's office. As we entered, the smell of cigarettes and stale air hit us. People stood wherever they could find room. We found an empty space along the wall and began our wait, which turned out to be more than three hours. On a chair next to me, a woman sat with her little girl who showed all the symptoms of a child tired of waiting beyond a reasonable length of time. She whined, fidgeted, and moved off and on her mother's lap. I didn't need to speak Russian to understand that she wanted to know, "How much longer?" In my bag, I had a handful of McDonald's Happy Meal Toys to amuse Tyler on the flight home. I pulled out a little green frog. Pushing the frog's back down set a button located underneath. After a few seconds, he popped up into the air. The little girl watched as I set the frog down on a table next to her. When it popped up into the air, she jumped. Delight crossed her face and she giggled. I showed her how to work the frog and gave it to her. Every time it popped up, she looked as surprised as she had the first time. Her mother smiled gratefully at me.

I turned to Peter. "Do people here know we are Americans?" I asked.

"Well, yes," he said. "You don't look different than most of the people here, but you smile more. You also wear brighter clothing. Look around you. Most of the people here are dressed in variations of gray, black or brown."

I wore a teal green coat with khaki pants and a red scarf. I had not seen any bright colors since we stepped off the plane. Maybe that contributed to the dismal feeling permeating the Russian air. When we finally got into the mayor's office, we came across the first of many "problems." Nothing happened in the corrupt Russian government without palms being greased. Peter had warned us about this fact and we had extra cash and other gifts to ensure our paperwork "problems" could be fixed.

After clearing the mayor's office, we returned to the hotel to have dinner with Ivan, the director of the orphanage, and Olga, the young translator for our home study, Immigration and Naturalization papers, birth certificates, and all other paperwork, necessary to complete the adoption, a task that would take days to complete.

The next week crawled by. The gloomy hotel offered no entertainment. We visited Tyler every day at the orphanage, but I missed Trevor and Jonathan terribly. Almost two weeks had passed since we left home. The government in Ukraine required both parents travel to appear in their court and we had met that requirement. The last of the paperwork could be finished without my presence. I decided to return to America and leave Roger with Peter to finish the paperwork.

On December 10th, we went to the train station in Harkov to buy my ticket to Moscow. The station bustled with people. Another of those buildings that was probably grand in its day, the train station needed major renovations and a good cleaning. I leaned against a wall coming away with a layer of soot on my coat. Tickets for the train were sold out, but groups of scalpers moved through the crowds selling tickets at outrageously high prices. Peter negotiated with several people to secure four beds, so I would not have to share my cabin with anyone, an unheard of luxury in Russia. As Roger and I watched Peter maneuver through the crowds, two men got into a fight. One of them pulled a knife and stabbed the other, who fell to the ground. A scurry ensued and two policemen dragged them out of the station. I gathered the strength to ignore what I had just seen because I just needed to go home. Peter returned with four tickets in his hand. We approached the train and he paid the conductor to watch out for me and make sure I was left alone at all times.

"Patty, this is Alexei," said Peter. "He has promised to take care of you. If you need anything at all, he will help you. When you get to Moscow, a man named Yuri will meet you. I've worked with him in the past and he'll take you to the airport. He'll be holding a sign with your name on it. He's been very reliable and you shouldn't have any problems."

I leaned over and kissed Peter on the check. "Thank-you so much for everything. I can't wait until we're all back in the states. We'll have to get together with your family after everything settles down."

"I'd like that," he said. "Good luck on your trip."

Peter walked away and left Roger and me standing in front of the train. "Give the boys hugs and kisses for me and hopefully I'll be right behind you bringing Tyler home," Roger said.

"It can't be soon enough," I said. Torn between wanting to stay and help finish the adoption and knowing my boys needed me back at home, I reached up, put my arms around Roger's neck and kissed him. "I love you," I said.

"Me too. Please be careful and stay alert while traveling."

"Don't worry. I'll be all right. Just take care of yourself and get home as soon as you can." I stepped onto the train and the conductor led me to my cabin.

I closed the heavy cabin door and locked it behind me. I lay down on one of the beds and marveled at the speed with which the events of the past few weeks had happened. A month ago, I didn't know Peter and now here I was traveling alone across the former Soviet Union. Shortly after the train rumbled out of the station, exhaustion overtook me and I fell fast asleep. Before I knew it, the train arrived in Moscow. As I stepped down from the train, I saw a large man with a rugged beard and unkempt hair holding up a sign with my name on it.

"I'm Mrs. Havlicek," I told him.

"Yuri," he said with a toothless smile, motioning towards his cab. I followed him and got in. It should have been more than a little scary to get in a car with a stranger in a foreign country, but by this time I trusted the decisions Peter made. We drove in silence unable to communicate in each other's language. At the airport, I checked in, boarded the plane and finally felt safe. I couldn't wait to be home with Trevor and Jonathan.

CHAPTER 3
DECEMBER 1992

With Christmas just two weeks away, I arrived home and threw myself into shopping and decorating. I waited everyday to hear from Roger, hoping for news of his homecoming, but the Russian government moved slowly and everyday he faced new "problems." Then, in a brief, static filled call on December 23rd, Roger announced that he and Tyler would arrive in New York at 11:00 p.m. on Christmas Eve.

"Trevor! Jonathan!" I shouted. "Daddy and Tyler are coming home for Christmas!"

"An extra special Christmas present," said Trevor. "I don't know anyone else who is getting a brother for Christmas." I laughed and hugged both boys.

So this was how Trevor, Jonathan and I came to be in a limo traveling to the airport on Christmas Eve. The plane arrived on time and we waited for the passengers to disembark. I thought about how much we had all missed Roger. Peter emerged from the door first looking fatigued, but grinning. Then my heart jumped as I saw Roger following behind holding Tyler firmly in his strong arms.

The boys yelled, "Daddy! Daddy!"

Roger spotted us in the crowd and waved as Tyler wriggled against his grasp trying to get down and explore the new environment. I squeezed through the crowd dragging the boys behind me. When I reached the guardrail where Roger stood, he leaned over and kissed me.

"Merry Christmas," he said. "It feels so good to be home. I missed you all so much."

"We missed you too," I said tears of joy slipping from my eyes.

Roger passed Tyler to me and said, "Trevor, Jonathan, this is your new brother, Tyler." They checked him out as we moved to pick up the luggage.

"How was the flight?" I asked staring at Roger who looked like someone who had crossed a desert and finally found water.

"We almost didn't make it," he said wearily. "We were held up by our visas. At the last minute, the Russian officials said, 'visas no good'. Fortunately, Peter got us through it with some negotiations and a large payoff."

I put Tyler down as I reached for a piece of luggage. "I'm so glad you made it home for Christmas. I can't imagine what it would have been like without you."

"Mom, Tyler is climbing on the luggage!" cried Trevor.

I turned to see Tyler sitting on a piece of luggage and moving away from us on the conveyor belt. I ran after him, snatched him off the belt and held on to him.

"He's fast," said Roger. "If you look away for a minute, he's gone."

We collected the kids and luggage, said good-bye to Peter and moved to the waiting limo. Seeing Tyler experience the world as fresh and new was fun. He never stopped smiling and laughing. We climbed into the limo and I asked Roger, "When was the last time you two ate?"

"They served food on the plane, but Tyler didn't eat much. We slept through most of the flight."

"I brought some juice and snacks." I pulled out a large box of animal crackers and some juice boxes. Jonathan and Trevor grabbed their drinks and put straws in them. I put a straw in a juice box for Tyler. "Here you go Tyler," I said passing him the container. I gave the box of cookies to Trevor and Jonathan and they each took a couple.

Suddenly Jonathan yelled, "Look, Mom!"

I turned around to see Tyler spraying juice all over the limo from his straw. He had removed it from the juice box and was using it to propel the liquid into the air.

"Oh, Tyler," I said softly, not wanting to upset him. "We don't do that with the juice." But, of course, he had no idea what I said. I tried something else. "Nyet."

He laughed at me and continued to spray away as Jonathan and Trevor tried to hide their giggles. I took the juice box from Tyler and handed him a couple of cookies. Putting one in his mouth, he made eye contact with me and then spit it out. He threw the rest of the cookies into the air chasing after the one that had just flown from his mouth. In a flash, he jumped up from his seat, went to where the cookies had fallen and stomped them into the carpet with his shoes. With each crunch, Trevor and Jonathan giggled louder. I turned to see Jonathan cock his cookie loaded hand into to the air, ready to catapult it into space.

"Don't you dare," I laughed.

"Mom, is Tyler on Santa's naughty list?" asked Trevor.

"I don't think so," I said. "He just doesn't know how to behave in a car. He's never traveled like this before." I turned to Roger and whispered, "Was he like this during the plane trip?"

"No, I was lucky," he said. "He slept most of the way and only woke up twice to have a snack. I held his drink for him and only allowed him small sips."

Of course, I thought. After seeing the children eating in the orphanage, I should have known he wouldn't be able to handle food without restrictions. I handed him one cookie at a time, but he still seemed to think they were for throwing. Without warning, he reached over and grabbed the box of cookies, dumping the contents on the plush rug of the limo.

"Are you *sure* he's not on Santa's naughty list?" Trevor asked.

Roger and I both laughed. Tyler was having a grand old time and we had plenty of time to teach him the proper etiquette for traveling in a limousine. The important thing was we were all together. As we sped along the Long Island Expressway, Roger filled me in on what I had missed in the last two weeks in Russia. Before we knew it, we arrived home. It was 2:00 a.m. on Christmas morning.

Santa had come to our house while we were at the airport. Tyler, a child who never owned toys, came home to Christmas in America. Anyone with experience in adoption knows that the Christmas season is the worst time of the year to bring home an adopted child. Decorations fill the house. Visitors come and go. Routines are broken. We didn't choose this time of year, but we needed to make the best of it.

Trevor found a present with his name on it and tore it open eagerly. I gave Jonathan a gift and he ripped it open with all the dexterity of a chubby two- year old. Tyler sat down on the floor and watched until I handed him a gift. I gave him a start by putting my hands over his and helping him tug at the paper. His first gift was a little black and white cow that walked forward, stopped, mooed and then repeated the process. He loved it. He lay on the floor with his face next to it and slid his body along as it made its way across the floor. I gave him another gift, but he just put it down and continued to follow the cow. Meanwhile Trevor lost himself defending Super Mario against his evil foes and Jonathan delighted in a brio train set. My exhausted family didn't get to bed until 4:30a.m.

I showed Tyler to his new room. We have a colonial house with four bedrooms which meant each of our sons had his own room. Tyler's room had bunk beds, two dressers and a large bookcase filled with age appropriate books. A burlap textured paneling in a gray blue color covered the lower half of the walls. The top half was freshly painted in a light blue. A royal blue carpet covered the floor and a border of trains ran around the middle of the walls.

I put Tyler into one of Jonathan's sleepers, still amazed that although he was chronologically twenty-one months older than Jonathan, he actually stood at the same height and weighed less. I tucked him into bed and he fell asleep quickly. Roger and

I stood in the doorway and watched as he slept. "Our family is complete," I whispered. "Tomorrow we start the rest of our lives."

CHAPTER 4
CHRISTMAS DAY 1992

The next morning as I enjoyed the warmth of Roger's body against mine, I heard the sound of little feet jumping down the stairs. I followed the sound and found Tyler stretched out under the Christmas tree sitting in front of the bay window of the living room with his face close to the little toy cow, watching it inch along. Our tree was artificial, but our decorations told the unique and personal story of our family by marking every special event. An ornament hung to commemorate each Christmas Roger and I had spent together. Two bulbs designated "Baby's First Christmas" for Trevor and Jonathan. Trevor had hung Teenage Mutant Ninja Turtles and Mario Brothers ornaments while Jonathan had hung a Barney the Purple Dinosaur ornament. A souvenir bulb marked every family vacation we had taken and I had hung a pair of wooden shoes I purchased during my stopover in Holland on the way home from Russia. Tyler lay under the family tree without a clue to the significance of its ornaments. A shiver of delight traveled through his body every time the cow made its moo sound and swooshed its hooves over the carpeting.

"Good morning, Tyler," I whispered softly not wanting to wake anyone else up.

He smiled at me briefly and returned to the movements of the mechanical cow. He had reduced his world to the space occupied by the small bovine. Nothing else in the house, including his other Christmas presents, held any interest for him. I sat on the sofa content to watch him, taking in his face, his body and his gestures.

When I heard movement upstairs, I started breakfast. I assumed everyone would be hungry since we hadn't eaten anything the night before except the flying cookies in the limo. The kitchen was the first room Roger had remodeled when we bought the house. He put in new countertops, oak cabinets and ceramic tile flooring. The eating area has room for a table with six chairs and faces a large bay window overlooking a shady, wooded yard. Over the kitchen table, hangs a tiffany style lamp that Roger made before we married. I cooked a big breakfast of bacon, eggs, French toast and pancakes. The delicious aromas called everyone to the table except Tyler. Roger carried him in from the living room and we sat down to our first meal as a family.

"I'm hungry," said Jonathan.

"I'm starving," said Trevor reaching for the French toast.

"What would you like, Jonathan," I asked.

"Pancakes," he replied.

I fixed Tyler a plate with a small sample of everything and put it in front of him. "Here you go, Tyler."

He studied the plate for a few seconds, then slid off the chair like a slippery eel and ran to play with the cow. I brought him back to the table, but allowed him to bring the cow with him. He still didn't eat.

"I'm surprised he isn't hungry," I said to Roger. "He really didn't eat any of those cookies last night."

"He's probably just overwhelmed," Roger said. "Besides, from what I saw at the orphanage, he only ate soup and some dry bread. He'll have to develop a taste for our foods. Give him some time and he'll find something he likes to eat."

"I suppose you're right," I said. "It's just that he's so small." Jonathan and Trevor devoured their breakfasts while Tyler remained enchanted by the little cow.

Don't worry about it," said Roger. "When he gets hungry, he'll eat. Boy, I really missed good old fatty American food."

"Don't you mean my superb cooking?" I teased.

"Oh yeah, of course," he said sarcastically.

Normally on Christmas day, the family traveled to Roger's mother's house for dinner, but everything was different this year. We needed time alone as a family to get to know Tyler and for him to get to know us. Besides, last night's trip to the airport had left us all too exhausted to go anywhere. Shortly after breakfast, Roger went back to bed. He needed time to recover from jet lag and the month overseas. I spent the better part of the day on the floor in the den playing with the boys and their new toys always encouraging Tyler to join in, but only the cow held interest for him.

The friends and family who played Santa and his elves the night before had left us lots of food and I heated some of it for dinner. Again, Tyler sat at the table refusing to eat. I put some chicken on a fork and offered it to him, but he looked away. I would have to be patient. Common sense said he would eat when he got hungry.

After dinner, I led him to the upstairs bathroom for his first bath at home. I helped him get out of his clothes, lifted him up and put him into the tub as the water rushed from the tap. As soon as his little toes touched the water, he screamed wildly and fought to climb out, sloshing water over the sides of the tub. Steadying him so he would not slip, I spoke to him gently, trying to soothe him, but he continued to wail like an animal caught in a trap. Roger woke up and the boys rushed upstairs to see what torture was being visited upon poor Tyler. I lifted him out of the tub.

"What's going on?" Roger asked.

"While you were in the Ukraine, did you hear how they bathed the children at the orphanage?" I asked as Tyler howled.

"No," said Roger. "I just assumed it was part of the routine."

"You would think so," I said trying to keep Tyler from slipping, "but he's obviously terrified of the water."

"Why would he be afraid to take a bath?" asked Trevor.

"I can't imagine," I said. "Maybe he had a bad experience like falling in the water or maybe his bathtub at the orphanage didn't look anything like this one and he doesn't understand what's happening."

"I have an idea. Why don't Jonathan and I get into the tub with him and show him that it's safe," Trevor suggested.

"That's a great idea," said Roger.

In a matter of seconds, Trevor and Jonathan had ripped off their clothes, hopped in the tub and splashed each other with a collection of tub toys that hung in a sack on the faucet. I gently lifted Tyler and put him back into the tub, but he refused to sit. He quieted down as he watched his brothers, but when I reached over to clean him with a washrag, he screamed again, protesting with animal-like screeches. For the first time, I noticed he really didn't speak in sentences. He used some words, but certainly not enough language to explain why the water frightened him, relying instead on guttural and pained noises. I took him out of the tub, put on his pajamas and resolved to sponge bathe him until he came to know and trust us.

Roger put his arm around me and said, "It's only his first day. He'll learn."

Shortly after the stressful bath, Tyler fell asleep on the floor in his room and Roger moved him to the bed. Trevor and Jonathan went to bed a little later. As Roger and I settled in for the night, we heard a series of loud thuds coming from Tyler's room. We rushed to his room and found him on all fours on the bed in the darkness. As we entered the room, he thrust his body backwards away from the headboard slamming his behind on his heels. In an instant, he sprang back up, rested on all fours for a second before throwing his behind back on his heels again. The strong movement pushed the bed and the thud we heard was the sound of the headboard hitting the wall. I gently called his name, but he did not respond. I moved closer to the bed and touched his back softly, repeating his name. He jumped towards the wall and away from my touch with a look of terror on his face.

"It's okay, Tyler," I said. He relaxed his body, but looked at me as if he had never seen me before. "I think he was dreaming," I said to Roger. I settled him back into his bed and started to rub his back as I had done so many times when Trevor and Jonathan awoke from nightmares. Tyler resisted my touch, arching his back and sliding across the bed away from me.

"Why don't you go back to bed," I said to Roger. "I'll stay here with him until he falls asleep again."

"Are you sure?" Roger asked.

"I've had more sleep than you in the last two weeks," I said. "Go Ahead."

I went to Jonathan's room and got the rocking chair. When I returned, Tyler lay on his back thrashing his head from side to side on his pillow. He didn't notice I had come back. His head flopped back and forth like a windshield wiper on high speed. I whispered his name again, but he didn't respond. I moved closer and said it a little louder, but he still didn't react. He had slipped away to a dream in a distant land. I touched his arm and he jumped looking at me through startled blue eyes. He paused for a second. Then his head began to thrash back and forth again. After a few minutes the pace of his head movements slowed like a motor running out of gas. Somehow this disconcerting movement had put him to sleep. I sat on the rocker for a long time wondering about what I had just seen. I wondered about a little boy who put himself to sleep with strange movements and rejected the touch of another person. I wondered how long it would take to familiarize him with my voice and touch and how long it would take for him to reach out and accept us. I wondered how long it would take, but I never doubted that eventually he would be just fine.

CHAPTER 5
DECEMBER 26, 1992

On the day after Christmas, I woke to the sound of Tyler opening our bedroom door. He stood in the doorway looking bewildered. I had no idea what he had been told by the orphanage staff, so it was impossible to know what was going on in his head. Did he understand that we were his forever family and that this was his home?

"Good morning, Tyler," I said. He smiled, turned around and headed towards the stairs. I followed closely behind him, wishing I were still in bed.

"C'mon Tyler, let's go eat," I said. I picked him up and carried him to the kitchen. His back stiffened, but he did not try to leave my arms. I poured some cheerios in milk and took out a spoon, but before I could sit him at the table, he slipped out of my arms heading for the living room in search of his little cow. I picked up the toy and brought it back to the table as he followed. I spoon fed him as he played at the table. I felt relieved to finally see him eat something.

Later that morning, I scheduled a visit to the pediatrician's office because I was anxious to have Tyler checked out physically. When we adopted Jonathan, he came home with scabies which are gross, little, itch mites that live and breed under the skin. They are highly contagious, but easily treated. Before Jonathan was diagnosed, he had been passed around to family and friends who all had to be treated for the parasites. I wanted to make sure we didn't have a surprise like that with Tyler. The doctor's nurse, Sheila, a pudgy, little woman in her fifties who always seemed to be in the middle of a hot flash, escorted us to the treatment room to wait for the doctor.

"Gee, Patty, now you have a son with black hair, blond hair and brown hair. Are you planning to look for a redhead?" she teased.

"I think we're done," I said laughing. "Three sons under the age of seven will keep me very busy. Besides, we just got Tyler home. Another adoption is the last thing on our minds."

Sheila left us in the treatment room to wait for the doctor. On one side of the room sat the examining table. A counter and cabinets held supplies on the other side of the room. I put Tyler on the examining table, but he slithered off like a shapeless ghost taking the sanitary paper with him. I put the paper in the trash can and spread out a clean piece as he dumped a jar of cotton swabs on the floor bursting into laughter. As I collected the swabs from the floor, I heard a series of squeaks and thuds. Tyler was jumping on the scale right in front of the "PLEASE DO NOT LET CHILDREN PLAY ON THE SCALE" sign. I picked him up and returned him to the examining table as the doctor came into the room

"Congratulations, Patty," said Dr. Hollweg, our family pediatrician. "I guess this is Tyler. How's he doing?"

"Well, he's been with us for only two days, but he's a very busy boy. You're going to have to put some new cotton swabs in your jar because Tyler just dumped them on the floor," I said. "He's curious about everything, but I'm sure that's just because everything is so new to him."

"Sure, he's probably so over stimulated he can't rest," said

Dr. Holweg. He weighed and measured Tyler. "He falls below the charts in both height and weight. He only weighs 30 lbs. He's very small for his age."

"I know," I said. "Tyler is almost two years older than Jonathan, but he fits into Jon's clothing."

"He has poor muscle tone," said the doctor. "His body is shaped more like that of a toddler with a round tummy, flabby arms and a chubby chin. That should improve with regular activity and exercise. Otherwise he seems okay. Do you know where he got the scar on his head?"

Tyler had a large, jagged, Frankenstein scar running across the center of his forehead from one side to the other. Like something from a horror movie, the entry and exit point of each stitch was clearly visible. "I don't know," I said as the doctor examined the scar closely. "We asked about it at the orphanage, but they didn't know how it happened. We weren't given much information about him."

"I'm sure a plastic surgeon can make that look much better," he said. "When you are ready, I'll give you the name of a good pediatric plastic surgeon. Today we'll give him the first of his shots."

The orphanage had provided very little information about Tyler's record of inoculations, so he had to receive all his shots as if he were a newborn infant. Dr. Hollweg rolled Tyler's sleeve up and quickly inserted the needle so the first shot would happen before he could protest. Tyler giggled as if he had been tickled. The second shot went in just as easily and received the same reaction.

"I've never seen a child enjoy getting a shot before," I said.

"It would make my job easier if all children reacted that way," said Dr. Hollweg.

We left the doctor's office and drove to a children's shoe store in town. Tyler had left Russia wearing a cheap pair of maroon, plastic boots that were too big for him, causing him to trip over his own feet. He stood in the middle of the store with his mouth open scanning the wide selection of shoes covering the walls and display stands. The shoe salesman was very interested when I told him Tyler had just arrived from Ukraine.

"Does he speak any English?" he asked.

"No," I answered. "Not yet."

"Come here, Tyler," he said helping him into a chair so his feet could be measured.

Everything was going well until the salesman tried to remove the boots. Tyler struggled to keep them on making feral noises.

"Calm down. Nobody is going to hurt you," said the salesman, but Tyler's noises just got louder.

I stepped in and pulled one boot off and quickly put it into Tyler's hand so he would know he could keep them. Then I pulled the other one off and gave it to him. He hugged the little boots close to his chest as if he were ready to fight anyone who touched them. The salesman measured his feet, and suggested a pair of sneakers with lots of support because he said Tyler had flat feet. As he laced the sneakers up, it became obvious that this was the first time Tyler had worn any shoes with support because he wobbled around like a newborn foal. He was accustomed to wearing the soft soled shoes we had seen in the orphanage. The new shoes fit well, so I told the salesman to write them up. He reached over to take the boots and put them in a box, but Tyler screeched and screamed.

"It's all right, Tyler," I said trying to calm him. "He's just putting them in a box for you." But, of course, Tyler didn't understand me. Speaking calmly would have assured my other two sons who had formed a deep bond with me during infancy, but Tyler found no comfort in my voice. He dropped off the chair and fell to the floor in what would be the first of many meltdowns. Unable to communicate his needs, he lay there grieving the loss of the little, red boots. I told the salesman to give Tyler the boots and he carried them as if they were the necessary floating device to escape a sinking ship.

In the days that followed, I was often at a loss to know what Tyler wanted. Everyone knows what a parent does when a newborn cries. The parent runs through the list. Is he hungry? Does he need to be changed? Maybe he's tired or sick. The infant lies there giving few clues as to why he might be crying. Eventually the parents learn that certain cries mean different things and they can determine what the baby needs. The baby is not yet mobile and by the time he becomes mobile he will have some language to help him communicate, but Tyler was not a baby. He moved through the world with the speed of a three-year old, but with the experience and wobbliness of an infant. He needed constant supervision to ensure his safety.

At the end of the week, Roger and I took the three boys to our local Toys 'R' Us. Trevor needed a controller for his Super Nintendo and Jonathan had a toy that had to be returned. I had purchased a twin stroller for Jonathan and Tyler and I put them in it to shop. Even though Christmas was over, the store was packed. The line for returns was long and the lines to purchase new merchandise were even longer. It seemed as though every child who had received a gift certificate or money for Christmas had chosen this day to shop. Roger waited on line to make the exchange while I took the three boys to purchase the new controller. As I pushed the stroller through the crowded store, Tyler stared up at the tall, colorful boxes of toys piled from floor to the ceiling. People moving through the aisles banged into the stroller and their coats brushed past Tyler at eye level. Noisy kids and the sound of video game battles pierced the air. A store manager called extra cashiers over the public address system to assist at the registers. Bombarded with sensory input Tyler cried loudly. I tried to reassure him by speaking to him, but he looked around in terror at the towers of boxes surrounding him as if he expected them to crash down on him at any moment. His cries got louder by the minute and people stopped and stared at us. He wasn't just crying. He keened in a piercingly high voice like an animal being skinned alive. I rocked the stroller back and forth, but that just agitated him. I saw the anxiety building in Trevor and Jonathan.

"Mom, can Jon and I go find Dad?" Trevor asked.

"No, Trevor," I said. "I don't want you guys getting lost in this crowd."

"Well, can we go to the car?" he asked. "We can get the controller some other time."

Suddenly Tyler stopped crying. He thrashed his head back and forth as I had seen him do in his bed the night before, but something about this was more dramatic. I gently called his name, but there was no reaction. His little head just kept slamming from side to side like a metronome keeping a steady beat. I realized he wasn't really with us anymore. He had gone into some deep recess of his mind to get away from the stress of being in this new situation. I took the boys back to the car to wait for Roger. I put Tyler into his car seat where he continued to thrash his head back and forth. In a matter of minutes, he fell into a deep sleep and I was left to ponder what was going on with this little boy.

Over the next few days, our friends and neighbors stopped by to meet Tyler. Always interested in meeting new people, he greeted them with direct eye contact and a smile. Nobody noticed anything unusual about Tyler and I told myself, "He just needs time. He'll be fine."

CHAPTER 6
DECEMBER 31, 1992

On New Year's Eve, we went to Roger's childhood home for a celebration. The family couldn't wait to meet Tyler. Roger's mother, Lois, lived alone in the six-bedroom colonial where along with her late husband she had raised five children. The house was purchased in the post WWII era as a three bedroom ranch. Roger, his three brothers and sister had helped their father remodel the house. Roger and his siblings all learned carpentry from their father. The house was full of personal touches, including built in bookcases, custom room dividers and a finished basement where the family would gather on this day. The basement was typical of basements where baby boomers across America had played board games, celebrated holidays, stolen first kisses, and listened to 45's. On one side of the room stood a bar where many a drink had been hoisted as the children came of age. Knotty pine paneling covered the walls and a tone-on-tone blue rug lay over linoleum tiles.

Roger's mother, Lois, a fiercely independent woman, lived alone even though her aging body threatened to steal that independence. Both of her hips had been replaced and she had a chronically swollen ankle making a simple walk across the room painful. She moved with a severe hitch to her step always trying to minimize the pain. Despite this, she refused to accept assistance from any of her children. She did her own laundry, shopped weekly for food and kept a clean home. She was active in her church, attending bible studies, sewing circles and the garden club. Most people hope they will be able to manage such a life at the age of seventy-five. Lois, with her curly white hair, steel rimmed glasses and plump figure recalled a Norman Rockwell image of a grandmother, but things are not always what they seem.

Lois's children admired her independence, but independence taken too far can become selfishness. Lois never put her children first and feelings were often hurt. Her busy schedule rarely left time for them. My niece once asked Lois to attend a Grandparent's Day at her elementary school, but Lois turned her down because it was the day of her garden club meeting. However, on holidays, Lois expected her children and their families to flock to her house and live up to her image of the perfect family. I joined the family at I was thirty-five years old with my own strong sense of independence. I did not share the resentments the family had built up over the years for Lois. I was happy to be left alone to raise my family, glad not to have a meddlesome mother-in-law. But on this day, Lois's old-fashioned values and selfishness led me to wonder how she reconciled the teachings of her church with her own narrow values.

The last to arrive for the late afternoon dinner, we pulled up to the house and saw Roger's sister, Rosemary, waiting at the door anxious to meet her new nephew. Jonathan and Trevor jumped out of the car and ran into the house as I took Tyler's hand and led him up the driveway.

"Hi Tyler," Rosemary said. "It's so nice to meet you."

"Da," said Tyler.

"He's adorable," Rosemary said kissing my cheek. "Everyone's downstairs waiting to meet him."

We moved to the basement where Lois was setting up a buffet on a long metal folding table with a vinyl tablecloth on it. A Christmas tree stood in the corner of the basement, a pile of gifts at its feet. My twelve nieces and nephews crowded around the tree shaking presents and trying to guess the contents. Jonathan and Trevor searched for gifts with their names on them. Roger and I led Tyler into the room as everyone crowded around him, wanting to get a look at the newest member of the family. Tyler made eye contact with confidence and smiled at everyone who spoke to him. He seemed to enjoy receiving so much attention. Lois turned around from the buffet table and smiled. "Oh, my, is this Tyler?" she asked.

"This is him," said Roger with a big grin.

"Well now, *HE* really *fits* in the family!" She exclaimed. "Hi, Tyler."

"Da," he said pulling on the buckles of his Oshkosh overalls.

"He looks like a Havlicek," she said. "He could be the twins' older brother."

The twins were Rosemary's eighteen month old children. They had blond hair and blue eyes and did look like Tyler, but I was concerned about what her comments might really mean. The family moved to the buffet table and began to fix plates.

"Are you hungry?' I asked Tyler. I made an eating sign at my mouth with my fingers.

"Nyet," he said. He ran across the room to join Trevor and

Jonathan at the tree. Lois came up behind me.

"Oh, Patty, Tyler is so cute," she said. "He will really *fit* in the family." I wanted to ask her what that meant, but unfortunately I already knew. She felt Tyler would *fit* better in the family than Jonathan because of his coloring. Jonathan had lived with us for eighteen months and we were only cognizant of the differences in his appearance when other people reminded us. He was our baby and we loved him as much as we loved Trevor. I didn't know what to say to Lois. My eyes searched the room for Trevor and Jonathan. I feared they might have heard her insensitive comments. Fortunately they were too engrossed in play to notice.

"Is Tyler going to eat?" Lois asked me.

"He's probably too excited," I said burying my anger. "He can always eat later."

"I'll fix him a plate," she said ignoring me. "He can sit next to me at the table." She limped across the room, took him by the hand, fixed him a plate and led him to the table. I knew she would proudly show her friends the pictures of the adorable little Russian boy her son had adopted, but I wondered if she had shown her friends the pictures of Jonathan when he joined our family.

"Anna," Lois said to my other sister-in-law. "Doesn't Tyler *fit* beautifully in the family?"

"He's very cute," said Anna, not wanting to acknowledge what Lois meant.

I felt saddened and outraged at the same time. Roger and Rosemary must have sensed my emotion and came over to me.

"Can you believe what she's saying?" I asked feeling my blood pressure rising. "What an insult!"

"Ignore her," said Rosemary. "She's an old lady with the values of bygone generations. Nothing you say will change her attitudes. You know how stubborn she can be."

"Rosemary's right," said Roger. "Nothing will be gained by squaring off with her.

"Do you think Trevor heard her?" I asked knowing how Trevor adored Jonathan.

"No, he's too busy having fun with his cousins," said Roger. "And even if he did, he wouldn't understand what she's really saying."

"You know she's the only one in this room who thinks that way," said Rosemary. "The rest of us adore Jonathan."

The rest of the family had embraced Jonathan with his constant smile and outgoing personality from the moment he came home. I had never seen anyone in the family slight him in any way. If I started an argument over Lois's comments, I could ruin this day for everyone. I would also have to explain to Trevor why we had decided to go home. I didn't think this was a lesson I wanted to teach my six-year old yet. I decided to calm myself and make the most of it. Roger and I joined the family at the table. Throughout the afternoon, Lois never stopped fussing over Tyler as if he were the only grandchild she had. I realized her behavior was not just leaving Jonathan out, but every other child in the room. As I look back on the photos taken that afternoon, Lois was never far from Tyler. I knew how she felt about Jonathan, but I didn't have to accept it. I thought it might be time to distance my family from Lois and her narrow ideas.

CHAPTER 7
JANUARY 1993

      ` In the weeks that followed the holidays, new sights, sounds, tastes, scents and feelings bombarded Tyler. One day we awoke to a foot of snow glistening on the ground outside. I couldn't explain to children who hadn't seen snow since last year that it was too cold to be outside. I knew Tyler had seen snow before, but I didn't know if he had ever played in it. I suited the three boys up in snow pants, gloves, hats, scarves, coats and boots, knowing that within twenty minutes I would reverse the process and hang wet clothing all over the laundry room.

      Trevor wanted to build a snow fort and recruited Tyler and Jonathan as assistant masons of the snow. Tyler played with his brothers for about five minutes before the new environment stole his attention. A plane flew overhead and he turned towards the sky. A snow plow downshifted on the next block and he wondered what had caused the noise. Children in front of our house had a snowball fight and Tyler was drawn towards their laughter. He darted around the fenced yard following each sound, hoping to get closer to determine its source. As I had expected, the chill soon took hold of Trevor and Jonathan. Abandoning the fort, they came into the house removing clothing into a wet pile crusted with snow and ice. Tyler, however, remained outside, seemingly unaffected by the cold. Watching from the bay window in the kitchen, I saw him engage in a bizarre behavior. He put his face close to the chain link fence surrounding our pool and moved from one end of it to the other and back again like a caged circus tiger. Back and forth he went for about twenty minutes, until the snow plow arrived in front of our house and the noise stole his attention. He rushed to the stockade fence separating the backyard from the front and peered through the slats hoping to catch a glimpse of the big truck. I called him to come inside as the temperature dropped, but he ignored me until I went out into the frigid air and carried him into the house. He threw himself on the floor crying, kicking and screaming. He had learned the word "no" and used it over and over. His clothing was wet and tiny snowballs crusted on his gloves and hat. Little icicles on his hair peeked out from under his hat. The cold should have stung at every nerve in his body, but he showed no signs of discomfort. I peeled the layers of clothing off as he resisted, squirming and twisting away from me until the wet clothes were off and he was dressed in dry clothes.

He took off for the den, flung himself onto the couch and sat in an upright position rocking back and forth from the waist. Images of the 20/20 ABC News Program that had aired the previous year showing Romanian children suffering in orphanages sprang to mind. The naked Romanian children huddled together on the concrete floor, struggling to keep warm. Many of them engaged in rocking behaviors. For the first time, I wondered if the pristine little beds with the matching blue bedspreads had been a front for a much more sinister existence. Could it be that, Tyler, like the Romanian children, had been warehoused in neglectful conditions?

During the winter months, I introduced Tyler to toys, but he never sat still long enough to play with them. He never watched television or movies and most nights he didn't sleep more than five hours. I often awoke during the night to the sounds of his restless thrashing and rocking. He usually woke by 5:00 a.m. and I had no hope of returning him to bed. I tried to understand what it was like for him, living in a constant state of excitement. Every day he awoke to new experiences and a freedom that never existed in the orphanage. For him, sleep meant the possibility of missing out on a new adventure, but sleep was not the only difficulty we experienced with Tyler.

He drained Roger and me of our energy with his demand to be the center of attention at all times. When the family watched television, he blocked everyone's view, forcing Roger or me to get up and move him. When Trevor needed our help with homework, Tyler did something disruptive to draw us to him. He grabbed Jonathan's toys and ran away with them. He stood in the doorways of his brothers' rooms and made faces at them, but then he made faces all the time. He twisted his lower lip up over his upper lip and squinted like Popeye. We tried to help him break the habit by reminding him, "No faces, Tyler," but he seemed to do it unconsciously.

Trevor returned to school after his Christmas break and I searched for activities to burn off Tyler's excess energy. We have a large in-ground pool in our backyard and Tyler needed to learn to swim before the summer, so I enrolled both Tyler and Jonathan in swimming lessons. Jonathan hated the lessons, but Tyler loved the water. By the end of the first lesson Tyler was diving under the water and holding his breath for long periods of time. At one point, he swam to the bottom of the pool and stayed there long enough to make everyone watching so nervous that the instructor dove to the bottom and pulled him to the surface. Tyler emerged from the water beaming. After that, it was tough to keep him off the bottom of the pool, but at least he learned to swim and I would have one less worry when the summer came. Leaving the pool after a lesson, however, was never easy as it was difficult for Tyler to transition to any new activity.

One incident in particular sticks in my mind. Tyler had lived with us for about three months when I took the boys to Chuck E Cheese's for lunch. Trevor pumped coins into the video games as Jonathan danced with the costumed characters and other kids. Tyler crawled through the maze and played in the ball pit. After a couple of hours of play, I told the boys we would be leaving soon. When it was time to go, Trevor and Jonathan put their coats on, but Tyler ran away from me. I caught him and tried to slip his arm into the sleeve of his coat. He screamed, "I need help!" I had been working on that phrase with him encouraging him to ask for help at home with daily activities rather than becoming frustrated and going into a meltdown. Now he beseeched other people to help him. Parents stared at me as I struggled to get Tyler's arm into the sleeve of his coat. "I need help!" he yelled, twisting his body away from the coat. Several well-intentioned people drew closer as he continued to fight and scream. Other moms eyed me as if to accuse me of doing something to cause the panic in the innocent looking child's eyes. I handed the coat to Trevor, picked Tyler up, and went to the exit with Trevor and Jonathan following closely behind. Tyler grabbed on to tables and chairs as if his very life depended on not exiting the building. I tried to contain his arms within mine, but he worked every muscle in his body which proved challenging even though he was small and thin. The mothers watching us grew into a crowd. Trevor, a shy child, hated having attention called to him. Jonathan looked plain scared. Neither boy was accustomed to seeing me in a situation I could not control. Near the exit, a hostess greeted the incoming children from a small, wooden podium. As we passed her, Tyler arched his back and flung his arms out to the side in a last ditch effort to avoid the exit, driving the back of my hand into the sharp corner of the podium causing a deep gash. My hand bled down towards my wrist, but I ignored it and put all my effort into securing Tyler and getting out the door. I held him tighter, put my shoulder to the door, gave a hard push and we were out. I carried him to the car with a sigh of relief, but this episode wasn't over yet. Three parents followed us outside as his desperate cries for help continued. They watched as I buckled him into his car seat waiting to see if I was going to hurt him. Trevor quietly settled Jonathan in his car seat and sat between them. I climbed into the car and wiped the blood from my hand with a napkin as the other parents drifted back into the restaurant. My hands trembled, my chest felt tight and I couldn't catch my breath. I turned my attention to Trevor and Jonathan who were visibly upset.

"Are you guys okay?" I asked.

"We're okay," said Trevor as tears ran down his face. "How is your hand?"

"Oh, I'm okay," I said applying pressure to the bloody cut on my hand. "I'm just worried about you and Jonathan. Are you guys okay?"

"Yeah," said Trevor grabbing hold of Jonathan's little hand. "We're okay."

I looked into the rearview mirror. Tyler sat calmly looking out the window at passing traffic, the only one in the car who seemed to be at peace.

From the minute Tyler joined our family, teaching him language was a priority. Roger and I knew life would get easier if we could communicate with him. As we taught him words, we showed him an object, such as a ball, and said, "Look, Tyler, this is a ball." When we wanted to explain a movement such as running, we acted it out and said, "Tyler, watch this." Unfortunately, he latched on to those two little phrases, "look" and "watch this" in a very negative way.

One day Tyler took notice of the electrical outlet wiggling a baby proof cover off one of them.

"No, Tyler," I said replacing the cover. He looked at me and giggled. Over the days that followed, he focused on the outlet covers and pulled them off all day long. He removed them and said, "Mom, watch this," or "Mom, look." I tried to redirect him to other activities, but nothing held his interest like the outlet covers.

Children who live in institutions such as Tyler's orphanage often develop negative attention-seeking behaviors. Caregivers are spread thin and a child learns that acting out is the only way to get attention. This learned behavior was deeply etched in Tyler's personality. If I told him knives were dangerous, he spent the day trying to get one from the kitchen draw. If he managed to get hold of one, he rushed to notify me saying, "Look, Mom," to make sure I knew what he was doing. Roger and I encouraged him when he engaged in positive activities, but that didn't give him the same satisfaction. In fact, if we praised him for a particular activity, he stopped the activity immediately. With limited language skills, explaining to him how certain things were just plain dangerous was impossible. I took a deep breath every time I heard Tyler say, "Look Mom" or

"Watch this" because it always meant he was doing something he shouldn't.

By March, we felt like prisoners trapped in our home because whenever we went out, Tyler exploded into a tantrum before going home. At home, we were just an audience to his negative-attention seeking behaviors. Roger and I decided to enroll him in preschool.

We hoped preschool would help him with language and give him an opportunity to interact with children his own age. I felt nervous about leaving him at the preschool because I couldn't explain to him that I would be back in three hours and I feared he might think he had been left in another orphanage. When I dropped him off for his first day of school, I stayed for about an hour to make sure he felt comfortable. I visited the different play areas with him and showed him the toys. He found a rocking horse and settled on it moving back and forth. As the other children came in, I noticed how much smaller he was than they were. His thin frame looked frail compared with those of the vigorous children entering the classroom. When it was time for me to leave, he showed no signs of fear, doubt or anxiety. He just smiled and said, "good-bye." I set off to spend some one on-one-time with Jonathan.

We live near a seaport town with a great park near the water. I went down the big slide with Jonathan and pushed him on the swings. After the park we walked along the shore and threw stones at the incoming waves of the Long Island Sound. We sat together in the sand, built a castle and poured water into its center enjoying the luxury of being alone together.

When I returned to pick Tyler up, the teachers told me he had done okay, although they said he spent some time running his eyes along the walls. Tyler smiled when he saw me, took my hand and we left for home as if preschool were something he did every day. I couldn't understand how the transition from home to preschool had not caused any stress for Tyler, but I was relieved to see him smiling as he left the school.

CHAPTER 8
APRIL 1993

A soft breeze crossed the air making it smell clean and fresh as if winter had been laundered away. The children couldn't wait to play outside. Trevor pedaled his bike to a friend's house to play baseball. I gave Jonathan and Tyler each a bottle of bubbles and sent them out to play on the deck running along the back of our house. Tyler loved blowing bubbles and watching them drift off into the sky. He acted as if each puffy bubble was the first he had seen. Jonathan jumped after his bubbles, popping them in the air as they floated above his head. Folding laundry in the kitchen, I watched them from the bay window as they played with the floating bits of suds. Suddenly Tyler burst into the den next to the kitchen and said, "Look, Mom. Bubbles. Watch me."

"I *am* watching you," I assured him. Tyler always wanted my eyes glued on him.

"Good," he said, but as he turned to run out the door, he tripped over his feet and stumbled backwards onto the oak coffee table in the den, slamming his head with a thud.

"Are you okay?" I asked rushing towards him.

"Yeah," he answered. He ran out the door before I could get to him. Tyler was always falling and banging into things, as if he didn't know where his arms and legs began and ended. I returned to folding the clothes, but after a few minutes, I glanced up, looked out and saw blood running down the back of his head, onto his neck and down his shirt. I gasped, realizing he had been seriously injured. I ran outside with a towel to stop the bleeding and told Jonathan to get Daddy who came to the deck within seconds.

"What happened?" Roger asked.

"He fell on the table in the den," I said struggling to catch my breath and stay calm. "Trevor is at Tommy's house. Stay here with Jonathan and I'll take Tyler to the hospital."

"I want to come," Jonathan whined.

"It's okay, Jon," I said. "Tyler has a boo-boo that the doctor needs to fix. Daddy will stay here with you and watch you play with the bubbles."

"Are you sure you don't want me to come?" Roger asked scooping Jonathan up in his arms. "How are you going to manage this alone?"

"Someone has to be here when Trevor comes back," I said applying pressure to the wound. "I'll take him."

Roger helped me get Tyler into the car and I drove to the hospital, keeping one hand extended across the front seat pressing the towel against the open wound. Within minutes, we arrived at the hospital and fortunately Tyler showed no signs of being in any discomfort or pain, but rather enjoyed my undivided attention. At the hospital, an ambulance pulled up to the emergency door. "Look, mom! Wee-ooo! Wee-ooo!" Tyler cried imitating the sounds of the ambulance unaware of the large amount of blood that now crusted his shirt.

We checked in and a nurse led us to a room surrounded with medical supplies and instruments. Tyler looked around the room with wide eyes.

"Who do we have here?" The doctor asked entering the cubicle.

"This is Tyler," I said. "He fell backwards on a coffee table." Suddenly I felt dizzy and wished Roger had come with me to explain the accident and take charge.

"That's a pretty good sized gash he has," the doctor said as he examined the wound. Rather than crying or pulling away, Tyler giggled every time the doctor came near the deep cut which measured over an inch long.

"He's going to need a few stitches. I can see he's had stitches before," said the doctor, pointing to the scar running along Tyler's forehead. "How did he react to having that injury sewn up?"

"I don't know. We adopted him from Ukraine a few months ago." I explained. "I don't know how he got that scar."

"Well, since we don't know how he'll react, it's probably best to belt him onto a papoose board to hold him still," said the doctor. "Is that okay with you?"

"Sure, I don't think he'll mind. He seems to delight in attention of any kind," I said, although I really had no idea how he might react.

The doctor strapped Tyler down on the board and a nurse came in to assist. With the attention of two adults, Tyler was happy. He snickered as they stitched up the wound.

"You're a great little patient, Tyler," said the doctor, but I wondered why my little boy didn't react to pain and hadn't cried at all. The sight of so much blood would have been enough to terrify Trevor or Jonathan, but Tyler wasn't scared at all. It wasn't just his lack of reaction to physical pain. He seemed immune to the emotions that should have gone along with being hurt. He was blowing bubbles one minute and visiting the emergency room the next and reacting just as happily to both scenarios.

The doctor finished stitching the wound and helped Tyler to sit up. He looked from the doctor to the nurse with a big smile. The doctor gave me instructions to keep the wound dry and clean and to see the pediatrician in a week to have the stitches taken out.

As we left the hospital, Tyler pointed to the bandage on his head and called out to people in the parking lot, "Look!" Several people stopped to look at his bandage and comment on how brave he was. He loved grabbing the attention of strangers.

When we got home, he raced into the house to find Roger to tell him about the adventure. "Look, stitches!" he exclaimed. "Fun!"

CHAPTER 9
MAY, 1993

On a warm day, Jonathan and Tyler played tag in the cul-de-sac with several of the neighborhood children. Their laughter permeated the air. I sat on the front lawn watching their activities enjoying the warm sun when I noticed something odd about the way Tyler ran. His movement appeared to be normal for the most part, but every now and then, he kicked his right foot out at an angle as if he expected to stop a pass from a soccer ball. I watched as he resumed running, only to stop after a few minutes and stick his little foot out again. The errant leg seemed to have a mind of its own, jumping out unexpectedly. Tyler continued to play unaware of the strange movement threatening his balance as Roger came outside ready to go to work.

"Do you know how sexy you look in that uniform?" I asked.

"You only tell me every time I'm ready to go to work," he said.

"Watch Tyler run and tell me if you see anything odd."

He watched for a few minutes. "What's he doing with his right leg?"

"I don't know. It's strange, isn't it?"

"Yeah, why don't you ask Dr. Hollweg about it?"

The next day I called the doctor who suggested I have Tyler looked at by a pediatric neurologist at University Hospital. Dr.

Ibab asked Tyler to perform some simple movements.

"Tyler, can you touch your toes?" he asked.

"Oh, he can do that," I said, anxious to talk to the doctor about what I saw as Tyler's troubling behaviors.

"Good Tyler," said the doctor. "Now can you hop on your right foot? Good, now your other foot." Tyler had no difficulty, treating the exam like a big game.

"He can easily copy movement," I explained. "I'm concerned about some other odd behavior he engages in from time to time."

"I understand. We'll get to that," said Dr. Ibab as Tyler stood there beaming, waiting for the game to begin again. "I just need to make sure there is nothing odd about his general movements. We'll get to your concerns in a minute. Now, Tyler, watch me." The doctor stood with his arms outstretched to his sides. He closed his eyes and touched his nose. "Can you do this?"

Tyler snorted a giggle and performed the task.

"Okay, let's see how you walk, Tyler. Come out here in the hall. Walk to the end and come back again."

I watched Tyler walk back and forth looking steady. Each step looked normal and the little leg that concerned me never went astray.

"You're not seeing what I've been seeing," I said. "He's been kicking his right leg out intermittently when he's moving."

"Well, he's not doing that now," said the doctor. "In fact,

his movements seem to be quite normal, especially considering he spent his early years in a Ukrainian orphanage."

"What about the habit he has of running his eyes along the walls and fences," I asked growing impatient. "That can't be normal.

"It may not be, but I think he's still adjusting to his new life," said Dr. Ibab. "Tyler probably spent most of his early years in a crib. He's not like normal children who reached for mobiles as infants and scampered after balls as toddlers. He was probably not exposed to toys that forced him to reach, swing, jump and spin in his environment, helping his brain to develop. Children who are neglected during their early years use their bodies for entertainment. They rock, flap their hands, or as you have seen, run their eyes along walls. They pull objects in and out of focus to keep from being bored often the only stimulation their brains receive and necessary for their survival."

"Watch me," said Tyler walking down the hall again wanting to keep the attention on him at all times.

"I see," I said. "Do you think the problems with his balance are also the result of neglect during those early years?"

"I do," he said. "A child who spends his early years in a crib without physical activity or stimulation will have difficulty with spatial awareness or what is called proprioception. That means he will have a hard time knowing where his body is in relationship to things around him. He'll trip, stumble and bang into every object he encounters. When he reaches for objects, they're not exactly where his brain tells him they should be. When Tyler first came home, he may often have felt as if he were free falling through space."

"That's really interesting," I said thinking about the trouble Tyler had with his first bath, the colors at the toy store and his clumsiness as he moved. Then I asked the question that had been running through my head since he started talking. "Do you expect he'll improve in time?"

"It's hard to say for sure because it's impossible to know how much his development will remain stunted due to the neglect he suffered in the orphanage. However, he should make gains living in a loving family," he said. "Just remember that play is very important for him and he'll learn by moving through his environment. Make sure he gets exercise that includes gross motor movement."

"What about ADHD?" I asked. "*Everything* is a distraction to Tyler."

"I would guess he is still trying to process his new world. I wouldn't want to label him with anything just yet nor would I want to prescribe any medication at this time," he said. "Why don't I see Tyler again in six months?"

As we left the office, my mind reeled with what the doctor had said. I had a new perspective on Tyler's behavior and what he must have felt like during those first weeks at home. I tried to reconcile his behavior with what I had just learned. For the first time, I allowed myself to consider the possibility that Tyler's delays might be permanent, but I still hoped the doctor was right and Tyler would improve with time and experience. Unfortunately, he had not seen the broken gait as Tyler walked and I still had no explanation for the little leg that kicked out of step.

CHAPTER 10
JUNE 1993

Roger and I sat on the bleachers of a Little League ball field watching Trevor play while Jonathan ran on the playground with a friend. Tyler wandered around the perimeter of the field gazing up at the sky as a flock of geese passed overhead. One of the other parents, Laura, joined us on the bleachers. She worked in our school district as a reading teacher, helping students with learning disabilities.

"How's it going?" she asked, looking over at Tyler whose little hands flapped up and down. He walked along distracted by every sound traveling through his space.

"It's okay," I said. "He's really a handful though. He needs to be watched constantly."

"Have you had him evaluated by the school district for disabilities?" She asked.

Disabilities? Tyler had many problems, but I believed they were the result of his early years in an institution. Hadn't the pediatrician and neurologist said he would probably improve with time? To me, the word disabilities signified more physical limitations and a permanent condition.

"You know," Laura said. "He probably should be receiving speech therapy, occupational therapy and psychological services."

"Do you really think he would qualify for all of that?" Roger asked sounding a little defensive about Tyler. "He's been learning language very quickly."

"He could learn faster with some professional help and I'm sure he would qualify for services," she said. "My daughter attends a special preschool for children with developmental disabilities and she's seen great progress. You should call the school district and have him evaluated. You have nothing to lose."

"I suppose you're right," I said.

"Oh, there's Jack," said Laura as her husband pulled up in the parking lot. "I've got to go."

I turned to Roger. "What do you think? Should we have him tested?"

"If he could receive those services, it might make life easier not just for him, but for the whole family."

"I suppose we could use some help. I just still see Tyler as a child full of possibilities not as a child with disabilities. I really would hate to label him so quickly.

He hasn't been home that long."

"Laura is sending her daughter to a special preschool and she thinks the staff there is very good."

"I suppose we have nothing to lose by having him tested. If he can learn faster, life for the family will improve. I'll call the school district tomorrow."

The district arranged for Tyler to take a battery of tests at the special education preschool that Laura had recommended. The first person we met with was one of the school psychologists. She wanted to know about Tyler's development up to this point, but, of course, when she asked questions about him, my answer was often, "I don't know." I had no idea what life had been like for him in the first years of his life. I could only offer information on his behavior since coming to live with us. I told her about his strange attractions to noise, his caged behavior along walls, his frequent meltdowns and his erratic sleeping and eating patterns. I described the bizarre thrashing in bed that put him to sleep and the faces he made at us. I told her how he flapped his hands when he walked.

"Will he qualify for services?" I asked, but what I really wanted to know was whether or not I could expect him to catch up, and if not, what could Roger and I expect from him?

"It's impossible to know at this point," she said.

"I understand," I said. I knew she really couldn't give me a more definitive answer. She escorted us down the hall to the speech department.

Speech was the area that interested me the most. In the few months since Tyler had been home, he had absorbed language like a sponge, but I knew he was still significantly delayed. If Tyler improved his deficits in language, he could express his needs and hopefully reduce his frustration and difficult behavior. The speech therapist presented Tyler with a list of items that are familiar to all preschoolers, but he had never seen most of them before. We did not own a toy fire truck, so he could not identify the one in the picture. Our sandbox had been put away for the winter, so he did not recognize the pictures of the pail or shovel. He was unable to name any colors. In another part of the testing, Tyler was shown drawings of happy and sad faces. He smiled at each sketch without discerning any emotions. I asked the therapist about an annoying habit Tyler had of repeating every word we said.

"That's known as echolalia. We often see this in children who have difficulty with speech," she explained.

"I see," I said wanting to tell her how very annoying it was to live with someone who repeated everything you said and how his brothers wanted to kill him whenever he did it. "Is there anything we can do about it?"

"Hopefully as he learns more language, the habit will fade," she said.

We moved on to the gym to see if Tyler would qualify for physical therapy. He ran, hopped, skipped and jumped as the physical therapist, modeled the movements for him. He had no problem with any of these activities and enjoyed performing them. His balance wobbled from time to time in a drunken fashion, but he just laughed. The therapist set up an obstacle course. Jumping over blocks of wood and zig-zagging around cones, Tyler sailed through this part of the test. He fell down a couple of times, but he got right back up and kept going. Except for the fact he was clumsy, he didn't seem to have any physical limitations.

Our last stop was the occupational therapy department. At the time, I had no idea what occupational therapy was, but I would soon learn that in this area Tyler was severely delayed. The therapist, Jane, had straight blond hair and blue eyes and looked like she could have been Tyler's biological mother which I think drew her to him from the start. She led us to the occupational therapy room as Tyler ran ahead of us. I called out to him to slow down, but he just looked over his shoulder, laughed and continued running down the hall.

"Is he always moving?' Jane asked.

"Yes and he's always ignoring me too," I laughed

"How is his balance"?

"Not good. He's always bumping into things and tripping over his own feet. It doesn't seem to bother him though. Even if he hurts himself and is bleeding, he just keeps going."

"So he doesn't react to pain. How does he feel about being touched?"

"It's funny. When he first came home he arched his back whenever anyone touched him, but now he enjoys having his back rubbed and he loves to be tickled."

"How does he feel about his clothes? Does he resist certain fabrics or clothing in general?"

"I haven't noticed anything like that. I think he likes many different types of clothing because he never had much choice in Ukraine."

"What about noises? Does he cover his ears or shy away from noises?"

"No, on the contrary. He craves noises. The louder the better. If he hears a vacuum, a lawn mower, or a loud truck, he forgets everything around him and rushes to the sound. Then he spends hours mimicking the sound. It drives us all nuts."

"What about sensitivity to light?"

'I don't know. He certainly doesn't shy away from light. He likes to put his dad's flash light against his eyes."

"How is his appetite?"

"That's an area of great concern for me. He never seems hungry and eating is nothing but a chore for him."

"Is it just certain textures he resists?"

"I don't think so. I've tried many different types of food, but nothing interests him."

As we reached the occupational therapy room, Jane asked Tyler to walk a balance beam which proved difficult for him. She presented him with some large beads and a string and asked him to string them.

"This is going to be very hard for him," I said. "Tyler doesn't separate his fingers. His uses his hands like little lobster claws picking up items with his thumb as one part of the claw and all of his fingers joined together to form the other part of the claw."

"He probably didn't have opportunities in the orphanage to develop his fine motor skills," said Jane. Tyler picked up the beads, but didn't understand what he was supposed to do with them. Jane asked him to copy horizontal and vertical lines as she drew them, but he scribbled in frustration. She moved him to a sandbox, where he relaxed and enjoyed himself pouring sand in and out of a cup over and over again.

"I think Tyler would benefit greatly from occupational therapy," Jane said as she concluded the testing. "I see several areas in which he has difficulty. When the results of all the tests are put together, I'll go over what I think can be done for him through occupational therapy.

We returned to the office where the director of the school told us our school's district office would contact us with the findings, but she was sure Tyler would qualify for services. My feelings were mixed. I was glad to hear that Roger and I would get some help because we needed it, but I was also being forced to face the fact that time and love alone would not be enough for Tyler to overcome his delays.

Within a week, we were notified that Tyler did indeed qualify for services. He was delayed over two years in the areas of eye hand coordination, expressive language and fine motor skills. He began classes in July.

CHAPTER 11
JULY 1993

When Trevor began school three years earlier, I was reluctant to see him set out into the world. I knew he would lose a little innocence every time he went out the door. I wanted to keep him home a little longer to preserve his childhood for as long as I could. I wish I had felt the same way when Tyler began school, but I didn't. I looked forward to the time when he would be in school. I needed some time away from his constant demands for attention and I wanted to spend time with my family the way I had before he turned our lives upside down. I blamed myself for not doing a better job of keeping things running as smoothly as it had in the past. Logically, I knew Tyler didn't understand what he did to the family nor could he control it, but I still yearned for the old days before he joined the family. I wasn't proud of these feelings. I needed to remind myself Tyler hadn't asked to come here and it wasn't his fault he had such a difficult time fitting in.

At the preschool, Tyler ran happily up to the door, his new white sneakers smacking on the concrete. His skinny little legs stuck out from a pair of crisp, white, shorts held up by red suspenders with little sailboats on them. His blond hair, in a mushroom cut, bobbed up and down with each bounce of his tiny frame.

Tyler was in a classroom with five other children who all had difficulty learning and staying focused. From the start, the teacher, Celeste, became the target of Tyler's constant demand for attention.

"Hi, Tyler," she said. "Welcome to school. Would you like to walk to the classroom with me?"

"Yes," said Tyler as he fidgeted with his suspenders.

"Say good-bye to mom and let's go," she said taking his little hand in hers.

Tyler turned and smiled at me. "Bye mom," he said. I watched as the two of them walked down the hallway and marveled at how easily he walked off with people he did not know. At home, he spent his time getting me to watch his every move, but now he left me without a glance backward.

"Do you want to watch your son in the classroom for a while?" a voice from behind me asked. It was the psychologist who had tested Tyler.

"Can I do that?"

"The classroom doors have windows and we can watch from outside. He doesn't have to know we're there."

"Great. I'm curious to see how he'll behave in a structured classroom setting. He just walked away from me as if he has been coming to this school forever."

"He may not miss you until he settles down and realizes you're not there."

We observed from the doorway as Tyler sat at a little table watching the movements of the other children. He appeared relaxed and happy. Suddenly he sensed we were watching him and turned around. He twisted his face, sucking his top lip in on one side in the now familiar Popeye grimace. As we watched, he made another bizarre face putting his fingers in his mouth and puffing his cheeks.

"He does that a lot. Why do you think he makes faces at me?"

"Perhaps he wants to connect with you and this is the only way he knows how."

"Do you really think so? Sometimes it seems he's deliberately trying to annoy me or his brothers."

"I doubt that. He probably just doesn't have any other way to communicate with you. He knows he gets your attention when he does it, doesn't he?"

"Sure. We're always telling him, 'No faces, Tyler.' Look, he's still doing it."

"It might be a habit he acquired at the orphanage to fight boredom. Why don't we leave him alone? I didn't think he would notice us, but now we're distracting him."

"Okay. I'm going home to spend some time with his brothers, Jonathan and Trevor. It's been hard for them. They really need more of my attention."

"That sounds good. Go enjoy yourself and don't worry about anything."

I returned four hours later. Celeste told me Tyler had a good day, although he needed to work on sitting in a chair and attending to task. A good day? What did that mean? I had hoped he would demonstrate some of the disruptive behavior we saw continuously at home so the staff might offer us some advice.

When I dropped him off on the second day, Jane, the occupational therapist was waiting for us at the door. "I observed Tyler in the classroom yesterday and I'd like to talk with you if you have some time. During our initial interview, you told me Tyler craves noises and likes to be close to lights. I think he was deprived of sensory input such as sound, light and touch as an infant. Now, his brain craves that input."

"Is that why he runs towards noises that he hears?" I asked.

"Yes. Tyler may have been left for many hours in a crib without stimulation which caused him to develop self-stimulating behaviors such as rocking or flapping his hands. He didn't have toys to play with or the touch of an adult to stimulate him, so he used his body to provide the stimulation his brain needed to thrive. He developed the habit of running his eyes along objects to stimulate the brain. Twisting his face and making noises were other ways to pass the periods of boredom. I think Tyler suffers from sensory deprivation."

"Can he overcome that?"

"I want to start treating him for Sensory Integration Dysfunction."

"How do you treat someone for that?"

"I'm going to bombard him with sensory input. Hopefully his brain will process that input more normally in time. I'm going to set up a program for him here and give you some suggestions of things that may help him at home."

"That would be great. I'll do anything that will help life with him improve." I finally had an explanation for some of Tyler's behavior and some concrete suggestions to help him.

When I picked Tyler up, he bounced down the hall wearing a little khaki colored safari vest with lots of pockets on it.

"Hi," Jane said. "How was your afternoon?'

"Great!" I said. "I took Jonathan to the park with a couple of his friends. How did things go here?"

"Things went well. Tyler is wearing a weighted vest to help him relax and concentrate. Children with sensory integration problems enjoy the feeling of deep pressure they get from weight on the body because it helps them with proprioception or knowing where their bodies are in relationship to the world around them. They enjoy activities like swimming or being wrapped up tightly in blankets and deep massages. Tyler will start by wearing the vest for about a half an hour every day and we'll increase the time as his behavior warrants."

"Is that why Tyler likes to swim to the bottom of the pool and stay there?"

"Exactly. The deep pressure of the water is very calming for him. At night you might want to try to wrap him up in blankets like a sausage to help him fall asleep."

"Really? I'll give it a try. We'll see you tomorrow."

In the weeks that followed, Jane exposed Tyler to different forms of sensory input throughout his day at school. He finger painted and ran his fingers through shaving cream and Jell-o. He played in a sand box and jumped on a small trampoline. He spent time in a little dark cave with neon lights that Jane had constructed in the occupational therapy room.

The speech teacher worked on language with Tyler three times a week exposing him to objects that four-year olds should easily recognize and taught him to make the different sounds of the English language.

The psychologist taught him to play with toys appropriately rather than using them as objects of self-stimulation. He learned to push a car along on the floor rather than turn it upside down and spin the wheels in front of his eyes. She showed him sketches of different expressions to teach him about emotions.

In the classroom, Celeste worked on getting Tyler to cooperate in a group, take turns and share. However, he focused on keeping Celeste's attention on him at all times. When she read a book to the class, he climbed into her lap. He always had to be "first" to try an activity or to head up a line. At circle time, he did not sit on the carpet like the other children, but instead jumped around making disruptive noises. He delighted in being carried back to the circle by the two classroom aides. He demanded to be the center of attention in the classroom just as he did at home.

While I hoped this school would effect a change in Tyler, it was going to take some time and it would take even longer to see the change in the less structured environment at home. In fact, at home, things were getting worse in many ways.

CHAPTER 12
AUGUST 1993

Our respite from Tyler extended over five blissful hours every day. I tried to regain the family life which had been stolen from us when he joined the family. I spent time with Trevor and Jon at the park, the pool, or the ice rink, savoring every precious moment, knowing it was destined to end when the school bus brought Tyler home.

From the minute Tyler arrived home, he made his presence known with noise. He developed an annoying little routine mimicking the sounds a truck makes as it goes through its gears. He started with a vroom noise and walked forward. Suddenly he stopped, hesitated, and then raised the level of the vroom noise and moved forward again, imitating a vehicle hitting first gear. As he passed through each gear, he raised the level of the sound. He did this activity over and over with the noise getting ever louder and the speed picking up. Unfortunately, many of Tyler's imaginary vehicles had as many as ten gears. The annoying little routine went on all day and just when it seemed he would finish, he started all over again.

"Mom, Jonathan and I are trying to play Nintendo and we can't hear anything but Tyler's noises," Trevor complained. "And he's walking back and forth in front of the T.V. Make him stop!"

"Tyler, can you use your inside voice?" I asked, handing him a few matchbox cars. "Take the cars and your noises to your room."

"Okay," he said, but after a few minutes, he returned making noises and moving in a circle from the den to the kitchen to the dining room and through the living room as if the first floor of our home were a race car speedway.

As a result of the sensory integration deprivation, Tyler had experienced during his early years, his brain now craved input from sounds of all kinds. Every sound was a treat to be savored. When the motor of the vacuum came to life, he forgot everything and ran to be as close to the vibrating appliance as possible, lying on the floor next to it and then walking around for hours copying the noise. Noises were like candy to his brain. While listening to the vacuum was a benign activity, sometimes when he followed noises, he put himself in danger.

One day as the kids played on the front lawn, the mail truck pulled up. As I walked down the driveway to retrieve the mail, a commercial landscaper with a big trailer pulled up in front of the house across the street. Tyler's attention quickly shifted to the landscaper and he dashed across the street, moving before I realized what was happening. The landscaper took the commercial-sized lawnmower off the trailer and drove across the lawn as Tyler ran next to the mower, trying to recreate the sounds of the powerful machine. I called out to him, but between the noise from the machine and the noises he was making, there was no way he could have heard me. Fear ran through me as I envisioned him slipping beneath the mower or getting hit with a flying piece of debris. I got there as fast as I could and grabbed him. It was only then that the landscaper noticed him.

"Tyler! What are you doing?" I yelled as my voice

trembled.

He didn't answer. He continued to stare at the mower, making vibrating engine noises, his mind consumed with fascination and excitement. I picked him up and carried him back to the house where I desperately tried to explain the danger of running in the street, not listening to me and chasing lawnmowers, but he just stared across the street at the humming lawn mower, transfixed and unable to be reached.

On another memorable day, Jonathan, Tyler and I waited with Trevor and three other neighborhood children at the bus stop, which was at the end of our driveway. The bus pulled up and the children boarded as Tyler stood next to me mimicking the humming sounds of the bus in neutral. The driver closed the door and pulled away from the curb. As I waved to Trevor, I realized Tyler was running alongside the bus very close to the wheels as it circled the court which had been sanded after a recent snowfall. My pulse raced. Terrified that he would slip on the sand and go under the wheels, I chased after him, but he ran far ahead of me. I yelled, "STOP", hoping the driver might hear me, but it was a futile effort. The bus finished circling the court, straightened out and accelerated. Falling behind, Tyler stood in the middle of the street watching the bus move away, still echoing the rumbles of the engine. I caught up to him and snatched him up in my arms. I looked at the departing bus and saw Trevor staring from the back door looking terrified. I was breathless, but Tyler smiled calmly and continued making the noises of the bus. I talked to him about running into the street and going near moving vehicles, but he didn't understand how dangerous it was. While Tyler moved as fast as a typical four-year old, his brain functioned at an age of much less experience. I knew I had to step up my vigilance to ensure his safety.

Because Roger worked as a police officer from 4:00 p.m. until 12:00 midnight he was often gone in the evenings and at dinner time. Getting Tyler to sit down and have dinner with Jonathan, Trevor and I was a challenge. He sat at the table. He just didn't eat. His focus was on disruption. He spilled his drink, dug his utensils into the table and made noises over our conversation, and other disruptive things to keep the audience seated at the table focused on him. If I let Tyler do something else while we ate, he inevitably found a way to drag me away from the table. For a while, I took the kids out for fast food at dinner time on the nights that Roger worked. If we went to MacDonald's, Roy Roger's or Burger King, Tyler played in the ball pit or on the playground while we ate. I knew this didn't teach Tyler to sit at the table, but at least it gave us some peace at dinner and I could talk with Trevor and Jonathan.

Of course, eating dinner out created another problem. At some point, we had to leave the ball pit or playground. Without fail, Tyler had to be physically removed and forcibly brought out to the car. For Trevor and Jonathan the process of getting into the car was more stressful than anything he might do at home at the dinner table. I gave up the idea of eating out. Instead, I allowed Trevor and Jonathan to take dinner to their rooms. It was not what I wanted, but it wasn't fair to force them to sit at the table and be the targets of Tyler's behavior. I tried to feed Tyler at the table, but without an audience to watch his antics, he engaged in self-stimulating behavior or simply fell asleep. He ate very little and I didn't accomplish anything by making him sit there. I wasn't trained in child psychology. I was just a frustrated mom trying to manage a very difficult situation in the best way I could. I was in way over my head.

Long before Tyler arrived at our home, I developed a bedtime routine for Jonathan and Trevor that started with Jonathan's bath. He was the youngest and went to bed first. I helped him into his pajamas and then we snuggled on his bed while I read him a story. I always loved the way his hair smelled after his bath and he felt extra cuddly in his soft pajamas.

Jonathan had little interest in listening to the story, but he loved our time alone and talked incessantly as I read. Usually his chatter was insignificant and filled with two-year old questions like, "Mom, why did Winnie the Pooh's mom give him a name with the word pooh in it?" Sometimes the questions provided opportunities for little lessons about life. I remember one such evening in particular. As I read to Jonathan, he put his little hand on top of mine and said, "Mom, I wish we matched," referring to the differences in our skin coloring. It was the first time I had a meaningful discussion with him about what it meant to be adopted.

Every night as we finished reading, I asked Jonathan two little questions, "What was the best part about today?" and "What was the worst part about today?" The answers always told me what was important to him on any given day and what was on his mind. Just before I left the room, he recited the opening line from his favorite book by Bill Martin, "Brown Bear, Brown Bear, what do you see?" I gave the expected answer, "I see a red bird looking at me." We went back and forth reciting the book from memory. Then I kissed him good night and tucked him into bed.

Next, it was Trevor's turn to get ready for bed. He took his bath independently and when he had his pajamas on, he met me in his room where we read together. Then I asked him the same two questions I had asked Jonathan, "What was the best part about today," and "What was the worst part about today?" and learned the most about what was going on in his life outside the house. "The best part about today was playing soccer at lunchtime." "The worst part about today was when the teacher was yelling at the class." "The best part about today was when we read aloud and I did really well." "The worst part about today was when Tommy punched me in the stomach." A special time for me to talk alone with Trevor without interruption, it gave me an opportunity to learn what really mattered to him. As I tucked him into bed, he recited a line from his favorite book by Robert Munsch that he loved as a baby, "I love you forever. I like you for always." He waited for my response which was the next line in the book, "as long as I'm living my baby you'll be." I kissed him good night and tucked him in. When Tyler came along, this routine was thrown into chaos.

Initially, I decided to set time aside for Tyler between Trevor and Jonathan's reading times, but Tyler had other plans. From the minute he came to live with us, he disrupted any time I had alone with his brothers. I explained to him that I would read with him when I finished with Jonathan, but he had no intention of taking turns.

One night as I read to Jonathan, Tyler opened and slammed the door to the bedroom. I invited him to sit with us, but as soon as I started to read again he grabbed the book from my hands and ran away laughing. I went after him and took the book back as his laughter increased.

"Tyler, this is Jonathan's time to read with me," I said. "You can sit and listen or go find something to do in your room."

He went to his room and took a couple of books off his shelf. He returned to where I was reading with Jonathan and shouted, "Watch this!" I looked up to see him ripping pages out of the books. I jumped up and snatched the books away from him and sat back down next to Jonathan. Tyler came into the room, stood next to me and spit on the book.

Trevor appeared in the doorway with a look of concern in his eyes. "Are you okay, mom?" he asked. He liked to think of himself as the man of the house when his dad worked late.

"I'm okay," I said. "Can you start filling the tub for Tyler's bath? I need to get him engaged in another activity."

'Sure, mom," he said.

I picked Tyler up and brought him to the bathroom where I helped him get undressed. Jonathan appeared in the doorway. "Mom, what about reading?" he asked.

"We'll have to wait for an evening when Daddy is home to read again," I said.

His little shoulders drooped and he looked at the floor. From the hallway, I heard Trevor say, "C'mon Jon. I'll read to you."

The two boys went to Jonathan's room. I felt a horrible pang of guilt as I was forced to concentrate on Tyler. I understood he needed my time and attention, but it broke my heart to think I had to short change Jonathan and Trevor to meet Tyler's demands. From that night on, reading only happened when Roger was home. He occupied Tyler while I spent special time with Jonathan and Trevor. Bit by bit, Tyler was altering every aspect of our family life.

CHAPTER 13
SEPTEMBER 1993

Tyler resumed classes for the fall with the same teachers and support staff he had throughout the summer. The school used a "team" approach to its staffing which meant each student was assigned a special education teacher, two classroom aides, a psychologist, a speech therapist, an occupational therapist, a physical therapist and a social worker to assist the family. With the start of the new school year, the staff invited Roger and me to take parent training classes offered by the school for children who had particularly difficult behaviors, many of whom had diagnoses along the autism spectrum. While Tyler had not been diagnosed as autistic, he had many behaviors that are characteristic of autistic children and the teaching staff thought our family would benefit from the training. However, unlike many autistic children, Tyler sought attention, made eye contact and learned language quickly.

The parent training classes used Applied Behavioral Analysis (ABA), a program commonly used to teach children with autism. ABA teachers look closely at the behaviors of the child and then create an individual program to target a specific behavior for improvement. For example, Tyler had difficulty sitting in a chair at school. The staff wrote a program to reward him for sitting in a chair for thirty seconds. After he mastered that behavior, the staff wrote a new program to increase his ability to sit for longer periods of time. ABA works best if it is continued in the home as well as in school. Roger and I needed to learn how to support and use the ABA program.

The classes, held for two hours every Monday evening, were run by Kelly, a teacher with extensive experience in behavioral approaches to dealing with difficult children. Our coordinator was Celeste, Tyler's teacher. Kelly began the classes by teaching the parents that to understand behavior one must understand the motivation behind the behavior. In Tyler's case, we needed to understand why he found the consequences of negative behavior so rewarding. After the first lecture, Kelly and Celeste made an appointment to meet Roger and me in our home to choose target behaviors.

When Celeste and Kelly arrived at our house to observe Tyler, he smiled and talked with our guests as if he were the most cooperative and delightful child on the face of the earth. He didn't fool Celeste and Kelly. They had seen Tyler in action at school and had a pretty good idea of what we faced at home.

"First of all, we must put a stop to Tyler's negative attention-seeking behaviors," Kelly grinned at the challenge Tyler's behavior gave her. "It won't be easy because that behavior is deeply ingrained into his personality."

"I know," I said. "Yesterday, I taped him at the dinner table so that you could see what we're up against. At one point, he picked up his fork and started to eat along with the family. I praised and encouraged him. His reaction was to drop the fork like a hot potato and stop eating anything more."

Kelly smiled. "Here's what we're going to do," she said. "From now on, I want you to ignore all of Tyler's negative behavior."

"You're kidding, right?" I asked. "Do you realize that may mean I will be ignoring him most of the time? There are very few moments in a day when he behaves in a positive manner.

"We know," said Celeste. "The idea is he will only be able to get your attention when he does what he's supposed to do."

"So we're supposed to just completely ignore him when he acts up?" asked Roger.

"That's right," answered Kelly. "When he's engaging in negative behavior, you must ignore him and make sure you show no emotion. Don't frown or look angry because that could be rewarding for him. Just stay stone-faced and ignore him. Eventually he'll learn the only way to get your attention is to do the right thing. And it will get worse before it gets better."

"I can't imagine that it could get worse," I said.

"Oh, it will," said Kelly. "Imagine you have a lawn mower that won't start. You pull the cord to start it and the engine won't kick over. You keep pulling at it with more force hoping that working harder at it will make it start. That's what's going to happen with Tyler's behavior. He'll work harder and harder to get a reaction from you before he gives up his negative behavior. This is known as extinction burst."

"I can't believe things could get any worse," said Roger.

"They will, but with time they will get better," said Celeste. "Eventually he'll learn the methods he used to get attention since he was born no longer work."

"Okay, we'll give it our best shot," I said.

"It's not going to be easy," said Celeste. "You'll have to stick to the plan and stay tough. If he throws a tantrum, you must ignore it, no matter how hard he kicks and screams. You must not acknowledge that he is behaving inappropriately. We'll have to try to explain to Trevor and Jonathan why you aren't reacting to Tyler anymore. If they can also ignore Tyler's antics it would be very helpful."

"I'm sure we can get Trevor involved, but it may be difficult to explain it to Jonathan," said Roger. "He's only two-years old."

"Just do the best you can," said Kelly. "The less Tyler can draw the family into his act, the better it will be for everyone and don't forget we are in this with you. We're available to talk to at any time."

"Thank-you," I said, that's good to know."

Celeste and Kelly wished us luck and left the house. Roger and I looked at each other. "What do you think?" he asked.

"I don't know," I said. "Ignoring is the last thing I would have thought of as a behavior management technique. Tyler was left alone and ignored in the orphanage throughout his early years which created most of his troubles. He's a wounded little soul as a result of lack of attention. I've been trying to give him as much attention as I can, hoping love and attention will help him to heal."

"Yeah, me too," said Roger. "We didn't bring him here to ignore him."

"But Celeste and Kelly are far more knowledgeable about behavior management than you or me," I said. "What we've been doing so far hasn't been working. We really have to give this a try, don't we?"

"At this point, I'm willing to try anything," said Roger. "We have no family life left. We're always going in two different directions and splitting the family. We can't go on like this."

Roger and I agreed to put our best effort into the program. We didn't know it, but we were about to kick Tyler's negative behaviors into high gear.

The following afternoon, Roger met Tyler's bus at the end of our driveway. "How was your day?" he asked.

"Good," Tyler said.

As they walked up the driveway to the house, Roger took Tyler's back pack and looked through it. Celeste usually wrote a little note to tell us how the day had gone, because if we asked Tyler about school he had very little to say. The note gave us a starting point for conversation with him about his day. As soon as Roger unzipped the back pack, Tyler tried to pull it away from him.

"NO! NO!" Tyler shouted. "Gimme the bag!"

"I'm looking for a note from Celeste," Roger explained.

Tyler cried and wailed, "Gimme the bag! Gimme the bag!"

"When I'm finished," said Roger. "You can have the bag."

Tyler's protests grew louder, but Roger ignored him as he had been instructed and stopped talking to him. By the time they reached the door, Tyler was in the middle of a full blown tantrum and Roger carried him into the house. He put him down in the center hall and continued to look through the back pack as Tyler screamed.

"Celeste's note says he had an okay day," said Roger over the ongoing outburst.

"Somehow I don't think we're going to have anything near an okay evening," I answered as the shrieking grew louder.

Trevor came downstairs looking worried. "What's going on?" he asked.

"Well, remember how I told you we're going to ignore Tyler's bad behavior and only give him attention when he's doing the right thing?' I asked.

"Yeah, I remember," he said as he pushed his eyebrows down in an expression of concern.

"Tyler doesn't like being ignored and it's making him very angry," I said.

"Can I eat in my room?" Trevor asked. "I'm getting a headache." Trevor was having frequent headaches as Tyler's behaviors escalated.

"No, we need to try to eat at the table when Daddy's home," I said. "If he doesn't settle down, maybe you and Jonathan can eat in the den where at least I can see you."

"Okay," said Trevor.

I returned to cooking at the stove. Tyler moved into the kitchen and lay on the floor between me and the stove. He cried, kicked his feet and shouted, "I'm not eating. I'm not eating."

I climbed back and forth over him as if he were not there. Every muscle in my body tightened, my blood pressure rose and the stress floated around the kitchen like a deep fog I could not see through. This was not going to be easy.

Jonathan came downstairs and hesitated in the doorway of the kitchen. "What's he doing?" He asked, staring at Tyler's body writhing on the floor.

"C'mon buddy," Roger said. "Don't worry about him. Let's eat dinner." He helped Jonathan get seated at the table.

Trevor took his place at the table, but he looked stressed. His eyes had darkened and his headache was getting worse. We ate dinner while Tyler repeatedly kicked my chair as he continued to cry and scream. I ignored him, but this was a terrible situation for my family. Nothing was going to be gained by making everyone stay in the room while he went wild. We couldn't even talk to each other so I relented and asked Roger to take the boys upstairs with their dinners while I stayed with Tyler. I ignored his tantrum which continued as I finished my dinner and cleaned up the kitchen. Upstairs the boys finished eating and I heard Roger running a bath for Jonathan. I assumed Trevor had gone to his room to do his homework.

I felt overwhelmed. I looked at Tyler who had flung himself on the floor yet again still crying. What motivated this little boy? He lived to disrupt our activities and wanted us to be angry with him. I wondered how long it might take to turn him around and what the cost might be to my family. Would it be worth it?

I finished cleaning the kitchen and picked Tyler up. He didn't resist as I moved him upstairs and put him on his bed. He was exhausted and began to rock himself to sleep with the now familiar thrashing back and forth of his head. In a matter of minutes, he fell asleep. Everyone went to bed early that night. Our first attempt at ignoring Tyler had worn the whole family out.

Within a few weeks, we saw a decrease in the intensity and duration of Tyler's tantrums, but we also saw an increase in other behaviors meant to rile us up. He spent more time teasing his brothers in their rooms, broke their toys and got up close to them and made faces. He constantly made noises and slammed doors. It got so bad that Trevor barricaded the door to his room. I didn't like having him shut in his room, so Roger designed new doors for him and Jonathan. He created a sort of Dutch door that was sliced in half horizontally just above the door knobs. These new doors had locks on them, so the boys could keep Tyler out, but I could still see what they were doing in their rooms. While not the best solution, it would work for the time being. It was one more concession we made to live in a house dominated by Tyler.

Roger and I continued to attend the parent training meetings. Kelly assured us that if we just stuck with the program to ignore the negative, it would get better each week. Her lectures included lessons on different aspects of behavior modification.

"All behavior serves a purpose," she explained at our second class. "I've passed out worksheets and I'm asking every parent to make a list of things that are rewarding to your child. It can be a favorite food, favorite toy or favorite activity."

The other parents filled their sheets out quickly, but Roger and I struggled to think of things that might be rewarding for

Tyler. He had no favorite toy. He enjoyed watching the ceiling fan spin or engaging in some other self-stimulating activity more than playing with a toy. Eating didn't interest him and he had no favorite food.

"Maybe since Tyler has a history of sensory deprivation, he might enjoy a sensory activity," suggested Kelly.

"Lately, he has enjoyed being tickled," said Roger.

"Good," said Kelly. "When he performs a target behavior, he will be rewarded with 30 seconds of tickling. It's not going to get better overnight, but if you stick with it, things will improve."

Week after week, we dissected Tyler's behaviors and our reactions to them. Then we set up programs to change them. We would never have survived without the support of the preschool staff. Their professional input gave us the strength to continue. More importantly, it gave us hope that things would improve.

Getting Tyler to eat a meal at the table with the family continued to be a big problem. He only ate enough to stay alive. He told us his stomach hurt, but he never connected the pain in his stomach with the hunger he experienced. Celeste and Kelly advised us to try a new technique. The plan was simple. A timer was to be set for twenty minutes and put on the table at meal time. We were to place his meal on the table and tell him to sit down. He would sit alone, so the rest of the family didn't have to watch his antics. At the end of twenty minutes, we were to remove the food from the table without any comments. In other words, we were to provide the food, but we were not supposed to show any emotion or interest in whether he ate or not. There was to be no cajoling, bribing or arguing. He would simply eat or not.

The first time we tried the new plan, Tyler was obviously confused. I explained a timer would determine when his meal was over. He couldn't understand why I stopped showing any interest in whether he ate or not. He sat at the table and tried his best to rile me up.

"I'm not eating," he said.

I ignored this.

He said it louder. "I'm not eating!"

Again, I had no response.

He yelled. "I'M NOT EATING!"

I reminded him about the plan. "That's okay, Tyler. When the timer goes off, you can leave the table."

I watched him as he wondered how he would deal with this new plan. To Tyler, everything was a war and he was determined to win. He sat there for a few minutes while I cleaned the kitchen. He reminded me several times that he was not eating, but he received no reaction from me. After twenty minutes, the timer went off.

"I didn't eat!" He proclaimed proudly.

"Okay, Tyler," I said. "You can go."

He stood at the table for a few minutes twisting his lip between his forefinger and his thumb, wondering whether he had won or not. Then he slowly left the room.

The next morning, I explained to him what I expected again.

"I'm putting your breakfast on the table and setting the timer. You have twenty minutes to sit and eat."

"I'm not eating," he said.

As I loaded the dishwasher, he got up from his chair and stood by the table. "Look, I'm not sitting," he said.

I ignored him as he tested the limits of what I would allow. He moved away from the table. "Look, I'm not near the table."

I took a deep breath and ignored him again although it wasn't easy. I knew arguing with him or doing things to make him eat were not working, but I felt like I had given up all control. He moved into the den which adjoins the kitchen and jumped up and down singing, "I'm not eating, I'm not eating." I considered returning him to the table, but that just would have led to a power struggle that he would have enjoyed. Finally he left the room and went upstairs. After twenty minutes the alarm went off and I threw out his breakfast.

He went off to school without eating. I had a lot of trouble with this. Wasn't breakfast supposed to be the most important meal of the day? Wasn't it a parent's responsibility to see that their children were properly nourished? Meal times should be something families build memories around. The foods that families eat are deeply woven into our childhood memories. Hadn't I just let him slip a little further out of our family circle? What else would I have to let go? How would I keep Jonathan and Trevor on track amid this chaos? Would Tyler ever really be a part of our family?

That night, things got worse. Once again, I put Tyler's dinner on the table. He sat down for a minute. Then he lay across the table with his legs dangling in mid air.

"Look at me," he said laughing.

This was just a new game to him. He had no idea how he isolated himself. He got off the table and went to the back of the chair. He stood on the rungs of the chair bouncing up and down. I knew it would be wrong to recognize this behavior so I left the room. I went into the den to help Trevor with his homework.

"Mom," Trevor whispered. "Shouldn't you stop him?"

"Not right now," I said softly. "His mealtime will be over soon."

I had explained the program to Trevor, but it was hard for a child to comprehend why his mom was not able to control his brother. I was the adult and he didn't understand why I wasn't taking charge of the situation. After twenty minutes, I removed the plate and Tyler left the room without eating. Day after day, I provided food for him and he refused to eat it. I knew he was eating a little at school, but it didn't seem like enough to sustain him. I worried constantly.

CHAPTER 14
SPRING 1993

Tyler had been attending the special-ed preschool for about six months when another parent told me about a child psychologist in the area. Dr. Finch had a good reputation with the school staff as well as the parents. I made an appointment for Tyler.

Dr. Finch reminded me of a kindly old grandfather with his soft eyes, grey hair and wire-rimmed glasses. His treatment focused on play. His office, located in a nearby medical complex, had a desk, a file cabinet, two arm chairs and endless shelves of toys. Every week the doctor played on the floor with four year-old Tyler, attempting to teach him to express his feelings. Although Tyler was learning language quickly, he still did not understand emotions or comprehend that a smile meant a person was happy or that a scowl meant a person was angry.

After a few months of treatment, Dr. Finch asked Roger and me to meet with him.

"Tyler is a very interesting child and I think both of you are doing a great job with him," said Dr Finch. "However, I do have some concerns. Do you know what Reactive Attachment Disorder or RAD is?"

My heart beat faster. Some of the staff at the preschool had suggested Tyler might have an attachment disorder, so I had visited the library and read many articles about the large numbers of adopted children from the former Soviet Union and Eastern European countries who suffered from attachment disorders.

"I do," I said. "It develops when an infant does not receive an opportunity to bond with a caregiver."

"That's right. The absence of consistent care at an early age is usually the cause," said Dr. Finch. "You see, the bond between parents and children is very important to human development. Your other children developed in a loving family and are learning to value what the family values. They naturally want to please you and behave in a way valued by the family. In Tyler's case, it's impossible to know what types of caregivers were there during his early years, but his self-stimulating behaviors are a strong indication that he was probably ignored and left alone for most of his early years."

"Tyler doesn't care whether he pleases us or not," said Roger. "He shows no remorse when we are displeased with his behavior. He just does whatever he wants to without any regard for the consequences. It's like he doesn't have a conscience."

"That's classic behavior for an unattached child," said Dr. Finch.

"He also doesn't seem to distinguish between what he feels for us and what he feels for strangers," I said. "He'll see someone at the mall, talk to them for a few minutes and then declare he loves them."

"Again," said Dr. Finch. "That's typical. As an infant, he never bonded with anyone and never had anyone he could count on. As a result, he has no reason to trust people or to allow them to get close to him."

I looked at Roger. He already looked tired and still faced a twelve hour shift at work later that night. "This is serious, isn't it?" I asked, turning back to Dr, Finch. "I mean, I've heard that family members of a child with attachment disorder face rage and aggression as they try to get close to the child. Many RAD children never bond with anyone."

"That's true," said Dr. Finch. "These children resist getting close to anyone and will particularly resist the efforts of the mother or primary caregiver. It's hard to know what the future will hold for Tyler because he fights any attempts you make to bond with him."

"So what do we do?" asked Roger with a deep sigh.

"In America, we do not see such dramatic cases of neglect as we've seen coming from these countries," said the doctor. "No one is sure how much brain damage such extreme neglect can cause. When the brain of an infant is not properly stimulated through use of the senses, parts of it, die off. All I can recommend is that you continue to do what you have been doing. Provide a loving and consistent environment for Tyler and hope he will bond with your family in time. I wish I could offer you more hope."

Roger and I left the office feeling defeated. We wanted to do whatever was necessary for Tyler to succeed, but now we were being told that no matter what we did, it might not be enough and there was no way of knowing what the toll might be on our other two children.

"Now what?" I asked Roger as we left the building.

"He's still our son and we have to do what we can to make him accept us," he said.

"And what if he never does?" I asked. "You're not with him as many hours as I am. He's relentless in his desire for negative attention. Are we going to give up everything, including the childhoods of Trevor and Jonathan in the hope that maybe someday he will care about us?"

"I don't have an answer," he said. "We can't just turn our backs on him. We have to give it more time."

Jonathan was now three, and attending preschool. I noticed that his left eye wandered a little, so I scheduled an early morning appointment with a pediatric eye doctor. Roger had worked the night before and needed to sleep before going out again that night so I had to take Tyler with us. Everything was fine until the doctor put Jonathan into a big chair to examine his eyes. He asked Jon to look at a series of arrows and move his hand up or down, right or left, imitating the direction of the arrows. Seeing Jonathan getting so much attention, Tyler diverted the attention to himself by touching the equipment in the room. I told him to stop.

"I can't see," he said.

"What did you say?" I asked trying not to laugh.

"I can't see," he repeated. He held his hands out in front of him as a visually impaired person might do.

"Oh, Tyler," I said. "You don't have a problem with your eyes. You've had several eye exams since you started

106

preschool."

"I need glasses," he said.

"No you don't," said Jonathan. "We're here to get *my* eyes checked!"

Jonathan was a model patient and I ignored Tyler's sudden transformation into Helen Keller. The doctor determined that Jonathan did need glasses and escorted us to the front of the building to the eyeglass showroom where Jonathan tried on several pairs.

"How do these look?" asked Jonathan.

"I need glasses," whined Tyler.

"No, Tyler, your eyes are fine," I said.

"But look," he said as he got up and walked into a wall. "I can't see."

I stifled a giggle and decided to ignore his behavior rather than feed into it, but by the time we chose a pair of glasses for Jonathan, the drama of Tyler's vision problems had escalated to complete blindness.

"Mom, can you help me?" he asked. "I can't see."

At home, Tyler's complaints about poor vision continued. He went to school, but had trouble finding the bus at the end of the driveway. I called the school and warned them not to get caught up in his desire to get glasses.

A few days later, Jonathan's glasses came in and the drama began all over again. Tyler was so jealous he couldn't think about anything else. As time went on, the family learned never to discuss any illnesses or impediments with Tyler because he was sure to develop the symptoms.

CHAPTER 15
SUMMER 1994

Tyler was making improvements in many areas. As he learned more language, communicating with him got easier, although he remained oppositional and defiant. His problems with sensory integration were abating and he processed the world around him more naturally. He still craved light and noises, but far less intensely than he had before he came to the preschool. He had difficulty with fine motor skills and was unable to copy shapes and letters, but he could visually identify them. His play skills had improved and he was learning how to play with toys, although he had little interest in the other children in his class. The staff at the preschool had helped Tyler make great strides towards improving his educational deficits, but he was turning five in October and aging out of the preschool.

I visited special education elementary schools with Tyler and Celeste looking for an appropriate kindergarten placement for him. The staff at the preschool proposed that he be placed in a class of twelve students instead of six as in his last placement. The recommendations called for him to have one classroom aide instead of two, based on testing. I worried because throughout his time as a preschool student, one staff member always gave individual attention to Tyler to keep him focused and on task. His need for negative attention remained constant and I didn't know how he would adapt to having fewer adults in the room.

In September 1994, Tyler began kindergarten classes with eleven other children. His teacher, Mrs. Grogan, a woman in her fifties, with many years of teaching experience, was a tall, stern looking woman with heavily sprayed shoulder length hair that flipped up neatly at the shoulders. She always wore a dress and high heels even though most teachers had long ago adopted more casual attire, especially in special education environments. Her classroom, the picture of order, was decorated with learning aides and motivational posters for her students. I met Mrs. Grogan at "Back to School Night" during the first week of school. When I saw her standing in the classroom of organization and neatness, I wanted to jump up and tell her some mistake had been made and my son would never last in this classroom. The teacher's aide, Mrs. Simpson, also in her fifties, had worked in the classroom with Mrs. Grogan for a number of years. She was shorter than Mrs. Grogan, but in every other way she was a duplicate of the teacher.

Tyler set out for his first day in his new school with all the usual trappings of a child entering kindergarten. He wore sneakers with lights that blinked when his feet met the ground, a red tee shirt with a fire engine on it, new jeans with a belt to hold them up on his slim frame and a fresh mushroom haircut. Inside his Power Rangers backpack, he had his lunch, pencils and a notebook. He jumped on the bus without looking back.

The first signs of trouble appeared that afternoon in his backpack. A little note from Mrs. Grogan said, "Tyler had a good day, although he needs to work on staying seated at his desk." The next day I received another note. "Tyler appears to be a friendly child, but he needs to work on not speaking out when I am talking." On the third day the note said, "Tyler seems eager to learn, but he has difficulty staying on task." And so it went until the end of the month when the note said, "Tyler is very disruptive and may not belong in this classroom. Please call me to make an appointment to discuss his behavior at your earliest convenience."

Two days later, Roger and I met with Mrs. Grogan and the school psychologist, Dr. Sherman who sat together on one side of the desk in cushioned rolling office chairs while we sat on two stiff wooden chairs facing the desk. The battle lines had been drawn.

"Has Tyler ever been evaluated by a neurologist?" asked Mrs. Grogan, getting right to the point.

"Yes," said Roger. "He's been seen by two different neurologists. Both times we were told that his behaviors are probably a result of his time in the orphanage and that he should improve with time."

"ADHD was never mentioned?" asked Dr. Sherman, not even trying to soft peddle the question. He was about thirty-five years old with jet black hair slicked straight back and he wore a starched blue oxford shirt and khakis.

"Well, yes," I said. "I asked both neurologists if they thought Tyler might have ADHD because he's more of a handful than my other two sons put together, but in both cases, the physicians were reluctant to diagnose him as a child with ADHD. They felt he was too young to be labeled."

"I guess I'm not surprised," said Dr. Sherman with an air of arrogance. "Few physicians will prescribe medications for a child under the age of five. I've observed Tyler in the classroom and both Mrs. Grogan and I feel he would benefit from medication. He should be reevaluated now that he is five years old." Dr. Sherman looked at Mrs. Grogan whose hair was sprayed so heavily that it never moved as she nodded her head vigorously.

"We would like you to see Dr. Kinney, a psychologist who has worked with many of our students. We'll put a report together about what we've seen in the classroom and you can take it with you when you see him," he said looking bored with the conversation.

"You two seemed to have already diagnosed him," Roger said. He stiffened his back and sat up straight in the wooden chair. "We're not opposed to having him take medication if it will help him to succeed because we know how difficult it is for him to get through the day at school and at home, but you've only known him a month and you're ready to medicate him. Have you tried any behavior management techniques?"

"That won't help," said Mrs. Grogan dismissively. "Tyler can't pay attention long enough to follow a behavior management program."

"Maybe you just don't have the patience or staff to meet his needs," I said.

"Staffing is not the problem," said Dr. Sherman. "Tyler needs help. You really need to take our recommendation to see Dr. Kinney"

I wondered why I felt so defensive. Roger and I both realized medication might be necessary for Tyler to succeed. It was just irritating to listen to these two people who had known him for a month, inferring we should be doing more.

"Okay," said Roger. "We'll make an appointment with your psychologist."

He took the information from Dr. Sherman, pushed his chair back and stood up. "I just hope you aren't expecting that medication will magically make Tyler a delightful child. C'mon Patty, let's go."

I got up and followed him out of the room. Medication or not, it was obvious Tyler was not going to do well in the classroom of this rigid woman. As we pulled away from the school, I imagined her on the phone calling the neurologist and telling him about the unusually difficult boy she was sending to him. When we got home, I made the appointment with Dr. Kinney.

This time, after collecting the usual background information, Doctor Kinney, a short, gray haired, middle aged man, talked specifically about Tyler's behavior.

"I've examined Tyler and read the reports the school sent outlining his delays, but now I'd like you to tell me about him," he said.

"Whew, I don't know where to begin," said Roger.

"Tell me about a typical day with him," Dr. Kinney suggested.

"He is oppositional from the minute I wake him up," I said. "He resists getting dressed and usually won't eat breakfast. He fights Roger and me on everything we ask him to do. If we catch him behaving appropriately and praise him, he immediately stops the activity for which he is being praised."

"What toys does he like to play with?" asked Dr. Kinney.

"His preschool has tried to teach him to play with toys

appropriately," said Roger, but he still enjoys spinning the wheels on cars or lining them up in patterns rather than pushing them around on the ground."

"What does he do when he doesn't have a toy to entertain him," asked the doctor.

"He engages in self-stimulating behaviors such as rocking, flapping his hands and running his eyes along walls or fences," I said. "We've been told he was probably isolated in a crib during the first few years of his life."

"That might be true," said Dr. Kinney. "He came from Ukraine, right? How is he doing with language?"

"He's learning language quickly and always makes direct eye contact when he speaks," I explained.

"Tell me about his social skills," Dr. Kinney said.

"He definitely needs work there," said Roger. "He doesn't understand basic emotions, like what makes a person happy or sad. Throughout the day, he focuses on getting the attention of all the adults that are near him, often getting that attention by doing things he shouldn't. He frequently tantrums and can get aggressive, endangering himself and my other two children. I worry about them constantly."

"Is there anything else that troubles you about his behavior?" asked Dr. Kinney.

"I'm frustrated by his eating and sleeping habits. He never seems hungry and he only sleeps about five hours a night," I said. He's frightfully thin and I often wonder if he might not be better behaved if he got more sleep."

"I see," said Dr. Kinney.   "Well, first of all, it seems apparent that Tyler has ADHD. I'm going to give you a prescription for Cylert, a medication similar to Ritalin. Initially, he should take it once a day and the effects should last for about four hours. I recommend giving it to him just before he goes off to school. I don't want you to tell his teacher when you give him the medication, because I want to see if she notices any changes without looking for them."

"Okay," said Roger. "But what about the hours that he's at home?"

"Well, if he does well on this initial dose, we may give him a second dose to use at another time during the day," said Dr. Kinney. "However I think ADHD is not his only problem. I think he has Pervasive Developmental Disorder or PDD-NOS."

"Oh, no," I said, knowing what that meant. Some of the students in Tyler's preschool had been diagnosed with the disorder.

"What's PDD?" asked Roger.

"PDD is an Autism Spectrum Disorder diagnosis given to children with developmental and social issues that are not classic autism," said the doctor.

Roger reached over and put his arm around me as I began to cry. It all seemed so hopeless. First, he was diagnosed with an attachment disorder which meant he might not ever be able to have a normal relationship with the family. I was ready to hear he had ADHD but now---a form of autism. It was all too much.

"But Tyler is very outgoing and constantly tries to engage

people," said Roger.

"That's what makes him different from other autistic children and why I'm diagnosing him as PDD-NOS. I'm sorry," said Dr. Kinney.

"It's okay," I said through tears. "I should have known when the preschool put us into parent training with the parents of autistic children."

"You're overwhelmed now," said the doctor. "You should go home and digest this. I'd like to see Tyler again in a month. I don't think you should give up on him. He has a very endearing personality and he's pretty bright. It's too soon to say how he will do with proper management. I'm glad to hear you've had parent training. It will help. Please feel free to call me with any concerns you might have."

When Roger and I got to the car, I sobbed openly. I just couldn't hold it in anymore. Roger didn't know what to say to me, so he just held me until my tears ran out.

Finally he said, "We don't know how far Tyler can go. Look how much he has learned in such a short time."

"I know, but what if he isn't capable of caring about us? What if he spends his whole life just trying to get us angry?"

"We can't look at the negative possibilities. We need to continue to see him as a child with possibilities, so he will become all he can."

"I know, but what about Trevor and Jonathan? Are they destined to be shortchanged throughout their childhoods?"

Roger didn't answer me. He couldn't. He started the car and headed home. The diagnosis of PDD-NOS seemed to override the diagnosis of RAD and became one of the diagnoses that would appear on Tyler's school records as we sought services in the future, although for me, as a mom, Tyler 's behavior often seemed more characteristic of RAD than PDD-NOS.

On Monday, I gave Tyler the medication just before the bus arrived at 8:00 a.m. By 10:00 a.m., Mrs. Grogan was calling the house.

"Mrs. Havlicek, Tyler is having a particularly difficult day," she said. "He's twitching all over the place. He can't seem to sit still. He's acting like he wants to crawl out of his skin. Did you give him something today?"

"He started on Cylert today," I said. "It's an ADHD medication."

"I thought so," she said in a smug tone. "You'd better come and pick him up because he can't stay here like this. His tongue is flailing around in his mouth, he looks itchy and his whole body appears to be in a spasm."

"I'll be right there," I told her, disappointed to hear he was having such a hard time. When I picked him up, I couldn't believe the effect the medication was having on him. His body was totally agitated. He fidgeted and couldn't stop moving. His little tongue darted in and out of his mouth. His limbs twitched and he looked very uncomfortable. I couldn't help but feel guilty for giving him the medication that had sent his nervous system into such distress. I took him home and let him rest until the medication wore off while I called the neurologist who said some children have an adverse reaction to ADHD medication. The medication was discontinued immediately. It was one more disappointment. I had hoped Tyler might receive some help at school by being medicated.

Mrs. Grogan continued to send her daily notes with increased exasperation as Tyler interfered with her plans for the perfect classroom. Even after seeing Tyler suffer a negative reaction to medication, she wasn't willing to cut him any slack.

"Tyler has been annoying the other students and instigating trouble."

"Tyler broke out of line today and ran away and refused to come back."

"Tyler keeps turning off the lights when I'm talking."

"Tyler got angry today and tore down the material on the bulletin board."

His frustration at his inability to succeed was growing. He pinched and hit other students. When I tried to discuss his school problems with him, he crossed his eyes and refused to look at me. By Christmas, the staff at school said it was time to find another school for him. Five-year old Tyler was being kicked out of his special-ed kindergarten.

CHAPTER 16
FALL 1994

One evening I took the boys to a fast food restaurant because Roger had to work. As always, Tyler refused to eat and was instead, racing around the play area. Suddenly, he walked to the restrooms. He studied the symbols of the man and the woman on the two doors, stepping closer to the door with the symbol for the men's room. He looked down comparing his own little body with the symbol, clearly unsure what to do. He moved over to the ladies' room door and considered that symbol. Again, he looked at himself and the door, but still, didn't know which picture looked like him. Without saying a word, Jonathan jumped up from the table, grabbed Tyler's hand and led him to the men's room door.

"It's this one!" he exclaimed turning to me with all of the indignation he could muster. "Do you believe this?" he asked. I had to laugh at Jonathan's confidence.

Four-year old Jonathan recognized the symbol for the men's room, but six-year old Tyler had difficulty understanding he was a male. Often, when Tyler saw little girls, he asked me to put ribbons or barrettes in his hair. In stores, he was drawn to girls' clothing and requested things like Little Mermaid shoes. Of course, Trevor and Jonathan were mortified every time Tyler crossed the aisle to the girls' department in search of pink and purple apparel.

"You're a boy. You can't wear girls' clothing," Trevor would tell him.

But for a boy who is still trying to understand the emotions that go along with the changes in a person's facial expression, understanding that society assigned different colors and styles to different genders was a concept that was out of reach. Peer pressure from his brothers didn't influence him because he didn't care whether they approved of him or not.

Roger was often at work by the time the kids got home from school, so I was the chauffeur for after school activities. When Trevor was nine, ice hockey became his passion and he skated several times a week. Each skating session was a four hour commitment, allowing time to travel to the rink, getting equipment on and off, and time on the ice. On the nights Roger worked, I packed all three boys into the van and off we went. Tyler didn't mind the ride in the car, but he couldn't sit still once we arrived. I brought etch-a-sketch, coloring books, matchbox cars and LEGOS for Jonathan and him to play with, but he wasn't able to do most of those activities because he lacked fine motor skills. From the minute we arrived at the rink, he was on the move. We watched the practice from the concrete stands running above the rink and over the locker rooms. He climbed the handrails, jumped off the steps and ran from one end of the stands to the other. He banged into people, smiled adorably at them and kept going. To an outsider, he probably looked like a typical, active little boy. I saw something very different.

Watching Tyler run back and forth, I cringed as he climbed on the railings of the stairs and often lost his footing. I constantly told him to slow down and stop climbing, but he just had to keep moving. To anyone watching, I probably sounded like an overly protective, nagging mother who wouldn't let her little boy play.

One evening, Jonathan and I were acting out a fun little

game that he loved. He sat next to me and pretended to be watching the game.

"Hey Jonathan," I whispered. "Wanna know a secret?"

"Yeah," he said as he put his ear close to my face with a giant smile.

"Don't tell anyone," I whispered. "Your mamma loves you SOOOO MUCH!"

He laughed and stood up on the bleachers next to me, lifting his head and throwing his arms out to his sides. "Hey everybody," he said loudly. "Guess what!"

Before he could say anything else, I pulled him down, tickled him and whispered, "It's supposed to be a secret." He laughed until he couldn't breathe. Then he sat next to me, waiting for me to ask again, "Hey Jonathan, wanna know a secret?"

From the corner of my eye, I watched as Tyler climbed on the railings on the steps of the bleachers. Suddenly, he slipped and slammed his chin on the metal rail with a loud chinging noise. Blood dripped from his chin, but he didn't react.

"Tyler, you're bleeding," I said. He looked down at his shirt and smiled.

"Can we go to the hospital?" he asked eagerly.

Tyler had enjoyed all the attention he had received when he went for his first set of stitches and was excited at the prospect of going back to the hospital.

"Let's go down to the first aid station and clean the cut," I said. "Then we'll decide if we need to go to the hospital. C'mon Jonathan, we have to go downstairs."

In the First-Aid station, I saw the wound more clearly. He definitely needed stitches. I left Tyler in the care of a rink worker and went back upstairs with Jonathan to gather up the toys. I tried to catch Trevor's eye, but he was too engrossed in skating to look up. Another mom volunteered to bring Trevor to her house after the practice. He could sleep there if we got home too late.

By the time we arrived at the hospital, the bleeding had just about stopped and Tyler was beyond excited. "This is great!" he exclaimed as we got out of the car.

Jonathan had fallen asleep. I carried him into the emergency room and settled him on a couch. We waited for two hours while Tyler ran around showing his wound to anyone who would look. We finally saw the doctor who stitched the wound while Tyler giggled with delight. It is hard enough to watch a child receive stitches under normal circumstances, but as I watched Tyler, my head was spinning with questions. Why didn't he react to pain? Why was he so pleasant with the doctor and other strangers when he was so difficult at home? Trevor and Jonathan would have been scared to have an injury that required stitches. Why wasn't Tyler? It was the second time he had received stitches in his head since he had come to live with us. How was I going to protect him from another injury and would it be more serious the next time? By the time we got home, it was after 11:00 p.m. and I was drained.

A few days later, I went to Tyler's bedroom to wake him up for school and noticed blood on his chin. He had pulled the stitches out. I can't say I was surprised. The stitches were just another annoyance to his already irritated body. Watching him every day was like watching someone whose skin did not fit well on his body. He seemed to always be fidgeting to adjust the fit. He wiggled, squirmed and twitched constantly. I called the doctor's office, but the wound was already partially closed and he didn't need a new set of stitches.

CHAPTER 17
WINTER 1994

During the winter months, I looked for ways to burn off Tyler's excess energy. In January, I took Tyler and Jonathan to an indoor playground in Port Jefferson where children played on slides, ran on the basketball court, jumped in the ball pit and played in the sandy beach room. It was a great place for kids. We met up with Colleen and her son Avery, a boy who had attended preschool with Tyler.

"How are things going with Tyler?" Colleen asked.

"We're still having a rough time," I said. "It seems that as we conquer one behavior, he comes up with something even more outrageous."

"Has the neurologist given him any medication since his diagnosis of PDD?" she asked.

"He tried cylert, but that was disastrous. Now he's taking risperdal, but nothing slows him down."

"How many neurologists has he seen now?"

"He's been to three. It's very frustrating because it's not as if you can just put up an x-ray of his brain and definitively make a diagnosis. It's a lot of conjecture."

"I recently heard about a neurologist at Children's Hospital who has helped some of the other families from the preschool," said Colleen. "She's supposed to be very good. Do you want her name and number?"

"Sure, why not?" I said. I wasn't too hopeful, but I took

the number and made an appointment for January 25.

Dr. Eva Ramon, the head of pediatric neurology at Children's Hospital sent me a five page questionnaire so she could familiarize herself with the case before the appointment. I answered every question thoroughly and added six type-written pages of information about life with Tyler. I described his noises, echolalia, ADHD, twitching, self-stimulating behaviors, negative attention-seeking, impulsivity and his failure to react to pain. I explained how he got stuck on an idea or an object and was unable to move on. I included a videotape of him in action and told her he had been diagnosed with PDD-NOS. I wanted to paint as clear a picture of Tyler as I could.

At the hospital, a nurse escorted us to an examining room where Tyler hopped up onto the table with a big smile. The doctor came in and introduced herself.

"I'm Dr. Eva Ramon," she said extending her hand to me. "I read all of the material that you sent me. It was very helpful. Does he often chew on his lip like that?"

"Yes," I said. "He always has his fingers in his mouth and likes to twist his lips and face into strange shapes."

"Has anyone ever told you he has Tourette Syndrome?"

"No," I said feeling lightheaded. "Are you sure?"

"Oh, yes. In the material you sent to me, you described a classic case of Tourette Syndrome. Tyler does have problems that are a result of early childhood neglect and I agree with the diagnosis of PDD, but he also has Tourette Syndome."

"I can't believe it has taken this long for anyone to see

this," I said, staring at Tyler. The only thing I knew about Tourette Syndrome was that it caused tics and vocal outbursts. I tried to match that knowledge with Tyler's behavior.

Dr. Ramon explained, "The lip biting is a tic, an involuntary movement that can take on many forms from facial grimaces to gross limb movements. The car noises he makes are a form of vocal tic which can include grunting, coughing or saying a particular word over and over. Another symptom of TS is Obsessive Compulsive Disorder and you said sometimes he gets an idea in his head and can't think of anything else. ADHD is also characteristic of TS as well as sensory integration problems and learning difficulties."

"This is a lot to take in," I said. "How does one treat Tourette Syndrome?"

"There is no cure for TS, but medication can lessen the intensity of the symptoms. You sent me a video of Tyler at the dinner table that was very helpful. I counted over thirty-seven tics in that video. He shrugs his shoulders, blinks his eyes, bites and twists his lips, kicks his legs and bends his torso."

"Tyler has taken medication for ADHD and it was disastrous."

"TS patients often have adverse reactions to ADHD medications which exacerbate the tics. There are other medications that may help to reduce the tics, but he will have to learn to live with his TS symptoms. A tic can be ignored for a while, but it is like an itch that must eventually be scratched. I'm going to refer you to a psychiatrist who has extensive experience with TS patients."

"Thanks," I said suddenly finding it difficult to breathe.

As Tyler and I headed out to the parking lot, I couldn't help but stare at him and wonder if we had been fair to him. Was his behavior more out of his control than we had thought? Would this new diagnosis help my family to regain its stability? We saw the recommended psychiatrist as soon as we possibly could and Tyler was put on medication. We did see some minor improvements in his focus, but not enough to make him a manageable little boy.

CHAPTER 18
SPRING 1995

Our school district found a new school which had other students with TS and offered a support group for parents. The new school used a behavioral plan that allowed Tyler to earn points for good behavior which he could trade in for merchandise at the school store. The classroom was smaller with only eight students instead of twelve. However, this school was about fifteen miles from our house and Tyler spent over an hour on the bus each way.

The bus trips were too long for Tyler and he had trouble sitting still. He acted up on the bus, refusing to sit and making loud noises. An aide was assigned to travel with him to ensure his safety, but she became a target for his behavior. He spit at her, pinched her and hit her. When I tried to explain to him it was dangerous to jump around on the bus, he crossed his eyes and laughed at me.

At the new school, Tyler did what he always did in a new setting. He presented himself as a model of good behavior. I was frustrated because it was apparent he knew how to behave and could do it for a while. However, after a few weeks, the honeymoon ended and Tyler challenged his teachers with disruption and defiance. He cried, had tantrums and refused to work. As always, he enjoyed the extra time an adult had to spend with him when he misbehaved, but Tyler's negative behavior could not always be ignored because safety was a concern.

The psychologist at the school tried to help Tyler deal with his TS symptoms. He was given time to relieve his tics and express his feelings about his disability. Unfortunately, he used his TS as an excuse for his behavior. One day he returned home from school with a particularly angry attitude.

"How was school, Tyler? I asked.

"I don't know," he said.

"Do you have homework?"

"Yeah, but I can't do it. I have tics."

"I know you have tics, but that doesn't mean you can't do your homework."

"Yes it does. I can't pay attention or concentrate!" he said, getting louder.

"I know it's hard for you, but you still must try."

"I can't! I can't!" he shouted. He ran upstairs and slammed the door to his room.

From then on, every time life got difficult, he told me he had tics and couldn't do the right thing. While I understood that his tics were a constant source of distraction, they were not an excuse for his angry and often deliberate behaviors.

The long bus trip meant Tyler was out of the house longer which I must say was a good thing for the family. He was the first of the boys to leave in the morning and the last to come home in the afternoon. It gave Roger and me time to get Trevor and Jonathan dressed in the mornings without Tyler. In the afternoons we could talk with the boys about their days before

Tyler burst in the door and disrupted everything.

Tyler arrived home daily at about 4:30 p.m. frustrated after the long ride. He became more antagonistic and unruly with each passing day coming in the door and announcing he was not going to do his homework or eat. I became less reactive to his behavior. He was difficult at school, difficult on the bus and difficult at home. I was just another of the caretakers that crossed his path during the day. I never really felt he regarded me as his mother or anyone special. In fact, I must admit as time as went on, hearing Tyler call me "Mom" made me cringe. I know that doesn't make me sound like a very nice person, but I couldn't help resenting the title when it came to him. He never let me be his mother and pushed me away at every chance. If only he could smile at me when I came into the room, instead of plotting to control me, I might have felt differently. I constantly fought an inner struggle to suppress my growing feelings of resentment for Tyler while remembering he was just a little boy who didn't know how to connect with others. I needed to remember that he had never asked to join our family.

At about this time, Tyler began to torment our two-year old English Springer Spaniel, Tootsie. He delighted in teasing or pinching her and then dashing away as she tried to snap at him. The more I told him to leave the dog alone, the more he harassed her. He pulled and stretched her ears, and yelled, "Look, mom," as she yelped in pain. He was especially tickled when she nipped at him or caught a piece of his clothing. Tootsie was just an animal. I couldn't say to her, "Look, Tootsie, this boy had a difficult beginning in life, can't you just ignore him?" Tootsie weighed more than Tyler and was capable of severely hurting him. It was only a matter of time before the instinct to protect herself took over. I worked hard to keep them apart, leaving Tootsie outside more.

Tyler was potty trained when he came home from Ukraine and just before bed, I made sure he went to the bathroom. One night I sent him to the bathroom and when he came out he said, "I don't have to go tonight."

"Are you sure?" I asked. "Did you try?"

"Yeah, I tried," he said. "I don't have to go."

"Okay, let's get into bed," I said. I led him to his bedroom and pulled his blankets back as he climbed into bed with a smile. When I reached to pull the blankets up over him, he suddenly pulled down his pants and urinated into the air. I jumped back to avoid the spray, shocked by what he had done. He looked at my face, realized I was stunned, and laughed deviously. He had succeeded in startling me and was triumphant.

"Tyler! What did you do?" I yelled.

He laughed so hard he couldn't answer. I got angrier with each passing second. For the first time, I wanted to hurt him. I wanted to pull him out of the bed and make him fear me. I took a deep breath and stepped out of the room. I went into the bathroom and locked the door. I sat on the floor thinking about how much I had to lose if I ever lost control with Tyler. I breathed deeply trying to calm myself before returning to Tyler's bedroom.

Tyler was still laughing when I handed him a dry pair of pajamas. I changed his sheets without saying a word to him as my hands trembled. I was dumbfounded. There was nothing I could say that would matter to him. I purchased rubber sheets for the bed the next day.

The next night, Roger was home and I suggested he get Tyler ready for bed. I was curious to see if he would do the same thing with Roger. He did not. It seemed that as time went on, I was the bull's eye for Tyler's outrageous behaviors. The next time I had to put him to bed, Roger was working and once again, Tyler chose to urinate in his bed rather than in the bathroom. Not wanting to play his game, I gave him dry pajamas but did not change the sheets. I told him to sleep on the floor. I wanted to love Tyler, but he made it harder each day since he made me the principal adversary in a battle neither of us could win.

CHAPTER 19
SUMMER 1995

Roger's mother, Lois, lived alone in the large house where she had raised her five children. She was in her seventies, had some heart problems and suffered with stiffening joints. The family worried about her rumbling around in the big house alone, but she stubbornly resisted any move that might in any way limit her independence or move her away from her church and lifelong friendships. Roger often stopped at her house on his way to work to check on her, doing household repairs and maintenance while visiting with her. Inevitably, the conversation turned to the family's struggle with Tyler. Lois refused to believe there was anything wrong with him that could not be resolved with love and prayer. Roger told her how difficult Tyler made it for us to have anything even closely resembling a normal family life. She recommended we hug him more.

One evening Roger stopped at Lois's house to repair her dishwasher and found himself in a recurring conversation.

"You just aren't giving him enough time," Lois told Roger as she sank into a living room chair off the kitchen taking the weight off her swollen ankle. "You're expecting too much from him."

"You don't understand," argued Roger from the kitchen floor in front of the dishwasher. "His behavior is all consuming and there's no time for Jonathan and Trevor. It isn't fair to them. Nothing we try with Tyler, despite our parent training, has any effect on him.

"You can't compare him to Trevor and Jonathan. His needs are much greater because of his early years. He just needs to be loved."

"I wish it was as simple as that. He has neurological problems and no matter how much we love him those problems will never go away. A recent study of the children adopted from Romanian orphanages found that those children had significantly smaller brains than normally developing American children. Without stimulation during the infant years, the brain of a child shrinks and parts of it called synapses die off never to be recovered. Simply loving Tyler will not change that."

"You're just feeling overwhelmed," she said, dismissing Roger's frustrations. She struggled to lift her bulky body from the chair and limped into the kitchen. "Would you like a glass of iced tea?"

"No, thanks. We *are* overwhelmed. We're not equipped to meet his needs and his behavior is often dangerous for him and his brothers. He simply doesn't listen to us. There's no desire on his part to please us because he has never bonded or attached to us. Patty and I have begun to discuss the possibility we may have to have him placed outside the home."

"I'll tell you what," Lois said as if she had not heard a word Roger was saying. "Bring him here for the weekend and you and Patty can have a break."

"You can't be serious," said Roger. "You won't be able to handle him."

"Oh, don't be silly," she said. "He's just a little boy. Remember I raised five children. He'll be just fine with me."

She had had this conversation with Roger many times before and she always denied our pain. She was saying that if only we were more patient and loving, everything would work out. We were pretty sure we were not the problem. On this day, Roger felt tired enough to let her find out for herself what it meant to spend a weekend with Tyler.

"Okay," he said. "You can have him for the weekend. We could use a break. I'll drop him off on my way to work on Friday as long as you promise to call us if he proves to be too much to handle."

"Oh, you worry too much," she said. "He'll be fine with me."

So that Friday, I packed a little bag of clothes for Tyler. Roger dropped him off at about 3:00 p.m. and we began a much needed weekend of peace with Trevor and Jonathan. Over the weekend, we called Lois several times to make sure she was doing okay with him. She repeatedly told us he was no problem and that she enjoyed his company. Roger picked Tyler up on Monday morning on his way home from work. Lois assured him that Tyler had been a delight and a pleasure to have at her house. My heart broke thinking that Tyler would have behaved well at her house and not at ours, but later that morning, I received a phone call from my sister-in-law, Rosemary.

"So how did Tyler enjoy his weekend at Grandma's?" she asked.

"He said he had fun," I said.

"I'm sure he did, but Mom didn't think it was so much fun."

"What do you mean? She told us everything went fine."

"Well, you know she isn't going to admit to you that he was difficult."

"I really don't understand that. What is she trying to prove?"

"I don't know, but I can tell you it was a rough weekend. She tried to take him to the park, but he kept running away from her. She filled a bath for him and left the room. He emptied the water onto the floor with a bathroom cup. He wouldn't stop playing with the pilots on the gas stove and he kept sticking his fingers into the floor fan. And to top it off, he put a towel into the bathroom sink, turned on the water and left the room."

"Now that's the Tyler I know and love. She must have been pulling her hair out."

"Definitely, but she's not going to tell you that. She's so stubborn she'll never admit she was wrong. She doesn't want you to place Tyler in a facility outside the home because she won't be able to brag to her church friends about what a wonderful thing her son has done by adopting a troubled child from overseas."

"I guess you're right," I said. "But in the end, we'll have to do what's right for Tyler and for our family."

"Of course," said Rosemary. "I know what you're going through and I don't know if I would have the strength to face it every day. Don't worry about her. Just do what's right for your family. We'll support you and Roger no matter what you decide."

"Thanks," I said. "And thanks for the information. I would

have loved to have been a fly on the wall as your mom tried to manage him. I do feel better in a strange way knowing he behaved in the same outrageous manner as he does at home."

I told Roger what Rosemary said and we agreed Tyler was too much for an elderly woman to handle and we were probably fortunate that nothing serious had happened. It would be the last time we would leave Tyler alone at her house.

CHAPTER 20
FALL 1995

Tyler's school had a program of rewards, but it didn't interest him. All of the students at this school had behavioral problems, giving Tyler an education in new ways to misbehave.

One day after school, he found me in the kitchen and danced around giving me the middle finger. He had no clue what the finger actually meant, just that it always got a reaction.

"Tyler," I said, "that's not a nice thing to do."

"I know," he said. "Does it make you angry?"

"No, it makes me sad to see you doing that."

"Good, I want you to be sad."

"Why would you want me to be sad?"

"Because it's fun."

I knew it would be best to not give him or his finger any further attention, so I started to unload the dishwasher.

"Look at me," he said. "I'm still doing it."

I didn't reply, but I felt the stress building in my body. As I bent over to grab another dish from the dishwasher, he poked me in the cheek with the finger, laughing. "Damn you!" he yelled.

"Where did you hear that word?" I asked.

"At school. It's bad, isn't it?" he asked still waving the little finger.

"It's not a nice thing to say."

"Does that make you sad too?"

"It does."

I looked at the little boy standing in the kitchen doing his best to get me riled and I did feel very sad. I thought about what life would hold for him if he continued to work so hard at being oppositional. He certainly wasn't being educated because he was too busy interfering with classroom instruction. He showed more signs of stress with each passing day that were reflected in his appearance. His shoes were untied, his fly was open, one shirt tail was hanging out of his pants and his shirt buttons were misaligned. He reminded me of a lanky scarecrow that had been poorly put together. He carried stains from his lunch on his face and clothes. His shoulders sagged as if he carried a heavy weight on them. Since he had started at this school, he had less tolerance for frustrating situations and flew off the handle when the least little demands were put on him. I knew that managing his tics and impulses was a lost cause when his mind was in such a state of constant confusion.

"Would you like something to eat?" I asked him.

"No," I'm going to go outside," he said dashing out the back door.

I watched as he walked around the backyard, a lonely little boy who could not be reached. He talked to himself and waved his hands about as if trying to understand why his behavior had not instilled rage in me.

During this school year, Tyler began to engage in sexually inappropriate behavior. At only six-years old, he had an unusual interest in his genitalia. He grabbed himself and thrust his hips forward with an unusually wicked laugh. He seemed to know how inappropriate this was for a little boy of his age and took pleasure in the shocked reaction of people who saw him. We knew this behavior was not a tic because it was only done when there was an audience. It was one of those things a little boy shouldn't be aware of unless he has been exposed to it somewhere.

Tyler also intentionally broke things or as the professionals say, "engaged in property destruction." He broke toys and household items. He developed a fascination for how things were made, taking things like radios, lamps and electronic toys apart.

The hardest part of these behaviors was trying to get him to understand why they were wrong or why people around him were unhappy when he did these things. He still hadn't developed empathy or the ability to understand another person's feelings.

He engaged in activities he knew were wrong and as he did them, he said, "I'm sorry." He knew what he did was wrong and the appropriate response was to apologize, but he didn't understand what the apology meant. Sometimes he announced he was "sorry" before he even began the offending activity.

Tyler took medication to calm him, but his body remained agitated. He had tics all day long and picked at his lips and the skin around his fingers constantly. No matter how many times the psychiatrist adjusted his medications he never looked comfortable or relaxed in his own little body.

CHAPTER 21
SPRING 1996

Like most parents, I believe books are important for children. Each of my boys had a rack of age appropriate books in his room. Tyler was no exception, although he was very rough on his books. He often tore the pages as he looked through the books, because he lacked the fine motor skills to turn them. Roger and I always encouraged Tyler when he showed any interest in books. We showed him how to turn the page carefully so as not to rip it, but his fingers always made a tear in the bottom of the page even if he tried to turn it carefully.

One morning I woke at 5:30 a.m. to noises coming from Tyler's room. I walked down the hall, opened the door to his bedroom and found him kneeling on the floor with books strewn around the room. He was ripping the pages out and tearing them into hundreds of little squares. He lined up the little pieces, creating a circle with the tiny blocks of paper that started at the center of his room and spiraled towards the outside of the room. He must have been working on the dizzying pattern for hours. When I entered the room, he had no reaction. He continued to tear the pages into pieces and arrange them. He was lost in his work, as if I were not there.

"What are you doing?" I asked.

He startled, but didn't answer.

"What are you doing?" I asked again.

He looked around as if looking at someone else's work. "I

don't know," he said.

"We don't do this with books," I said as calmly as I could, although I was anything but calm.

"I know," he answered looking dazed.

"Then why did you do this?"

"I don't know."

It seemed as if he really didn't know. I couldn't imagine what had motivated him to do this. I went back to the bedroom and woke Roger up.

"You've got to see this," I told him. He followed me into Tyler's room and looked as stunned as I was.

"Jesus, this isn't just haphazard destruction," he said. "I wonder what he was thinking as he created this pattern."

"I have no idea, but there's something scary about the thought of him destroying the books so methodically," I said. "This has to have taken him hours to do. He should have been sleeping, but he's obviously been up for hours."

"So now what?" Roger asked. "Do we have to sit up all night watching him?"

I cleaned up the mess, not knowing what to say to Tyler. My instincts told me that giving him an angry reaction would encourage him to do it again, so I tried to hide my emotions. I removed all the books from his room.

I went into Trevor's room and started to move his book rack to the top of his closet as quietly as I could, but he woke up.

"What are you doing with my books?" he asked.

"Tyler just ruined most of his books and I'm putting yours out of his reach."

"But what if I want to read a book?"

"Just call daddy or me and we'll help you get it."

"It's not fair that my books have to be out of reach because of Tyler."

"I know. I'll try to come up with a better plan, but for now I have to put them up in the closet. Please try to understand."

"I understand. I just don't like it."

"I know, buddy."

I left the room feeling totally inadequate as a parent. I couldn't control Tyler and his behavior kept spilling negative consequences on Trevor and Jonathan. I wanted so much more for my family, but I was at a loss to know how to achieve it. Tyler was like a little thief who stole bits of our family life every day.

CHAPTER 22
SUMMER 1996

I awoke to a noise coming from Tyler's room. FFFFTTT-snap! A few seconds passed and there it was again. FFFFTTT-snap! I went to his room and saw him playing with the window shade. He had climbed up onto a shaky bookcase next to the window and was pulling the shade down making it snap up again.

"Tyler, get down!" I shouted. "You're going to fall!"

"I hope I *do* fall," he answered teetering on the empty bookcase. Using the top of the bookcase like a springboard, he jumped from it like a cat, causing it to sway back and forth, finally crashing to the floor. He fell on top of it in a fit of laughter.

"Look what you did!" I shouted as he dashed past me and out of the room. I needed to calm down. Roger was still at work and Trevor had a 6:30 a.m. practice at the rink. I went to Trevor's room.

"It's time to get up for practice," I said trying to sound calm although my heart was racing.

"Okay. Mom," he said.

"Tyler is having a difficult morning, so I may need your help getting Jonathan ready to go," I said.

"Sure, Mom," he said pulling himself up from the bed, "I can take care of that."

Tyler appeared in the doorway and banged himself against the door, making a loud thumping sound. He laughed and stared at me, waiting for a reaction.

"Tyler," I said ignoring his behavior. "We're going to Trevor's hockey practice this morning and you need to get dressed."

"This noise bothers you. I can tell because you're trying to ignore me," he said.

He had heard me tell his brothers to ignore his actions and now he recognized that my efforts to ignore him meant he was annoying me. He grinned at me and continued to slam his skinny body against the door.

"I'm going downstairs to make breakfast now," I said. "I don't want you to come downstairs until you're dressed." After a few minutes, he came down all dressed, except for his left shoe which he held in his hand.

"Good job getting dressed, Tyler," I said tousling his hair.

"What should I do?" he asked smirking. I was supposed to tell him to put the other shoe on and begin the game. It was the only way he knew to interact with me. Trevor and Jonathan came down after awhile and had breakfast while Tyler jumped around on one foot making guttural, throaty noises.

"You need to put on your shoe, Tyler," I said finally.

He laughed, but at least he put the shoe on.

"Good job getting dressed, Tyler," I said again. "Let's get going boys. We all put our coats on except for Tyler, who held his coat in his hand.

"What should I do?" he asked, still playing the game that never ended for him.

"Put on your coat, Tyler," I said. He stared at me and sniggled. In his imaginary war, he scored a point every time I told him to do the obvious. I moved to the door and he followed, still carrying his coat. Eventually he got cold and put it on as we traveled toward the rink.

"Good job putting on your coat, Tyler," I said.

As soon as we arrived at the rink and he could be face to face with me, the coat came off. Ice rinks are cold places, often colder than the outside environment, but Tyler would ignore the cold if it meant he could push my buttons. Jonathan met up with several of the younger siblings from Trevor's team and went to play with them. A very social kid, he always met friends when we went out. Tyler picked up where he had left off at home.

"Look, mom. My coat is off," he said.

"You're going to catch a cold," I said. "Put it back on."

"No," he snickered. I knew it was pointless to repeat the command and give him another opportunity to laugh at me, so I ignored him. Throughout the practice, he climbed on the railing and jumped off the steps. I worried every time I saw him fly through the air.

"Tyler, you need to calm down," I said when I could no longer stand to watch him. "Remember you had to get stitches when you fell from the railings."

"I remember," he answered. "I want to get stitches. I like to be bloody and go to the hospital."

I tried to think of an appropriate response, but my parent training never taught me what to say when your child tells you he wants to be bloody. I felt inadequate and hopeless. I was not equipped to deal with this. I sat through the rest of the practice with one eye watching Trevor on the ice and the other eye watching Tyler jump around, hoping he would not get hurt either accidentally or intentionally.

At the end of the practice, Jonathan came upstairs.

"Tyler, it's time to get Trevor," I said. He smiled at me and climbed down from the railings. "Good boy, Tyler," I said happy to have a chance to recognize his good behavior. The three of us went downstairs to meet Trevor at the locker room.

"You skated well today," I said to Trevor. "You're skating backwards faster than ever."

"I know," he said. "But my skates are getting too tight and I have blisters on my toes."

Trevor had been telling me his skates were getting tight for weeks, but I had been reluctant to go skate shopping when Tyler was with us. Roger had been working a lot of overtime and there never seemed to be a good time to shop with Trevor alone.

"We can stop at Center Sports on the way home," I said.

"Great!" said Trevor.

Trevor and Jonathan headed for the back of the store

where the hockey equipment was, but Tyler stopped near the entry and picked up a small hand-held top that gave off friction sparks when it was pumped.

"Do you like that, Tyler?" I asked.

"Yeah," he said watching it spin around.

"If you're a good boy while we shop for Trevor's skates" I said, "I will buy it for you."

"I don't want to be good," he said. He dropped the top and turned to a nearby pile of weights. He picked up a five pound weight, hefted it to his chest and dropped it with a loud clang.

"Tyler," I groaned. "Don't touch those."

I grabbed his hand as he laughed and led him to the back of the store. Jonathan tested hockey sticks which were all too big for him as Trevor stared intently at the wall of skates trying to decide which ones would be best for him. I held tightly to Tyler's hand.

"What do you think of these?" Trevor asked pointing to a pair of CCM skates.

"If you're interested in those, you should try them on," I answered still clinging to Tyler who tried to escape my grasp by twisting and pulling his trapped hand. A salesman approached us.

"We're interested in these skates. Can you measure him for me?" I asked pointing at Trevor.

"Sure," said the salesman.

Just then, I felt a sharp pain at my wrist and looked down to see Tyler sinking his teeth into my skin. I let go of my grasp and he ran away. I looked at the wound. He had broken the skin and an imprint of his teeth was imbedded on the top of my hand. The salesman was busy measuring Trevor's foot and did not realize what happened. I did not chase Tyler. Trevor needed the skates and I had to concentrate on the task at hand. The salesman explained to us it was customary to buy skates a size or two smaller than your shoe size, but we already knew how the sizing worked. As the salesman disappeared into the stockroom, I heard basketballs bouncing on the other side of the large store followed by the voice of a female salesperson. "Stop throwing those balls!"

I knew it was Tyler. "Stay here and try on the skates when the salesman comes back," I said to Trevor. "I have to go find Tyler"

I looked around and saw Jonathan nearby staring at a poster of his hero, Mark Messier. "Watch Jon," I said. I followed the sound of Tyler's giggles to the area where the basketballs were. An exasperated saleswoman was putting the basketballs back into the bin just as Tyler prepared to throw another one.

"Tyler!" I yelled. "Stop that right now!"

He looked up and laughed, satisfied that he had gotten me away from his brothers and drawn my attention to him. I apologized to the salesperson and picked Tyler up. I carried him back to the area where the ice skates were as he kicked and bit me. I refused to give in and hung on tight. I felt his feet connecting with my body in painful jabs and I knew his teeth were breaking my skin, but I was determined to get the skates that Trevor needed. I did not let go. By the time I returned

Trevor had the skates on and was standing on the rubber floor testing the fit. He and Jonathan heard us coming from across the store. They were frozen in anticipation in front of the skate display as we emerged from the nearby racks of sweatshirts. I sat down on a bench, put Tyler on my lap and encircled him with my arms pinning him to my chest.

"How do those feel?" I asked Trevor as normally as I could while Tyler struggled for freedom in my lap.

"I like them," he said ignoring Tyler's behavior. "They feel much better than my other skates."

"Do you want to try on another pair?" I asked.

"No these are great," he said.

"We'll take those," I said to the salesman as I breathed heavily under the strain of keeping Tyler in my lap. I picked him up and proceeded across the store to the register in front of the store. Trevor held Jonathan's hand as they both took a cue from me, pretending nothing unusual was going on. In a matter of minutes, the transaction was completed and we went to the car.

Trevor helped Jonathan get into his car seat and I put Tyler into his seat. I could never have managed any of this without Trevor. He was always ready to please and to help.

As soon as Tyler was secured in his seat, he slammed his head back and forth in his customary rhythm. He shut down and left the stress of the moment to escape to some far away place where he could not be reached.

Trevor climbed into the front seat and closed the door

behind him. I looked over and saw the familiar dark circles around his eyes.

"Are you okay?" I asked him.

"I'm fine," he said.

"You have a headache, don't you?"

"I do, but I'm okay."

"I'm sorry."

"I know. It's not your fault. At least I got the skates." He struggled to smile at me. "I love you," he said.

"I love you too," I answered.

"What about me?" asked Jonathan from the back seat. "I love you too!"

"I know and I love you, Jonathan," I said. "You guys were really great in there. Thanks."

We drove home with the radio filling the silence too tired for mundane conversation.

CHAPTER 23
AUGUST 1996

I heard a story on the news that terrified me. A Colorado mother was accused of beating her two and half-year old son with a spatula and wooden spoons. The boy had been adopted from a Russian orphanage and had been diagnosed with Reactive Attachment Disorder (RAD). When the mother called the police on the morning of February 11, 1996, they found the boy's little body in a trash can outside the home. He appeared to have been beaten to death with a wooden spoon which was also found in the garbage. The mother was arrested and charged with murder. The media saw her as someone who had taken an innocent child from another country, brought him to America and then lost her temper, killing him.

The story shook me. I understood the public rage she faced. Her story was like a flashing red light in my mind. What if someday Tyler pushed me too far? Could I ever hurt him? I wanted to think it could never happen to me. I wanted to believe I would always be in control, but I wasn't so sure. Tyler's behavior was relentless and dominating every aspect of my family's life and I found myself getting angrier and angrier every day. Logically, I knew his behavior was not his fault, but it always seemed so intentional and was usually directed at me. The story sent chills of fear through my body. I needed to learn more about the story of this little boy and his mother.

I went to the library and spent the afternoon researching the story and found that the mother was at home alone with the boy that night. Her other child who was also adopted was away with her husband and she thought an evening alone with the little boy might give her a chance to bond with him. According to the mother, the little boy acted aggressively towards her, hitting her and lunging at her, throughout the evening. He took off his diaper and smeared feces on the wall of his room. She says she saw him put a spatula up into his rectum. She claimed he beat himself with the wooden spoon. Of course, the only witness to the activities of that evening was the mother. At some point during the evening she called her therapist and told him she had hurt her son. However, now, she denied she had killed him and was insisting his wounds were self-inflicted. The jury didn't show her any sympathy. She was convicted of murder and sentenced to eighteen years in prison in a Colorado correctional facility.

The story of the Colorado mother and her little boy haunted me. I often felt I was struggling not to lose control with Tyler. I tried to imagine what might happen if I ever snapped. I would lose Trevor and Jonathan. Even if society could understand how difficult it was to live with a child like Tyler, there would be no forgiveness. There simply was never an excuse to hurt a child even one who in no way behaved as a normal child. From that point on, I vowed to keep the Colorado woman in mind whenever things escalated. I feared that if I ever became physical with him, the day might come when I would not stop. I needed to concentrate on my other two children and on our survival when things got out of control. Somehow my family must survive the deluge of Tyler's behaviors until we found some sort of relief.

That night I sat up waiting for Roger to come home from work. I was sitting in the dark in the living room as he came through the door.

"Couldn't wait for me to come home?' he asked with a sly grin.

"I wish it were that simple," I said.

"What's wrong?"

"I heard a story about a woman who adopted a little boy from Russia. She snapped and killed him. Tyler is always pushing me. He never stops. What if..."

"Stop right there." He knelt in front of the chair and took my hands in his. "You would never hurt Tyler."

"How can you be sure?"

"Because I know you."

"But where will it end? He continues to threaten us and he's going to get bigger. You aren't with him as much as I am. You're at work in the evenings and then in the mornings, you need to sleep. When you are home, we separate Trevor and Jonathan from Tyler and you never have to handle all three boys together."

"You know," he said, "the Ukranian Embassy sent us paperwork after the adoption, saying Tyler would maintain his citizenship in the Ukraine as well as in the United States. Perhaps, we could put him on a one way flight back to Russia."

"Don't joke around," I said. "I think we probably should start thinking seriously about having him placed outside the home."

"But what will become of him?" He asked. "Can we really give up on him? I mean, we love him. He's just a little boy and..."

"I didn't say we should pack his clothes tonight," I said choking on the words. "I just think we should see what options we have. We can't wait until the day he's too big for us to handle and one of us gets hurt. We have to think of keeping our family in tact and stop sacrificing everything for Tyler. We need help."

"I know, you're right," he said. "We'll start making some phone calls and explore our options. It's just so sad to think about giving up."

"Try not to think of it as giving up," I said. "Try to think of it as doing the right thing for Tyler. He really needs serious psychological treatment. We aren't helping him by keeping him here."

"I know," he said. "I just need some time to adjust to the whole idea of letting go of one of my children."

"Me too," I said.

CHAPTER 24
SEPTEMBER 1996

By the fall, things were escalating out of control at a dangerous pace. I felt as though I had driven my car onto train tracks with Jonathan and Trevor in the back seat. Everyday, Tyler became more aggressive, abusive and self-injurious. He talked daily about death--his and ours. Roger and I gave up the hope of effecting a change in him. We were all treading water and hoping not to be pulled down by the undertow that was Tyler. It became apparent that for any of us to survive emotionally and possibly physically, the family would have to separate from him. We made the difficult call to the Department of Social Services to have Tyler removed from the home.

In November, a social worker, Leslie Starret, was sent to our home. Roger and I presented our story to her and told her how the tensions and dangers were growing on a daily basis.

"Perhaps, if Tyler were the only child in a family, he might do better," suggested Roger.

"Probably, but it's not that easy. Children who are over the age of five with handicapping conditions are very hard to place," Ms. Starret explained. "It could take a long time to find another family for him."

"I see," said Roger. "What about foster care? Perhaps, if we had some time to catch our breath… "

"Once again, it would be difficult to find a family that

would accept him," she said.

"Can we have him placed in the blue books?" I asked. I had learned about the blue books through adoption support groups. They listed children throughout New York State who were available for adoption, but were difficult to place. The books carried pictures and brief descriptions of the children and were maintained by the local libraries.

"Sure, but again, that could take quite a long time," Ms. Starret said. "I'll look into that for you, but your best bet would be to have him placed in a residential treatment facility where he could receive treatment in a structured environment."

"How do we do that?" I asked choking on the words. It was such a difficult conversation to have. I never expected to be making plans to move one of my children out of our home.

"You must contact your local school district" Ms. Starret explained. "It's their job to assist you in finding a residential placement that will meet his needs. However, I must tell you it is very unusual to place a child who is under the age of eight. Tyler is only seven and it may be difficult to find a placement for him at such a young age. I wish I could offer you more hope."

"So what are we supposed to do? I hope you understand we're afraid of what he might do next," I said. "Isn't social services supposed to protect children? What if Tyler hurts one of my other children?"

"I'm sorry to say it's the job of social services to protect children from adults," she said. "It's the job of the parents to protect children from each other."

"You can't be serious," said Roger. "You're saying you can't help us protect Trevor and Jonathan from Tyler."

"I'm so sorry. I want to help, but everything I could do to help you would take time you may not have." she said. "I really do sympathize with you. I'll go back and talk to my supervisor. Maybe listing him in the blue books is a possibility, but I would contact the school district if I were you. A residential treatment facility will probably be your best bet. I wish I could offer you more hope."

When she left, I turned to Roger. "It was hard enough to face the fact that we might have to give Tyler up, but now we're being told it may be impossible to make it happen. I feel like I can't breathe."

"There has to be an answer," he said, trying to calm me. "We'll contact the school district and maybe when Ms. Starret explains our situation to her supervisor he or she will have a suggestion."

"I hope so. I'm so afraid that someone is going to get hurt if things don't change soon," I said.

Roger put his arms around me. "We'll find a solution. We have to for the sake of Trevor and Jonathan."

CHAPTER 25
NOVEMBER 1996

The week before Thanksgiving, life with Tyler reached a crisis point. I met his bus at the end of our driveway as usual, but when he jumped off, he was enraged.

"How was school?" I asked as he flung his backpack skidding up the driveway.

"Shut up! You're stupid!" He shouted pushing past me and through the doorway. I followed him to the house and he met me at the door, standing in the foyer with his legs spread apart in a stance of defiance, holding a large ceramic vase from the dining room over his head. As I entered the doorway, he threw it at me. I ducked as it crashed into the door behind me.

Jonathan came downstairs, "What happened?" he asked looking at the broken chips of ceramic on the floor.

Tyler turned to him with fierce anger in his eyes. "You're going to die, Jonathan!" he shouted.

"Go back upstairs, Jon," I said. "Tyler is having a bad day."

"A bad day?" yelled Tyler. "Watch this!" His eyes darted around as he searched for something else to throw at me. He ran into the kitchen where I had been cutting fabric at the table to make Christmas curtains. I followed him with Jonathan close on my heels. Tyler reached across the table, grabbed the fabric shears and rushed passed me, lunging at Jonathan who jumped out of his way just in time.

"I'm going to kill you, Jonathan!" he yelled waving the shears in front of him.

Jonathan turned and scrambled for the stairs with Tyler following closely behind threatening with the shears. I caught up to Tyler, wrested the shears away from him and dragged him back downstairs into the foyer.

I yelled up the stairs, "Trevor! Please keep Jon upstairs with you! Tyler is trying to hurt him!"

"Jonathan! Quick! Come into my room," I heard Trevor say and then the door to his room slammed.

I turned to find Tyler glowering at me with a challenging expression. He appeared to be out of breath and I wondered if he was hyperventilating. My own breath was ragged and my hands trembled as I stared back at him. He had tried to attack Jonathan and now I felt defensive and protective. Anxiety captured my brain and threatened to steal my sense of reason. From somewhere deep inside I felt a deep animal instinct to protect Trevor and Jonathan rising in me. I expect a mother animal feels this instinct towards her young in the wild, but we were not in the wild and I needed to calm down. I needed to remember the Colorado mom.

Just then Roger walked in the front door from a Police Officer's meeting. He saw the tension between Tyler and me. "What's going on?" he asked.

"Tyler threatened to hurt Jonathan with a pair of shears," I said as my voice trembled with trepidation.

"No, I didn't! She's lying!" yelled Tyler never breaking eye contact with me. "Jonathan tried to hurt *me* with the shears. He wanted to kill me."

Roger grabbed Tyler's hand and brought him into the den, pointing at the couch. "Sit there and don't move," he said.

"No! No! No!" Tyler shouted. "She's lying! She always lies!"

Roger bent down and got close to his face, "Stop! No more!"

Tyler slid to the corner of the couch cowering. "Are you going to hurt me?"

"No. I'm not going to hurt you."

"Oh, but I want you to hurt me."

Roger looked at me dumbfounded. He turned back to Tyler. "No one here is going to hurt you."

"I'm going to call Dr Kant," I said. He was Tyler's current psychiatrist and had increased Tyler's medications over the past few weeks in the hope that if he were more sedated, we might be able to manage him until he was removed from the home. Tyler was taking enough medication to put a large man to sleep for days, but it had little effect on his small body. I reached the psychiatrist's office and fortunately he was free and his receptionist put me right through.

"We're in trouble, Dr. Kant. Tyler just threw a ceramic vase at me and then chased Jon up the stairs with a pair of shears threatening to kill him. Now he's asking Roger to hurt him."

"We've talked about how things have been getting worse over the past few weeks and I'd hoped that medicating him might prevent it from getting to this point," he said, "but he seems to be more dangerous to himself and the family every day."

"The medications have little effect on him. What am I supposed to do now?" I asked, my voice unraveling with despair.

"I think Tyler needs to be hospitalized," said the doctor. "Take him to University Hospital Emergency Room right away for a complete psychiatric evaluation. Ask them to call me when you get there."

"Okay," I said. "Will they definitely admit him?"

"Oh, I think so," he answered. "He's becoming more psychotic everyday and he definitely needs to be separated from the family for a while."

"Thank-you, Dr. Kant," I said. "We'll go there right away"

"What did he say?" Roger asked.

"He said we should bring him to the Emergency Room at University Hospital to be admitted for psychiatric evaluation," I said.

"I'm going to the hospital?" asked Tyler brightening with anticipation.

"Yes," I said. "Roger, do you think Rosemary can stay with Trevor and Jonathan?"

"I'll call her," he said.

"I love going to the hospital," said Tyler excitement

growing in his voice.

In the past, he enjoyed the attention he received at the hospital. Now, he ran out to the car and bounced in with a big grin. He sat in the back seat talking and singing while Roger and I sat in the front. We both felt numb. We were taking our seven-year old to the hospital for psychiatric evaluation. Neither one of us knew how to respond to that. On one hand, it was sad to think that a child so young might need to be hospitalized for psychiatric treatment, but on the other hand, if he were admitted to the hospital. perhaps the whole family could catch its collective breath. We were discouraged and hopeful at the same time. When we arrived at the hospital, Tyler skipped happily into the emergency room. In the waiting room, he moved from one person to the next, cheerfully introducing himself and talking to everyone. After waiting two long hours, we were led into the psychiatric center. Two middle-aged female nurses came into the waiting room and greeted Tyler as if we were not there.

"Hi, are you Tyler?" one of the nurses asked warmly.

"Yes," he answered cocking his head adorably. "Are you a doctor?'

"No," I'm a nurse," she said, laughing, obviously taken in by his confidence and cute appearance.

"We're going to talk to Tyler," the other nurse said to me. "We'll be back soon."

I watched as he grabbed a hand of each nurse and walked away between them. As he reached the swinging doors with the words "Psychiatric Center" overhead, he looked back over his shoulder at me as if to say, "See? They love me." Tyler often professed love for new acquaintances, but was unable to have normal relationships with anyone who actually tried to get close to him.

"I guess they'll send someone out to talk to us," Roger said. We waited, but no one came. After more than two hours, one of the nurses returned and led us to an office. The other nurse joined her as we sat down.

"Tyler is quite chatty," she said in a voice that made me worry that she had been taken in by his charm.

"Yes, he is," I said.

"What medications is he on?" she asked.

I listed the medications and the dosages. She smiled and looked at the other nurse. "Are you sure you're following the schedule for these prescribed medications?" she asked.

"Of course," I said wondering where this was going. "We're very careful with his medications."

"If medications are not administered correctly, or if a dosage is skipped, there can be serious problems," she said in a clinical tone. "You really should be very careful to administer medications properly."

"We understand that," said Roger, not hiding the annoyance in his voice.

The other nurse broke in. "I understand your son is adopted from Ukraine," she said.

"Yes," I answered. "He's been with us for almost four

years. Did you read the paperwork we filled out? He has many behavioral problems."

"A child who has lived in an orphanage for the first few years of his life can be expected to have problems," she continued. "Sometimes we just have to accept children as they are."

I couldn't believe what I was hearing. They had talked to Tyler and he appeared to be a pleasant little boy to them, so they decided we must be the problem. I was furious. "The psychiatrist who is treating my son told us to bring him here." I said. "He thought it would be good for Tyler to be evaluated and spend some time away from the family"

"This is not a respite center," she said. "We have patients here who need the bed more than your son and we feel that if you are careful to administer his medications correctly and try harder to accept him as he is, you'll be able to manage him at home. We'll send him out to you in a few minutes. I'm sorry we can't help you."

Roger and I looked at each other in disbelief. How could we convince them that living with Tyler had become dangerous? They hadn't even asked about the events of the evening that had caused us to bring him here.

"Wait a minute," I said. "Dr. Kant said you should call him as soon as we got here."

"Dr. Kant is not on staff here and we can't help you," said the nurse dismissively.

Why did they see Tyler as harmless just because he was small and cute? He was still a threat to Trevor and Jonathan. I shuddered to think of what would have to happen before someone in a position to help us would understand the danger of the situation. My head felt light as I struggled to deal with the moment.

Tyler came into the office to join us and the nurse said, "Think about what we said."

"I love you," Tyler said to the nurse.

"I love you too," said the nurse in a sugary voice as she and her coworker left the room smiling at him.

"C'mon Tyler," said Roger.

"Can't I stay here?" asked Tyler. "I love *them* now!"

"No, we have to go home," said Roger.

We drove home in silence, not knowing what to say to each other. Tyler resumed singing and chattering to himself in the back seat. I felt as if a heavy weight was pressing down on my shoulders. When we got home Roger went straight to the cabinet in the den under the TV. He dug out the video camera and set it up on the bricks in front of the fireplace facing the couch.

"What are you doing?" I asked.

"We don't seem to be able to convey the seriousness of Tyler's behavior to anyone because he's so angelic around strangers. If we tape him, we'll be able to show what he's really like at home."

"That's a great idea," I said allowing hope to return. I'm an optimistic person by nature and I was unable to accept that we would not find help for Tyler.

The next afternoon when Tyler returned from school, Roger turned the camera on and went upstairs to stay with Trevor and Jonathan. Tyler found me in the kitchen and asked, "Can we go back to the hospital?"

"No. Tonight we're staying home," I said.

Before I even finished the sentence, he caught me off guard and lunged at me, slamming his body into mine with all his force. I fell backwards into the kitchen counter banging my hip. He jumped away from me, laughing so hard that he had trouble catching his breath.

"Where is everybody?" he asked.

"Trevor and Jonathan are upstairs with daddy," I said.

He pivoted on his heels, darted out of the room and headed for the stairs. I was right behind him. I caught him before he could go up and brought him into the den.

"You can't stop me!" he shouted biting my arms. Tootsie barked and nipped at his feet, sensing my exasperation. I put Tyler on the couch and said, "Don't move!"

He stuck his tongue out at me and gave me the middle finger. "Damn you! I'm going to kill you all!" He rolled off the couch and ran for the stairs, glancing back over his shoulder to make sure I was following him. I caught him before he reached the stairs. He slapped me, kicked me and spit as I returned him to the couch. It was the kind of physical encounter I feared the most.

"When can I go upstairs?" he demanded.

"When you fall asleep, I'll move you up to your bed. Until then you must stay down here. I don't want you to be anywhere near Trevor or Jonathan after what you did last night." I struggled to keep it together and thought to myself, "Don't let your anger make you do something you will regret." Stay in control. Think of Jonathan and Trevor. No matter what happens, remember the Colorado mom and stay in control.

"You mean when I tried to kill Jonathan with the scissors?" he asked with a mocking smile as he rolled off the couch again and lunged at Tootsie, grabbing a handful of her skin. She yelped in pain.

I pulled him away from the dog just in time to prevent her from biting him. "Why are you doing this?" I asked.

"I dunno." he answered as he always did. He never knew why he did the things he did. "I have to go to the bathroom."

"Okay, let's go," I said following him across the kitchen to the bathroom near the back door.

He ran ahead of me to the bathroom, pulled down his pants and urinated on the floor with fits of laughter.

"Roger, can you come down here?" I yelled as Tyler skirted past me and headed for the stairs. Roger met him on the stairs, picked him up and returned him to the couch.

"He peed on the bathroom floor," I said to Roger. Tyler laughed as he pulled off his shoes and socks and began to pick at his toenails.

"Can you stay with him while I clean this mess up?" I asked Roger.

"Sure," he said. "Tyler what are you doing to your toenails?"

"I'm pulling them off."

"Why are you doing that?"

"Because I want to be bloody."

"You want to be bloody?"

"Yeah, I want to be covered in blood."

"Why would you want that?"

"I dunno. I want to be dead." He jumped off the couch and ran for the stairs, but Roger quickly brought him back to the den.

"Let's do your homework," said Roger.

"No, I like to do it at recess. I hate to go outside now."

When Tyler refused to do his homework, he was not allowed to go outside for recess. Instead, he was rewarded by the undivided attention of an adult, who stayed indoors with him and helped him get the homework done.

"Let's try to do it here," said Roger as he brought him to the kitchen table. He opened the backpack and spread the homework on the table. "This looks easy enough. You just have to copy these four words three times each."

"I can't do that," Tyler said as he licked the kitchen table.

"I think you should try," said Roger.

I finished cleaning up the mess in the bathroom and watched Tyler take on Roger. He usually directed his worst behavior at me, but now he put up his middle finger and poked Roger in the face just below his eye. Roger pulled his hand away and gave him the pencil. Tyler thought for a second and then hit Roger on the arm. He paused and waited for a reaction.

"You need to stop that, Tyler," said Roger.

Tyler hit him two more times. "Aren't you going to hit me back?" He asked.

"No," said Roger, putting the homework assignment away. He knew it was a waste of time to try to get Tyler to focus at this point. He led him back to the couch in the den.

Tyler hit him again. "I want you to hit me. I want you to punch me. I want to be hurt."

"I'm not going to hurt you, Tyler" said Roger. "Why do you want me to hurt you?"

"Because I like to be hurt. What if I kill you?" he asked as he started to peel off his clothing.

"What are you doing, Tyler?" I asked.

"I'm getting naked," he said. "I want to be naked and bloody."

"Tyler," I said, "we don't walk around the house naked."

He ignored me and pulled off the rest of his clothes. He sat on the couch, lifted his penis and began to talk to it. "Hi, Little Roger," he said, addressing it. "What are you doing?"

"Tyler, put your clothes back on," said Roger.

"No, I'm talking to my friend, Little Roger. What should we do, Little Roger?" he asked his penis. Once again I wondered what horrors Tyler might have experienced as a baby to make him have these thoughts.

Suddenly Jonathan cried out from upstairs. "What's going on up there?" I yelled.

"Jonathan wants to go downstairs, but I won't let him," Trevor answered.

I turned back to Roger and Tyler. "This is getting us nowhere. Why don't you go back upstairs with Trevor and Jonathan and I'll stay with Tyler. We're only providing an audience for him now."

The phone rang and I answered it. It was Roger's sister. "He's having a tough time again," I said. "Do you think you can come over again and sit with the boys in case we need to go back to the hospital?"

"Who are you talking to?" Tyler asked. "Are you calling the police? I don't want anyone to come here." He scrambled to put his clothes back on as Roger went upstairs.

"Who's coming here?" he asked.

"Aunt Rosemary. Why?" I asked.

"I don't want the police here. I had a great day in school today. I got thirty points."

"That's not what your teacher said."

"She's lying. I had a good day. She always lies. I'm ready to go to sleep now. Can you take me upstairs?"

"You can sleep here on the couch and when you fall asleep I will carry you upstairs."

"I'm getting you killed."

"Is that what you want?'

"I'd like it."

"Why"

"I like it when I attack you." He spit at my face. "I'm going to tell daddy you're hitting me."

"That's not true."

"You're cheating."

"What does that mean?"

"You tell daddy everything. That's cheating. See this middle finger? This is mommy." He waved the finger in the air. "Hi, mommy," he said and then he asked, "When was I dead?"

"You were never dead, Tyler. If someone is dead, they stop breathing and never get up or move again."

"They don't?"

"No. They're finished moving forever."

"I have a headache from you. My stomach hurt in school

today."

"Did you eat? Your stomach will hurt if you don't eat."

"I didn't eat because lunch time was over."

"You mean you took too long to eat?"

"Fuck you."

The door bell rang. It was Rosemary, coming over to watch Trevor and Jonathan.

Roger came downstairs and popped out the video that had been running for over an hour. "Tyler, do you want to go back to the hospital?" he asked.

"Yeah, I love the hospital," Tyler said. "Let's go."

Twenty minutes later we arrived back at the emergency room of University Hospital.

"We were here last night," Roger told the staff. "Tonight we taped our son as he threatened the family and himself. He can be very manipulative and charming if you do not know him. Please look at the tape. It will give you a much better idea of what is going on than talking to him will."

The staff took the tape into the back room while we waited outside with Tyler. Forty-five minutes later they told us that they had secured a bed for Tyler at a psychiatric facility on the south shore. Tyler went by ambulance and we followed in our car to be available to fill out the necessary paperwork. Tyler was admitted two days before Thanksgiving.

CHAPTER 26
NOVEMBER 1996

Tyler was kept at the psychiatric hospital for two weeks. Although Roger and I visited him every day, it gave us a much needed respite at home. On the second day, when we visited Tyler, Mrs. Koch, a social worker, led us to her tiny office. She hoped to make a difference even though Tyler's stay was described as crisis intervention and was only expected to last for two weeks, the amount of time insurance would cover.

"Have a seat," she said pointing to two chairs that were squeezed in front of a desk. "Tell me what led you to have Tyler placed at this hospital?"

"Tyler is unmanageable at home and a threat to the family," Roger said.

"Can you tell me more about that?"

Roger let out a weary sigh. Tyler was only going to be here for a short stay and it was hard to imagine how the staff at the psychiatric hospital might accomplish anything in that short amount of time. After all, he only received about an hour of therapy a day.

"Tyler was adopted from a Ukrainian orphanage and has never bonded with any of us. He fights our every attempt to make him a part of the family," I said hearing the fatigue in my voice as I robotically told the story again. "He is verbally and physically abusive to us and has recently become self-abusive. He has an insatiable need for negative attention and gets satisfaction from property destruction. He has Tourette

Syndrome and PDD-NOS."

"I see," she said. "Sounds like you've really had your hands full. Can you describe a typical day with Tyler for me?"

I knew she meant well and was just trying to do her job, but I didn't see how going over all this again would help. I had not slept well since Tyler went into the hospital. I lay awake at night trying to understand why I could not reach this little boy. I went over the events of the last month wondering if I might have done things differently—if I might have been able to have a different outcome. "We gave that information to the intake coordinator when we checked Tyler into this hospital," I said. "Perhaps you can tell me how he is doing in this environment? Does he ask about us or why he is here?"

"I'm not sure," she said. "I haven't talked to him yet. I just received his case this morning."

"I see," I said, trying my best not to be rude. "I appreciate your interest in our case, but Roger has to be to work in an hour and my other children will be getting off the bus in two hours and I have to be home for them. Perhaps you could meet Tyler, spend some time with him and we could finish this conversation tomorrow. Right now, we would like to visit with him."

"I understand," Mrs. Koch said. "Come on, I'll take you to his room."

We got up and followed her down the hall to Tyler's room. He stood in the doorway looking agitated. His hair was a mess, he wore a stained long-sleeved tee shirt I had never seen before, and his jeans hung loosely at risk of falling off his bony hips because his belt was missing. His shoelaces had been removed and with each bounce of his frame, his feet slipped in and out of his sneakers. He turned, spotted us, smiled, and ran to us.

"Shit is a curse word, isn't it?" he asked as his eyes darted back and forth between Roger and me searching our faces for confirmation. He wasn't missing us or thinking about coming home, but rather adding to his arsenal of inappropriate behavior. I stared at him in disbelief.

"What about asshole?" he asked excitedly bobbing up and down on the balls of his feet. "That's a bad word, isn't it? A kid in my room says it's a bad word. Is it? Fuck-you is bad too, isn't it?"

He was waiting for us to come to the hospital and verify that he had discovered some new words that would evoke displeasure from those who heard them. He held his hand up in front of my face with the middle finger extended. "This is a bad thing, isn't it?" Although he had used the middle finger before, we had not reacted to it. Now other kids reacted and he realized just how nasty a thing it was. I looked over at Roger struggling with every ounce of energy to remain calm. I felt extremely sad and at a loss to know how to react.

"Tyler, can we see your room?" Roger asked as the doctor approached us.

"Are you Tyler's parents?" asked the doctor. "I'm Dr. Frescia."

"Nice to meet you," said Roger. "How's Tyler doing?"

"He's doing fine," he said. "Tyler, Mrs. Koch is going to take you to the lunch room now. You can see your mom and dad in a little while. Mr. and Mrs. Havlicek, let's go to my office." We followed him down the hall.

"I've read what you reported about Tyler and I obtained his school records. I think I have a pretty good idea of how hard this has been for you. Tyler's multiple diagnoses make it very difficult for him and I'm sure, for your family. I'm going to add the diagnosis of Intermittent Explosive Disorder because Tyler flies off the handle and becomes enraged for no apparent reason. I understand you're considering having him placed in a residential facility. As difficult as that may be for you, it probably would be best for Tyler and your family. In the proper setting, he would receive psychiatric help to deal with the issues that make it difficult for him to succeed. I'm going to write a strong recommendation that he be placed as soon as possible. I hope that will help."

"Thank-you." was all I could say.

"How long will he be here?" asked Roger.

"Your insurance company has approved a two week stay," said the doctor. "He will get therapy here, but I'm sure you realize that just as he gets to know the staff here, he'll be home."

"I understand," said Roger.

"I wish I could do more for you," said Dr. Frescia.

We left the hospital feeling more hopeless than when we had arrived. Exactly fourteen days later, Tyler was released and returned home.

CHAPTER 27
DECEMBER 6, 1996

At home, Tyler picked up where he had left off. The first afternoon as he returned from school, I met him at the end of the driveway.

"Hi, Tyler," I said, but he brushed past me. When I caught up with him, he was standing in the den holding a poker from the fireplace over his head. He tossed it across the room where it hit the couch with a dull thud. He paused momentarily to take in my reaction, before dashing towards the staircase. I grabbed him before his little feet hit the second step and brought him to the kitchen table. I took his homework from his back pack and placed it in front of him.

"Do not go upstairs again!" I shouted.

"Okay," he answered, grinning as if to say, "I accept your challenge."

"You can play with the toys in the den," I told him. "But you must stay down here. I don't want you to go upstairs."

"Okay," he said, but even as the words came from his mouth, he bolted out of the kitchen and ran to the stairs. I chased after him and brought him back to the den feeling more like a jailer than a mother. It was all just a big game for him and he was in charge of scripting the role I would play.

"Fuck you," he said. I ignored him.

"FUCK YOU!" he yelled, lunging at me and scratching my

arm with his nails.

Jonathan came downstairs, heard what Tyler was saying and said, "Fuck you, Tyler," giggling as the words slid out of his five-year old mouth.

"Jonathan!" I shouted. "That's not a nice word and I don't want you to use it!"

"Okay," said Jonathan. "I'm sorry. Can I go across the street to Timmy's house?"

"Sure," I said. "I'll call you at dinnertime."

"Fuck you! Fuck you!" Tyler shouted over and over again, happy that Jonathan had been pulled into the game. I ignored him, but the fact that I had told Jonathan not to use that word had given him some sort of perverse satisfaction. "I know you're angry because you're ignoring me," he said, turning his attention to Tootsie.

Dogs can sense tension in their owners. Tootsie knew the family was under stress whenever Tyler was home and she knew he often hurt her. She followed his every move with her eyes, ready to protect any member of the family who might need her help. Tyler ran over to her and twisted the skin on her back until she yelped. She turned, snapped at him and caught two fingers on his right hand. He let out a scream as if she had taken off his arm, although she had not even broken the skin. At that moment, I wanted to root for Tootsie. I briefly allowed myself to imagine telling a courtroom of my peers that I had allowed Tootsie to eat Tyler because he had asked for it, but I knew it was my job to protect my son from harm no matter what and I pulled the dog away from him and put her into her crate.

"I'm hungry, mom," said Tyler.

"What would you like to eat?" I asked.

"I want waffles," he said as he shook his head like a wet dog after a bath, a tic I had been seeing for the past week.

"You had waffles for breakfast. Wouldn't you like something else?"

"No, I want waffles."

At least he was going to eat something. I heated the waffles, put them on a paper plate, buttered them and poured syrup over them. I called him to the table and put the plate in front of him.

He looked at me with an evil grin. "I'm not hungry," he said. With that, he turned the plate over and smeared the food across the table. I should have known this was going to happen. He burst into manic laughter. I was so weary that I no longer had the energy to dance the endless Tyler tango. I wondered what gave him the strength to continue in his anguish. As I tried to catch my breath and slow my growing frustration, he spread his body across the table and began to lick the food and syrup from it, through crazed giggles. I peeled his body off the table, cleaned his face and hands and directed him towards the den. "Go watch T.V." I told him.

"Okay," he said. He sat on the couch staring at the T.V. and picking at his lip. I could see the wheels clicking in his head. He had not received the desired response to the mess in the kitchen. "Mom, can I go back to the hospital?" he asked.

"No," I said. "The hospital is not a place to live. It's a place to go when you need a rest, to think about what is happening in your life," I explained.

"I want to live there," he said.

"You can't live there," I sat down on the couch next to him. "You need to live in our family. Why would you want to live in a hospital? We love you. You can have a good life here with daddy, Trevor, Jonathan and me."

"I don't want to live in a DAMN family!" he snapped jumping up from the couch to get away from me."

I understood this. Tyler was having no success at living in a family. He just didn't understand what it was all about. At the hospital, fewer demands were put on him and he could hide in the dark alleys of his mind rocking and engaging in self-stimulating behaviors. I think Tyler had been happy to be away from a situation in which he always seemed to be failing.

"Did you hear me?" he asked raising his voice. "I don't want to live in a DAMN family!"

I heard you Tyler," I said. "But for now, you have no choice."

The doctors at the hospital had given us some medications that were supposed to help him relax at bedtime. I was to start with one pill and move up to three pills if necessary. This seemed like a good time to start.

He went back to Tootsie's crate and banged on it as she snarled and snapped at him. I pulled him away from the crate.

"We don't do that to the dog," I said.

He laughed as I picked him up and moved him to the couch in the den again. I couldn't believe he had been returned to our home. Nothing had changed. We were at the same point as before he was hospitalized. What was I going to do? How much longer could this go on? Just then Trevor and Steven came downstairs. Steven had been Trevor's best friend for years and was like another son because he spent so much time with our family. As they entered the kitchen, they were hit with an onslaught of, "Fuck you! Fuck you!"

Trevor took in the situation and said, "Oh, fuck this!"

I knew he was embarrassed and trying to ease the tension by making his friend laugh. He succeeded. Steven laughed out loud, knowing how unusual it was for Trevor to behave inappropriately. I ignored Trevor, but I thought, "Oh great. Now I'm losing control of my other children."

After a few minutes, Trevor came into the den where I was sitting and said, "I'm sorry about what I said. I was just trying to be funny."

"I know, Trevor. Don't worry about it. Just don't say that again."

Steven needed a ride home, but I couldn't take him in the middle of a Tyler breakdown. I told him to call home and see if his mother could come to pick him up.

Trevor came back into the den while Steven was on the phone and said, "I really am sorry about what I said." Trevor understood how important it was for me to know that even if Tyler's behavior was out of control, I could count on the rest of my family to remain steady.

"It's O.K.," I said and pulled him close for a hug. "I know you won't say it again. It's just very hard to know how to act around Tyler when he gets like this."

"Mom, I need to use the bathroom," interrupted Tyler.

"Okay," I said. "Let's go." I followed him into the bathroom and stood at the doorway watching as he reached for the toilet paper to wipe himself. Suddenly he took the paper away from his bottom and smeared feces on the bathroom wall. I pulled him out of the bathroom and cleaned him up.

"Pull up your pants," I said trying to maintain my composure.

"No," he said laughing so hard he could not stand up.

I grabbed him and pulled up his pants and returned him to the couch in the den. What, I wondered, motivated this child? Was there any possibility he would ever get past his thirst for negative behavior? He was sitting on the couch when he came up with a new idea. He leaned over the couch and blew his nose into the sofa. I was flabbergasted. It wasn't even safe to let him sit on the couch.

"Can I go to the bathroom again?" he giggled.

"No, you're finished in the bathroom," I said.

"But now I'm ready to do the right thing."

"It's too late. I don't believe you."

"I'm taking a time-out. One, two, three, four, five. Okay,

I'm ready. Can I go now?"

"No Tyler. You're finished in the bathroom."

"I'm going to count to five again and then I'm going to kill you."

I ignored what he said, sat down and stared blankly at the T.V. Suddenly he shifted gears. "I'm sick. I have a fever and a cold. I threw up in school," he said.

"You're fine. Your teacher would have written a note to me if you had been sick in school."

"She's stupid like you."

Trevor came into the room and spread out his homework.

"Fuck you, Trevor," Tyler said.

"Trevor, do you really want to do your homework here?" I asked.

"I want to be here. I'm afraid Tyler is going to hurt you," Trevor said. "I want to stay here just in case."

"I can handle Tyler," I said to reassure him. "You don't need to worry about me."

"I can't help it," said Trevor. "Can't I stay?"

"Okay, but why don't you put on your headphones so you will not hear him cursing at you," I said. "I don't want you to get a headache."

"Fuck you, Trevor. Fuck you," Tyler chanted.

"Trevor has his headphones on and he can't hear you," I said. He stopped talking and looked at Trevor as if trying to come up with a new way to get to him. It had been an hour since Tyler took his first dose of medication and he still showed no signs of fatigue. I decided to give him another dose with the hope he would settle down and move towards sleep.

"Fuck you," he said as he swallowed the pill.

Trevor came to me with his homework. "I need help with this problem," he said. "They are asking me for the area of this rectangle. I just add up the lengths of the sides, right?"

"No," I said. "That will give you the perimeter. To get the area, you must multiply the width times the length."

"Fuck you, Trevor!" shouted Tyler disrupting our conversation. "Fuck you, mom."

Trevor and I ignored his outburst. "That's right. I forgot," said Trevor. "Now I remember."

"What if I stick this middle finger in your face?" Tyler asked as he jumped off the couch. He started to wave his finger in front of my face. I felt my body grow tense. I picked him up and moved him back to the couch. I put him face down on it and held him there with my hand on his back.

"Tyler," I said. "If you calm down and behave, I will take you upstairs for a bath."

"Yes, bath. No, bath," he said.

"Who are you talking to?" I asked.

"I'm arguing with my brain in my head. Why are you

185

holding me down?"

"I don't know."

"That's right. You don't know anything."

I was holding him down because I hoped he would settle down. By holding him down, I exercised the one thing that gave me some control over his actions—I was physically stronger. I was also walking that very dangerous thin line between being in control of my behavior and losing control. If I physically took control of the situation, there was always a chance that anger would take over and I wouldn't be able to stop. If I gave in to the anger I felt for Tyler, I was sure I could hurt him. I must remember the Colorado mom. I moved away from him. I stood across the room looking at him. I looked at Trevor lying on the floor doing his homework. He deserved much more. It was so unfair to him and Jonathan.

Just then, Tyler jumped up from the couch and poked at me with his finger again. He jabbed at me repeatedly. At the same time he said, "I'm ready to take my bath now."

I told Trevor to call Timmy's house and tell Jonathan that it was time to come home. Jonathan came in the door and seemed to sense the tension immediately. He came to me, reached up on his tiptoes and said, "Can I have a kiss?" I leaned forward and kissed him. I knew that I must never forget how lucky I was to have two fine sons. I could never give up hope that we would find an answer to the situation with Tyler. The phone rang and I went to the kitchen to answer it. Tyler followed me and continued to poke at me and stick his tongue out. It was Roger, calling from work to see how things were going.

"He's back and stronger than ever," I said.

"Well tonight's my last night of work and then I'll be home for a few days," he said. "I'll be able to give you some relief then. Just hang in there."

When I finished the phone call, I noticed Tyler was finally slowing down. I took him upstairs for a bath after which he became drowsy and I put him into bed. I closed the door to his bedroom and breathed a sigh of relief. I had made it through another day.

CHAPTER 28
DECEMBER 9, 1996

Tyler returned home from school full of anger.

"Why don't you have the Christmas decorations up?" he demanded. Apparently he had seen Christmas lights on houses he passed on the bus ride home.

"We'll probably put the lights up this weekend," I said.

"You won't put up the lights. Dad will. You can't do anything right," he barked at me as his shoulders rolled in his newest tic. "I want the lights up tomorrow. Dad will be home in the morning and he'll put the lights up."

"Maybe you can talk with him about that tomorrow," I said.

"You're stupid," he said. I thought a change of scenery might stop him from perseverating about the lights.

"Trevor! Jonathan!" I called. "Let's go to Mc Donald's for dinner." They came downstairs and got their coats on.

"I'm not going to eat," said Tyler.

"That's okay," I told him flatly. "You can go to the play area while we eat."

"I'm hungry," said Trevor. "I want chicken nuggets."

"Me too," chimed in Jonathan. "And I want a milkshake."

"Fuck you Trevor! Fuck you Jonathan!" shouted Tyler.

"Put your coat on Tyler," I said.

"No, I'm not wearing a coat," said Tyler.

"Okay, well let's go then," I said.

By this time Trevor and Jonathan knew the rules just didn't apply to Tyler. Wrestling with him, forcing him to wear a coat would only force me into a physical battle and leave me drained. Trevor and Jonathan didn't question why Tyler was heading out into cold without a coat. Instead, they snapped on their coats and moved to the car. As we stepped into the cold night air, I felt a shiver run through my body, but Tyler showed no reaction to the chill.

We pulled up to McDonald's as Tyler reiterated defiantly, "I'm not going to eat!"

"Okay," I said. "Why don't you go play in the ball pit?"

I knew it was wrong to let him do whatever he wanted, but my goals had changed. Since I couldn't effect a change in him, I was intent on buying some peace for my other two sons. Tyler twisted his lip with his fingers, thought for a moment, then ran toward the play area, his little nylon running suit rustling as he ran. I turned to Trevor and Jonathan, "Let's go eat."

We ordered our food and sat down. "Hey mom," Trevor said. "My team is playing the Piranhas this weekend. I can't wait. They're in first place, but I bet we can beat them."

"I'm sure you can," I said amazed at how he was able to discuss normal kid things in the midst of this chaos.

"Am I playing this weekend?" Jonathan asked. He was almost five now and looked forward to his hockey games as much as Trevor did.

"I'll have to check the schedule," I said. 'I think you have a game on Friday."

"Good," said Jonathan. "Can we leave Tyler at home?"

"If dad isn't working one of us can stay with Tyler," I said.

"I hate to bring Tyler," said Jonathan. "He always embarrasses me in front of my friends."

"I know," I said. "We'll work something out."

I glanced over towards the ball pit where Tyler played with a little girl who appeared to be about two years younger than him. They chatted and jumped around and from where I sat he looked like an adorable little boy who was playing appropriately with another child. I so wanted to get inside that little head and see what motivated him.

When we got home, Tyler followed me into the kitchen and said, "I'm hungry."

I had expected this. It was his way of being in control. He would decide when it was time to eat. I fixed him a salad which was one thing he might eat. He ate two bites and said he was finished with a Cheshire cat grin on his face. I was becoming more resigned to the fact that I was just a slave to the life that Tyler sketched out for me. I emptied his plate into the garbage and loaded the dishwasher.

When I finished, I looked up to see him standing naked in

the laundry room adjoining our kitchen with a pair of his father's underwear that he had taken from the hamper in his hand.

"What are you doing?" I asked.

"I like to smell daddy's underwear," he said.

As I stared at him in disbelief, he put the underwear on his head. I picked him up, returned the underwear to the hamper and carried him upstairs. He scratched me, leaving bright red tracks on my arm. I pulled my arm away and shifted him to my other hip. He turned his head and sank his teeth into my other arm. A rush of pain ran through my arm. I put him in the tub as the water flowed in. I had cups and sponges in the tub for the kids to play with and Tyler filled a sponge and squeezed it over a cup. He was engrossed with this activity, so I left the room to get his pajamas. Trevor and Jonathan were doing homework together on the floor in Trevor's room. I was glad they had each other because Tyler took up so much of my time.

"Are you guys all right or do you need help?" I asked.

"We're good," said Trevor, smiling up at me. I ached to curl up on the floor and hang out with them, but it wasn't safe to leave Tyler alone for too long. I returned to the bathroom where Tyler still played with the sponges and cups which had calmed him down. I got him out of the tub and gave him his pajamas.

"Can I go back to the hospital?" he asked. "Chris, a boy at my school, was at that hospital and my teacher says if he doesn't behave he'll be sent back there. Can I go back there?"

"No, Tyler. You live with us."

"I don't want to live here. I hate you!"

He finished dressing and I escorted him to his room. I gave him some toys, left the room and went downstairs to start a load of laundry. I was only gone a few minutes when Trevor called me, "Mom, you better come up here!"

I ran upstairs to find Tyler at the bathroom sink. He was soaked from head to foot and water from the sink cascaded on the floor like a waterfall. When he saw my face, he exploded into laughter. I reached for the faucet as he streaked past me. I heard his feet thumping down the stairs followed by a loud thud as he jumped over the final five steps. As I mopped up the bathroom, I heard something crash. I ran downstairs to find Tyler flinging the dog's aluminum dish across the floor. I carried him back upstairs. Trevor was standing at the top of the stairs.

"Mom, are you all right?" he asked.

"I'm okay," I said. "I'm going to keep Tyler in his room until he falls asleep."

I put Tyler on his bed and held him there. He spit, kicked and scratched. There was nothing else to do. It was no longer a matter of finding a way for him to succeed. Now, what mattered was having my family survive in tact until Tyler was removed from the house. I was at my wits end. After about ten minutes he began to rock his head from side to side and I knew he was falling asleep. I covered him with a blanket and left the room.

Jonathan had fallen asleep on the floor in Trevor's room so I gathered him up and put him to bed. I returned to Trevor's room and lay down on the bed beside him.

"My head is splitting," Trevor said. "I took some Tylenol, but it isn't helping. I'm so angry at Tyler. I hate him when he hurts you."

"Don't worry about me. I'm tough," I told him as I rubbed his back. "He's not really hurting me. I can handle it. Dad and I are trying to have Tyler removed from the home. You just have to hang in there until we find another place for him to live."

"I know," he said. "It's just so hard. What if he seriously hurts you or dad or Jonathan? I'm afraid for my family."

"Dad and I will always watch out for you and Jonathan and we can take care of ourselves. You have to have confidence that this will all work out somehow. Try to relax now and get some rest. I'll stay here with you until you fall asleep."

CHAPTER 29
DECEMBER 10, 1996

I woke Tyler up for school and brought him downstairs for breakfast. I sat him at the table, but he hopped off the chair and ran to the den. I put a plate of pancakes on the table and brought him back to the chair.

"You need to eat breakfast, Tyler," I said.

He looked at me for a second, then put his feet against the table and rocketed the chair backwards. He jumped off the chair and ran to the den again. I followed him, took his hand and led him back to the table. A brick room divider separates the den from the kitchen in our house. As we passed it, Tyler pulled away from me, falling and banging his head on the brick wall.

"You hurt me!' he shouted with both of his hands gripping the back of his head. "My head hurts!"

I backed away. I should have just let him skip breakfast. I stared at him hoping he was not really hurt. He got up and ran from the room. I breathed a sigh of relief. There was no blood and he seemed fine. I followed him upstairs and laid his clothes out.

"I'm not getting dressed today," he said. "I'm going to school in my pajamas."

"You can't go to school in your pajamas," I said. "Everyone gets dressed for school."

The encounter downstairs had shaken me and I was not about to physically wrestle him into his clothes. The bus arrived a little later and Tyler put on his coat and left the house in his pajamas.

Trevor did not move on to the new day as easily. He had not forgotten any of last night's events.

"Mom, I still have a headache," he said when I went to his room to wake him up.

"Did Tyler leave for school yet?"

"Yes, he's gone," I said. "Come have breakfast. Maybe if you put something in your stomach, you'll feel better."

"I have to go to school today," he said. "I have a history report that Danny and I have been working on together and we have to present it to the class today."

"Well, take your time getting ready," I said. "You can always go in a little late. I'll talk to Mr. Parker for you"

"Thanks mom, but I don't want to go in late," he said. "I'll be all right."

Trevor's was a worrier under normal circumstances, but Tyler's behavior pushed his concerns to the limit. He had dark circles under his eyes and I could see pain permeating throughout his expression. I wanted to tell him to stay home and enjoy a day without Tyler. I wanted to watch T.V. or read books with him—to assure him that home was still a comfortable and safe place to be, but I knew that probably wasn't the best thing for him. If he went to school and got involved with the activities of the day, he might forget about the troubles at home for a while and that might be the best thing for his headache. However, I did go in to school to talk with Trevor's fifth grade teacher, Mr. Parker, and with the school nurse so they would know about his headaches and the problems at home. They both promised me they would keep an eye on Trevor and let me know how he was handling himself in school.

Later that morning, I got a call from the nurse at Tyler's school.

"Tyler was in my office today," she said. "He says you pushed him and he hurt his head."

I gasped. "I tried to move Tyler to the breakfast table.

"Don't worry," she said. "Everyone here knows that Tyler makes his own problems and that you wouldn't intentionally hurt him. We just thought you should know what he's saying."

I felt as if my legs would no longer support me. This was my worst nightmare. What if he had really hurt himself or what if the staff at his school thought I had hurt him? I would lose Trevor and Jonathan. I promised myself I was not going to let that happen. I resolved to avoid all physical encounters with him.

Jonathan went to school that afternoon, but I surprised him and picked him up after classes to grab some time alone with him. His kindergarten teacher, Mrs. Ball, met me near the buses. I had spoken with her before and she was familiar with the stress the family was under at home.

"How are things going with Tyler?" she asked.

"Not well," I said. "His negative behavior is increasing on a daily basis. We never know what he'll do next and I'm really worried he'll hurt himself or one of us."

"I ask because Jonathan is showing signs of a child under stress."

"Oh, what are you seeing?"

"Well, he seems to want to call attention to himself. He does things like calling out when I am talking."

I felt a pain in my heart as I looked over at Jonathan who was now playing with another student. "Jonathan is definitely being short changed when it comes to attention at home. Tyler takes up so much of my time it's impossible to find even five minutes to read a book with Jonathan. The whole family is stressed and living in a crisis situation. I don't know where it will all end. It's a terrifying way to live."

"I know you're doing the best you can. I just wanted to let you know about Jonathan. What have you heard about getting Tyler into a residential placement?"

"We've had the psychiatric recommendation since we left the hospital, but we seem to be the only ones who have a sense of urgency about the matter. No one else is living through this day after day. Please keep me informed of any other changes you see in Jonathan and I'll try to spend more time with him. Thanks so much for caring."

"Take care of yourself and hang in there."

"I will. C'mon Jonathan. It's time to go home."

Jonathan ran towards me with a big grin and grabbed my hand. As we walked towards the car, I said, "Jonathan, Mrs. Ball said you weren't following the classroom rules today. What's going on?" His little face grew serious.

"I don't know," he said. "I was just bored at school today. Tomorrow will be better."

"I hope so," I said. "It makes me sad to hear that you're not doing the right thing." I didn't want to make too big a deal out of this. I understood why he was acting out. We reached the car and got in. I changed the subject. "Are you going to play with Timmy today?"

"I don't know. Is Tyler home yet?"

"No. His bus won't be home for another half an hour."

"Maybe, I will play with Timmy. Turn the radio up, please. I like to listen to the Christmas music, especially this song, Grandma Got Run Over By a Reindeer."

"I like that song too." We drove home singing along with the radio.

Tyler arrived home, did his homework, ate dinner and took a bath without any major problems. I had no explanation why he was moving through the evening so well, but I welcomed it.

Later that evening, I went to Trevor's room to help him with his math homework. I was sitting on the floor with him when Tyler started to pull at the door knob.

"Tyler, I'm trying to help Trevor with his homework now," I said. "You need to leave the door alone and go back to your room. I'll be finished in a few minutes."

Tyler didn't like that answer. He threw the weight of his

body against the door screeching like a demon. Just like that, his mood had changed and we were in trouble again. I moved him away from the door as he yelled at me.

"Fuck you, you idiot," he said. "You want to hurt me? I'm going to kill you."

Just as I reached the door, he ran back to his room. I followed him and he got what he wanted which was to separate me from Trevor. As I reached the room, Tyler yelled, "You can't come in here! This is my room and I don't want you to touch my stuff."

As I stood in the doorway, he turned and faced the window overlooking the front lawn. He lunged towards the window.

"I don't want these curtains anymore!" he yelled.

He reached up and pulled at the curtains until the brackets for the rod separated from the wall with a snap and flew across the room. The curtains and the rod fell to the floor in front of the window.

"What are you doing?" I yelled. I moved him away from the window as I picked up the curtains. As I bent down, he flung himself at my bare feet and bit them. I felt his teeth tear into the flesh on top of my feet. I looked down at the impression of his teeth rising into little red welts. Trevor and Jonathan stood in the doorway watching the meltdown.

"Boys, go back to your rooms," I said. "There is no need for you to watch this."

"I'm afraid to leave you. What if he hurts you?" Trevor asked as his voice cracked.

"Yes!" Tyler shouted. "But I'm not going to just hurt her, I'm going to kill her!"

He spun around and pulled one of the drawers from his dresser. I moved across the room to stop him, but as I tried to close the drawer, he threw his weight against it and I heard a snap of wood.

"Tyler! You broke your dresser!" I yelled. I was just putting out little brush fires while the main fire still threatened to destroy everything I valued. Tyler ran into the master bedroom as I followed closely behind. He grabbed the phone and lifted it above his head.

"Put the phone down, Tyler," I said. He threw the phone at me, snapping the cord. Trevor and Jonathan watched from the hallway, looks of terror on their faces.

"Trevor, take Jonathan downstairs and watch a movie," I said. "I can handle this. Please, do this for me."

Trevor grabbed Jonathan's small hand and led him downstairs as Tyler ran back into his room. He fell on the floor and pulled at the baseboard heating surrounding his room.

"You want heat?" he shouted. "Watch this!"

He couldn't move the baseboard heating, so he attacked a growth chart I had glued to the back of his door. On it, I had recorded all the boys' milestones in height and weight on each birthday. It was glued on pretty firmly, so he didn't have much luck destroying it. He scratched wildly at the door as I went into the bathroom to get his evening medication. When I returned, I found him sitting on the floor with Jonathan's Yak-Bak, a toy that recorded a voice and then played it back every time a button was pushed. Tyler had recorded "Fuck you, baby! Fuck you!" He rolled on the floor, laughing every time he hit the button. I took the toy away, at a loss to know what to do now. I felt drained of energy and I just needed to stop him.

Suddenly, I remembered how well deep pressure calmed Tyler. I pulled the comforter off his bed, spread it on the floor and put him on top of it. I rolled him up like a little sausage in the blanket and tied it with the soft belt from my bathrobe, so he was immobile. Only his head was exposed. He continued to curse and spit at me, but after a few minutes, the pressure of being wrapped up relaxed him. Eventually his head rocked back and forth and he fell asleep. I untied him and put him into bed. I went down to see Jonathan and Trevor.

"Tyler is asleep," I said.

I sat down on the couch between them to watch the movie. Before it ended, they were both fast asleep. I carried them upstairs one at a time to their rooms and tucked them snugly in to bed.

I went to the closet of the master bedroom and pulled out the extra twin size bed we kept in the closet for sleepovers. I set it up on the landing of the second floor that led to all four bedrooms. I wanted to be there if Tyler woke up during the night and threatened the well-being of either of his brothers. Tootsie accepted this change and took a spot next to the bed in the hall. I knew she feared Tyler and would wake me the instant he stirred.

I lay awake for hours afraid to fall asleep. I couldn't give up hope that things would work out somehow. The next morning I took all the furniture, except the mattress, out of Tyler's room on the advice of his psychiatrist.

CHAPTER 30
DECEMBER 11, 1996

On Friday morning, I brought Tyler's clothes to the kitchen so he could get dressed while I fixed breakfast. He sat on the floor next to the clothes, content to sit there all day having a haunting conversation with an imaginary friend. Fear ran through my veins as I listened to him.

"We have to kill them," he said conspiratorially. Biting his lips, he answered himself. "I know, you're right."

I reminded him several times to get dressed, but he acted as if I were not there. He was like a person in a trance, so I dressed him as he continued to talk to himself.

"They all need to die," he said.

My hands trembled as I buttoned his coat. I told myself that he was a small boy with weak muscle tone and surely would not be able to overpower anyone in the family, but I was terrified.

As soon as he returned home, I administered his meds hoping he would be ready for bed at a reasonable hour. Of course, the flip side of giving him his meds early was that he would probably be up earlier than usual the next morning, but like Scarlett O' Hara, I would worry about that tomorrow.

"Tyler," I said. "You're homework seems easy tonight. You just have to write three sentences using your spelling words. Come sit here at the table next to me and we can work on it."

He dragged himself to the table, pulled out the chair and sat down. "I can't do this," he whined.

"The first word is jump. Can you think of a sentence using that word?"

"I can't."

"Sure you can. Think of a sentence with the word jump."

"I can jump." I knew I was worn out from months of struggle with Tyler, but he was burned out too.

"Good," I said putting my arm on the back of his chair. "I can jump. Now write it on the paper."

He looked at the paper. "What was the sentence?"

"I can jump."

He looked at the paper again and wrote the first word, 'I.' "What was the sentence?"

"I can jump. Write the word *can*."

"I can't."

"Sure you can. Try to focus. Write the word *can.*" I said coaching him from the chair next to him. Without warning, his little hand flew up and slapped me across the face.

"Fuck you!" He shouted.

A gasp erupted from my mouth and my hand flew to my stinging cheek. I could feel the impression of his fingers rising into red welts on my face. I stared at him in disbelief.

"I'm sorry," he said through giggles. So much was happening with Tyler that it was hard to know what caused any of his behavior. Perhaps, the slap was a response to an impulse of anger that he could not control. The giggles might have been a TS tic. It was impossible to know whether or not he was in control of anything he did. He had multiple diagnoses and I had no way of knowing how much of his behavior came from PDD, Tourette Syndrome, or Intermittent Explosive Disorder.

Tootsie sensed the mounting tension and snarled and nipped at his feet. She wasn't hurting him, but he howled, "Ow! Ow! Ow!"

Roger walked into the kitchen and boomed, "What are you doing?" The sound of Roger's voice startled Tyler.

"I'm doing my homework," he said as if everything were fine.

"I was helping him and he slapped me," I said to Roger moving away from the table.

"Why did you do that?" Roger asked.

Tyler sobbed pitifully, "I can't do it."

Roger picked up the home work and put it back into the back pack as I moved towards the stove to finish dinner. Tyler sat at the table crying, "I can't. I can't."

I believed Tyler was in such a state of distress and confusion that he really couldn't accomplish the assignments anymore. Interfering thoughts in his head made focusing impossible. After a few minutes, exhaustion overcame him. He put his head down and fell asleep at the table. Roger carried him upstairs and tucked him into bed.

On Saturday afternoon, Roger and I took the boys to

Wantagh to decorate Lois's tree. Rosemary was already there with her five kids when we arrived.

Tyler rushed ahead of us into the house. "Grandma! Grandma! I'm here to decorate your tree. What do you want me to do?"

"Oh, Tyler," she said from the living room. "I'm so happy to see you. Come to the living room and I'll show you where to start. The twins are stringing popcorn. Maybe you would like to help them?"

"I want to help *you*, Grandma," Tyler said eagerly as the rest of the family reached the front door.

I looked at Roger. "Well, isn't he just so cooperative?"

"Just be glad he's behaving and enjoy the afternoon," said Roger.

"You're right. It would be nice to pass an afternoon without confrontation." I turned to Trevor and Jonathan. "Go ask Grandma what she wants you to do."

"She doesn't care about us," said Trevor. "She just wants Tyler to help her."

"Well, maybe you could find Gregory and see what he's doing," I said. "Jonathan, look for Joseph and see if he needs help. Go on boys." Roger and I found Lois with Tyler in the living room.

"Tyler," she said. "Put this ornament on the tree. I made it at my sewing circle."

"That means it's special," said Tyler as he turned around

and gave me a Damian like grin. He was thrilled to receive the lion's share of Grandma's attention. Tyler hung the ornament on the tree and turned back to Grandma. "How does that look?" he asked as if pleasing her was the most important thing in his life.

"That looks great!" Grandma exclaimed looking at me. Her expression said, "Why do you have difficulty with this child? He's really easy to be with." No matter how many times I explained Tyler's difficulties to her, Lois never admitted that Tyler was highly manipulative. To her, he was just a cute little boy with blond hair and blue eyes who looked like her biological grandchildren.

"Tyler," I said. "Nice job."

He looked over at me, but didn't answer. "Grandma, which one do you want me to hang up next?" he asked.

"Well, let's see," she said as she looked into the box of ornaments. I knew Tyler and Lois would spend the afternoon together, so I moved on to the other kids.

"Hi Joseph, how's it going?" I asked.

"Good, Aunt Patty," he said. "Jonathan and I are stringing popcorn that my mom made."

I looked at Rosemary and smiled. "That's great!" I said. "I'm sure it will look great on the tree."

"Mom, can you help me?" Jonathan asked as he tried to pierce the popcorn with the needle. I sat on the floor next to him and put the popcorn on the string as he handed it to me. He ate two bites for every one he handed to me. Roger fished through a box of ornaments with Trevor and Gregory. We looked like an ideal family passing an afternoon decorating a tree. It was all I really wanted. Why wouldn't Tyler behave like this all the time? He was obviously capable of interacting appropriately when he wanted to. Why was he so intent on disrupting our family life? The rest of the afternoon proceeded pleasantly and we had a great time although Tyler monopolized all of Lois's time.

Grateful to have had an afternoon of peace we headed home at about 7:00p.m. All three boys fell asleep in the car on the way home listening to Christmas carols.

When we got home, Trevor and Jonathan ran for the den and sat down to watch a Christmas movie together. Tyler ran to his room. Within a matter of minutes, he was slamming doors upstairs. Roger looked at me and said, "I'll go. You've had him all week."

"Thanks," I said. "Call me if you need me."

Roger headed up the stairs as Tyler banged the doors fiercely. I heard Roger say, "Stop that now, Tyler. It's time to take a bath and get ready for bed."

"Fuck you!" Tyler screamed. "You can't tell me what to do!"

I turned my attention to the movie Trevor and Jonathan were watching. I sat down on the couch as they snuggled in on either side of me. Upstairs, I heard noise coming from the bathroom, but I really didn't want to know what was happening. I put my arms around the boys and felt the warmth of their bodies on either side of me. In that moment, I was overcome by a glimpse of what life would be like if our troubles with Tyler ever ended. I couldn't help but feel guilty about bringing Tyler into their innocent lives.

Suddenly Tyler burst into the room and the calm was over. He ran to the T.V. and stood in front of it blocking our view of the screen. Roger was right on his heels. He looked at me and said, "Did you hear the noise? He jumped off the side of the tub and into the water. I thought he was going to break his neck. I stopped him and bathed him as well as I could, but he just wouldn't stay still."

"Fuck you, Mom," said Tyler grinning.

Roger picked him up. "C'mon, Tyler. We're going upstairs. Say good-night."

"Fuck you! You're a shit!" Tyler responded as he pinched, bit and kicked Roger. "Why don't you hit me? I want you to hit me! I want to be hurt! Hit me! Hit me! I like to be hurt. I want you to hurt me!"

Roger didn't answer him, but rather showed incredible restraint and carried him quietly upstairs. I turned to the two wide eyed faces looking up at me. "It's okay, boys. Dad can handle Tyler. Let's watch the movie."

"Are you sure?" asked Trevor.

"I'm sure," I said.

Half an hour later, Roger reappeared in the doorway of the den. "He's asleep," he said. He found a place on the couch to watch the movie with us. Before the movie ended, both boys had fallen sound asleep.

CHAPTER 31
DECEMBER 17, 1996

When Tyler was at the hospital, the psychiatrist made the recommendation to have him placed in a residential treatment facility, but it was a long process that began with the school district. I sent copies of the video that had gotten him admitted to the psychiatric hospital along with the doctor's diagnoses to the district. They scheduled a CSE, a meeting of the Committee on Special Education. Before Tyler could be placed in a residential treatment facility, his status as a student with special needs had to include an update of his increasing list of disabilities. This change in status was sent to the Education Department of the State of New York in Albany which would be responsible for finding an appropriate placement for his needs. The CSE meeting was just the first step in having Tyler removed from the home and it took place in the office of the Superintendent of the District, Mr. Grace.

"Mr. and Mrs. Havlicek," he began, "I've reviewed the videotape of your son that you left with my office."

I was already nervous, but now my palms became sweaty. What if he failed to understand how desperate the situation was for us?

"I have to say," Mr. Grace continued, "I don't know how you've been doing this. There's a point at which any reasonable person would crack." He shook his head. "There seems to be no question that Tyler should be placed in a residential treatment facility as quickly as possible. His teachers at school find him to be as unmanageable in the classroom as he is at home and he's not learning in his current placement. We'll send our recommendations to Albany immediately. Do you have any questions?"

Finally, relief was in sight. Of course, I had one question. "How long will it take?"

"We'll move the paperwork along as quickly as we can from our end, but once the paperwork lands in Albany it's out of our hands. We'll stress to them how urgent the need is and we'll send along a copy of the video tape that got him admitted to the hospital if that's all right with you," Mr. Grace explained.

"I'd appreciate that," Roger said. "I feel as though we're racing closer towards disaster each day."

"I understand. Does anyone on the committee have any comments?" Mr. Grace asked looking around the room.

"I think we all want you to know that we hope everything will work out for you," said Dr. Hugo, the school psychologist.

"Thank-you," I said. "I appreciate that." This was a very big moment for us. I walked outside feeling optimistic.

"How are you?" asked Roger. At that point, I was sad for Tyler and what he was about to lose, but I needed to save my family.

"It looks like our nightmare may actually come to an end."

"Yeah, thank god. We just have to hang in there and keep everyone safe until it happens."

"It'll be a lot easier knowing our situation won't last forever."

That afternoon, Roger took Trevor to hockey practice and Jonathan tagged along with them, leaving me alone with Tyler. I walked down the driveway to meet him as he got off the bus in his pajamas. Evidently he had refused to change his clothes at school.

As soon as his feet touched the street, he looked at me and said, "I want to go back to the hospital."

"We've been over this, Tyler," I said. "The hospital is not a place to live. You live here."

"You're stupid," he said as he walked towards the house. "You should shut up."

I followed him into the house as he went to the Christmas tree and grabbed an ornament. "Do you like this?" he asked waving the ornament in my face. "I'm going to break it."

I jumped towards him, snatched the ornament and placed it high on a kitchen shelf. He seemed surprised I had taken the ornament away so easily and stood there looking bewildered for a moment sucking his thumb. I went to the kitchen to get his meds as he wandered into the den, slumped onto the couch and picked at the skin around his fingernails.

Suddenly, he jumped up and shouted, "Look! My fingers are bleeding!"

"What did you do?" I asked.

He ran to the dining room and stood next to the holiday tablecloth. "Isn't this new?" he asked. "I'm going to put blood on it!"

"No, Tyler," I said reaching the table just in time to stop him.

He laughed and skipped back to the den where he found a Christmas elf hat.

"This is Jonathan's isn't it?" he asked as he tried to smear blood from his fingers onto the white fleeced edges. I grabbed the hat away from him as he laughed with satisfaction, delighted to have me chasing him around.

"You really need to stop doing this," I told him. "Come to the kitchen and I'll put a band-aid on your fingers."

He grimaced and said, "Why don't you hit me? I like to be hit." His increasing requests to be abused unnerved me.

"I'm not going to hit you, Tyler," I said. "Let's work on your homework."

He jumped from the couch and ran at me with all his force. I picked him up, went into the den and turned on the T.V. I sat on the couch with him on my lap. His back was to me and I wrapped my arms around him tightly. At first, he struggled to get free, but after a few minutes he settled down and his body relaxed.

"I'm ready to do the right thing," he said.

I relaxed my arms for just a second when he suddenly slammed the back of his head into my chin. I tasted blood on my lower lip and felt pain race along my jaw. The area immediately swelled. He slid off my lap as I went to the kitchen to get ice. I was furious at myself for letting my guard down. He followed me to the kitchen.

"I have to go to the bathroom," he said.

I wrapped the ice in a small towel and gently put it against my chin. The chill of the ice sent pain coursing through my chin, but I knew it would help with the swelling. I walked to the bathroom to see what Tyler was doing. He stood in front of the toilet waiting for me. He wiped himself and then took the toilet paper and smeared feces all over the toilet seat.

"This is a mess," he said. "You should clean it up."

Oh, how I wanted to walk out of that house, get in the car and drive far away. I wanted to be out of Tyler's spotlight. He was relentless in his desire to rile me. I still had a few hours before Roger, Trevor and Jon returned—a few more hours alone with Tyler. I cleaned up the mess and waited for his next move. To fully understand my frustration is to fully understand Tyler's determination to keep coming at me every minute of every day. I was overwhelmed and burned out. I don't think I was mad when this happened. I just remember feeling weary and very, very sad. Of course, I couldn't just leave the scene. I had to stick it out. I was the adult and responsible for Tyler's safety even if I couldn't influence his behavior.

I went to the kitchen and returned with paper towels, a garbage bag and cleaning fluid. I reached under Tyler's armpits and made him clean the mess by putting my hands over his and moving them. Hand over hand we moved until the mess was cleaned up. I took a deep breath and waited to see what he would spring on me next.

CHAPTER 32
JANUARY 2, 1997

Trevor and Jonathan ended their Christmas vacation and went back to school, but Tyler had a few more days off. Jonathan's birthday was coming up and I took Tyler with me to shop for birthday presents. He behaved well until we approached the shoe store.

"I need new shoes," Tyler said, although he had on a new pair of shoes. Tyler collected shoes. No matter how many shoes he had, he always wanted new ones. When his brothers stopped wearing their shoes, he took them whether they fit or not.

"You just got those shoes. You don't need new ones," I explained. "We're shopping for Jonathan's birthday."

Tyler walked in front of me and tripped over his feet on purpose, falling to the ground. "Look, I can't walk in these. They don't fit me anymore," he whined.

I climbed over him and looked for the aisle with Jonathan's shoe size. Tyler caught up to me and flung himself on the floor, grabbing his feet and rolling on his back.

"Ow! Ow! Ow! My feet are killing me!" he cried. "These shoes hurt so much!"

"Your shoes are fine. I'm buying these for Jonathan," I said heading for the register. I put the shoes on the counter and reached into my bag for my wallet. Tyler came to the register and stood beside me. I glanced down and noticed that his shoes were gone.

"Where are your shoes?" I asked.

"I threw them in the garbage," he said. "They were no good."

I left the box with the shoes on the counter and headed back down the aisle to search for Tyler's shoes. I fished them out of a nearby garbage can, but he refused to wear them. I paid for Jonathan's shoes while the salesgirl, who appeared to be about twenty years-old wore an expression I had seen many times before. She thought she could do a better job with the adorable blond child. He looked innocent enough. She would have bought him the new shoes he obviously needed. She could not understand why I was being so hard nosed. I turned back to the job at hand. I knew there was no point in trying to get the shoes back on his feet. It would only result in a wrestling match that I was destined to lose as he continued to take the shoes off. I threw his shoes into the bag along with Jonathan's. He followed me out to the car in his stocking feet as other shoppers stared at the mom who let her seven-year old walk through the mall in his stocking feet.

The next day, I went to his room to wake him up. "Tyler, it's time to get up for school," I told him.

"Fuck you," he answered. "I'm not going back to school and you can't make me!"

I walked over to his bed. "Get up!" I bellowed. "You're going to school."

"Oh no, I'm not and you can't make me!" he shouted.

He wasn't even out of bed and he was acting as oppositional as a mule. I was not going to let him stay home from school, not only because it was important for him to go, but also because it was the only relief I got from his reign of terror.

"You're going to school," I said dragging him out of bed.

"You don't touch me!" You're hurting me!"

I didn't answer him, but rather went downstairs to prepare his breakfast.

"Don't ignore me!" He continued to yell at me as he followed me downstairs.

I made pancakes and put a plate in front of him. He dumped them onto the floor where Tootsie quickly gobbled them up. Then he licked the syrup from the plate making his face and hands sticky. I took the plate away from him, cleaned him up and removed him from the table. I carried him into the den and sat him down next to his clothes.

"It's time to get dressed," I said as calmly as I could.

He fell on the floor in a little heap and cried. "I'm sick. I can't stop coughing,"

"You were fine a minute ago."

"No, I wasn't. I've been coughing since yesterday. I can't go to school."

I went to the kitchen cabinet and found some cherry flavored children's cough syrup which I poured into a teaspoon and gave to him. He swallowed it quickly and said, "I'm all better now." Of course, the medication had not even had a chance to reach his bloodstream before he made this declaration, but he got dressed and within a half an hour he was out the door and on the bus.

In the afternoon, he came off the bus in tears. The bus driver said that he cried and screamed all the way home because she wouldn't change the radio station every time a song came on that he didn't like.

Later that evening, Tyler said something that scared me more than anything he had done previously. Trevor was watching T.V. in the den while I cleared the kitchen. Tyler was sitting on a cedar chest near the entry to the den and picking at his lip as if deep in thought.

He whispered softly, "It will be hard because Trevor is much bigger than me. I think I will get a hammer and bang him on the head while he is sleeping. Then I will get a knife and cut his head off."

I stood there horrified. "Tyler, what did you say?"

His head snapped up in surprise. "Oh, nothing. I'm watching T.V."

"I heard you, Tyler and I don't like what you said."

I wanted him away from Trevor so I led him upstairs and got him ready for bed. Fortunately, Trevor had not heard him, but I slept in the hallway that night with one eye fixed on the door to Tyler's room, alert for any sound of movement.

CHAPTER 33
JANUARY 8, 1997

Tyler's behavior became more erratic as I searched desperately for assistance. I contacted OMRDD, the Office of Mental Retardation and Developmental Disabilities and found a lifeline there in a woman named Cara Morgen. She supported and directed me as we waited to hear about Tyler's placement. She understood the growing danger my family faced and suggested I write a letter to my local congressman about our situation to see if he could make Tyler's placement happen faster. The letter explained my fear that someone was going to get hurt if my family continued on the current path.

Cara also suggested I call a local children's psychiatric hospital that had a mobile crisis unit that could come to the house and evaluate Tyler for a temporary placement. As I explained the urgency of our situation to the counselors from the mobile unit, Tyler returned home from school.

He burst into the house and yelled, "I want to play with my yak-bak!"

"Excuse me," I said into the phone turning to Tyler. "I'm on the phone now. I'll speak with you in a few minutes."

"No!" he yelled slamming his body into the dining room wall. "You talk to me right now!" He grabbed for the phone and scratched my hand as he did. I told the counselor I needed to get off the phone. I'm sure he heard what was going on and the urgency in my voice. He made an appointment to stop by the house the following day with the mobile crisis unit saying he might be able to get Tyler placed at children's hospital temporarily. I hung up the phone and turned to deal with Tyler. Again and again he slammed his body into the wall until he finally dropped to the rug crying, "I want to kill myself!"

"Why are you saying that?" I asked. "Did you have a bad day at school?"

"Everyday is a bad day," he answered as he got up and threw himself against the wall again. It was pitiful to see his mental anguish.

Trevor came downstairs to see what all the noise was about and as he stepped down the final step, Tyler jumped up and charged him like a ram. His head made contact with Trevor's stomach and both boys went sprawling across the floor. Trevor had the wind knocked out of him and lay on the floor under Tyler, gasping for breath. Tyler got back on his feet and looked down at Trevor sneering, "Good, I'm glad I hurt you. I'll kill you soon."

"Tyler, don't say that!" I yelled. I went to Trevor and helped him to his feet. "Are you all right?"

"I'm okay," Trevor said. He tried to sound brave, but I knew he was more scared of Tyler every day.

Later that evening, Trevor had hockey practice. Roger was working so I set out with the three boys. I dropped Trevor off at the rink a half hour before he was scheduled to skate, so he would have time to get dressed in his equipment. I took Jonathan and Tyler to the mall across the street to return a pair of boots I had gotten for Christmas. The exchange was a snap and we were walking out of the mall within fifteen minutes.

Great, I thought to myself, we can be back at the rink before Trevor hits the ice and we won't miss any of his practice. As we stepped out of the mall into the dark, cold evening air, I took Jonathan's hand and reached for Tyler's hand. Suddenly, he jumped away from me like a spooked horse.

"Jonathan!" he yelled. "Look out! The *REAL* man is coming to get us!"

I couldn't imagine what he meant. He sprang away from us and ran into the darkness across the parking lot. Twenty feet away from us a car's wheels screeched as he ran in front of it. For a few seconds I stood there stunned, holding Jonathan's hand tightly as I watched Tyler race further away from us. A second screech of tires against asphalt woke me up. I ran after Tyler, dragging Jonathan along behind me.

"Tyler, STOP!" I yelled frantically. "STOP!" I knew it was going to be impossible to catch Tyler while dragging Jonathan behind me so I picked him up in my arms. Customers moving across the parking lot heard my desperate cries. A man and his wife loading their trunk with parcels saw Tyler coming towards them. The man reached out and grabbed him in a bear hug.

"Where are you going little guy?" he asked as I caught up to them.

"The *REAL* man is coming!" Tyler yelled as he struggled to catch his breath and wiggle away from the stranger. "The *REAL* man is coming!

"Thank-you for stopping him," I said to the man as I caught up. "Tyler, you know it's dangerous to run in the parking lot. What were you thinking?"

He looked up at me with a smile and calmly said, "I'm ready to watch Trevor skate now."

I led Tyler and Jonathan back to the car. I was out of breath and my lungs burned from the chilly air. Adrenaline spiked through my body and I was shaking, but as was often the case, Tyler was calm. He created havoc with all of us and then as we reached a state of high anxiety, he acted as if everything was fine.

"Tyler," I asked, "who is the REAL man?"

"I dunno," he said.

"Who were you running from?"

"I dunno,"

I got Jonathan and Tyler into the car and drove back to the ice rink. Trevor was already skating and his eyes darted nervously around as he wondered where I was. When he saw me, he smiled with relief. I settled down on the bleachers.

"Tyler, I want you to sit with me and watch Trevor skate," I said.

Jonathan found a friend and the two of them played with matchbox cars along the bleachers. I was watching Trevor skate when I glanced at Tyler and noticed he had a book of matches in his hands.

"Where did you get those?" I asked.

"I found them on the ground at the mall," he answered. "I'm going to burn the house down when everyone is sleeping."

A new fear enveloped me. I snatched the matches from his hands before he could say another word. He ducked down and put his hands over his head as if he expected me to hit him. He slid off the bench onto the space between the seats of the bleachers and cowered on the ground.

"What are you doing?" I asked him.

He didn't answer me. I returned him to the seat next to me, but every time I looked in his direction he put his hands up like a boxer protecting himself. I had no idea what had spurred this behavior and I was scared to think what might happen next.

CHAPTER 34
JANUARY 11, 1997

As I put Tyler's clothes out for him, he whined, "I don't want to go to school. It's too boring."

"All children go to school," I said. "You must go to school to learn."

"I hate school," he moaned. "It's too hard."

"I know school is hard for you, Tyler. All students have problems at times."

"The bus trip is too long,"

"I'm sorry about the bus, Tyler, but you go to that school because you don't follow directions or do the right thing. You could attend a school closer to home if you behaved better."

"I can't do the work at school," he sobbed.

"You have to try, Tyler."

Tyler's interfering behavior kept him from staying on task so he rarely succeeded. He was on a program that reinforced his good behavior, but as far as he was concerned, they could keep their point system as long as they paid attention to him at all times. Of course, that meant the attention Tyler received was negative. I just didn't know how to make him see that he was the one making his life so difficult. Tyler was like a man who goes on a hunger strike and deprives himself of food to make a point. Rather than food, Tyler starved himself of a close relationship. To give up his fight and end the game, Tyler had to engage in the one thing which he was desperate to avoid, a relationship in which he depended on another human being.

Later that morning, I received a phone call from Tyler's social worker at school, Clara Frank.

"Tyler is having more difficulties at school," she said. "He's unable to cope with any of the classroom activities and lately he breaks down and cries whenever demands are put on him."

"He's been crying more frequently at home, too."

"He flies off the handle and overreacts to everything," said Miss Frank. "He loses control for no apparent reason."

"I don't know what to tell you. We're seeing his anger and frustration escalating on a daily basis. We've approached DSS to see if we can have Tyler placed in foster care until he is placed in a residential treatment facility, but they said it would be difficult to find a placement for him. Everything at home is so volatile, I'm afraid someone is going to be hurt and the whole family needs a major break."

"Well, I just wanted to let you know Tyler's behavioral problems in the classroom have been increasing. If there is anything we can do to help you, please let us know."

"Thanks. I'll keep in touch."

I knew Tyler was having more difficulty at school. While the family was feeling the stress of life with him, he was feeling the stress of being out of control. He broke down and cried more often and his tone was more and more hopeless as time went on. He wasn't happy, but he had no idea how to change things and I was at a loss to know how to bring him back from the dark hole he had sunken into. I knew that living with my family only provided a battleground for the invisible forces raging in him. With each passing day, Tyler moved closer to losing control over his thoughts and actions, yet he persisted in the behavior that left him so unhappy.

Later that day, I received a letter from DSS. They turned down our request to put Tyler into another family either as a foster child or through adoption because they knew we were working to have Tyler placed in a residential placement and that placing Tyler, even temporarily, would be a duplication of efforts. I was furious. It could take months for our application for residential placement to be approved if it ever was. I didn't think the family could survive much longer without something terrible happening. Hopefully, the mobile crisis unit from the children's hospital might have a solution for the situation.

Tyler had problems the minute he returned home from school. He had refused to eat his lunch at school and now his stomach hurt. I fed him early, but then he didn't know what to do for the rest of the evening.

"Mom," he whined. "Jonathan stole my pen. I saw it in his room."

"Tyler, I don't think Jonathan has your pen," I said with an exasperated sigh. "Come on, we'll look in his room."

"Oh, I know he has it," he said. "He's always stealing things from me."

I ignored that last statement and escorted him to Jonathan's room. "Jonathan, did you see Tyler's pen?" I asked.

"No, mom," said Jonathan.

"Tyler thinks you have it," I said. "Do you mind if we look around your room?"

"You can look, but I don't have it," said Jonathan.

Tyler and I looked around Jonathan's room, but not surprisingly, we did not find the pen.

"I know," said Tyler. "Trevor stole it."

"Tyler, nobody stole your pen," I said feeling exhausted. "I think you should search *your* room again."

"Nobody listens to me," Tyler said. "That's why I'm going to kill you all some day soon. Jonathan, I'm going to shoot you with Daddy's gun."

"Go to your room, Tyler!" I shouted. "I won't have you talking like that."

"No!" He shouted back.

Instinctively, I grabbed him and moved him to his room as he frantically scratched and bit at my arms. I put him on the floor in the middle of his room where he sobbed uncontrollably. He was ruthful to watch. I wanted to pick him up, hug him close to me and assure him that things would get better, but I knew he would resist any such effort because in his little world, I was the enemy.

I glanced at my watch and realized it was close to 5:10 p.m. The crisis unit was late, so I called their office. The man who answered the phone told me the unit had an emergency and he needed to cancel the appointment. He told me to call back the next day and reschedule. An emergency, I thought. What would have to happen for *our* situation to be treated as an emergency? Would we have to wait until Tyler seriously hurt one of us before we could get anyone's attention?

CHAPTER 35
JANUARY 14, 1997

Tyler refused to get dressed for school again today.

"I like to get dressed at school," he said. "Mrs. Meyers, the classroom aide, takes me to the nurse's office and I get dressed there. I like it that way."

I knew how appealing it would be for Tyler to have the undivided attention of an adult waiting for him to get dressed. Getting dressed in the nurse's office also meant less time he would be expected to sit in his seat in the classroom. This approach gave Tyler too much control over the situation. I called his teacher and left a message for her to call me.

I had met Mrs. Ross on several occasions since Tyler had joined her classroom in September. She was in her fifties and had been teaching for decades and struck me as a professional who worked well with children whose behaviors made learning difficult. I was sure she rarely showed anger or frustration in her classroom, but rather remained in control at all times. However, I was also pretty sure she had never met a child as destructive and difficult as Tyler. Every teacher who worked with Tyler learned that he did not respond to programs of positive reinforcement. He found his way around all the usual behavior management techniques. Despite her years of experience, Mrs. Ross struggled with managing Tyler just as all of his previous teachers had. She returned my call that afternoon.

"Mrs. Havlicek," she began. "We need to talk about Tyler.

He's showing irrational and fearful behavior lately. There's a little boy in the classroom who likes to blow his breath on the other students. Whenever this student blows on Tyler, he shrinks away from the boy as if he expects the little breaths to cause him great physical harm. He puts his hands over his head and cowers away from the boy."

"We're seeing that behavior at home too," I said. "For no apparent reason, Tyler shies away from certain activities as if he expects to be hit or beaten. I have no idea what is prompting this behavior."

"We also must talk about how he is coming to school in his pajamas. This cannot continue. You must get him dressed."

"I'm sorry, but he refuses to get dressed in the morning."

"Then you should just dress him."

"I would, but I think it would lead to a wrestling match between us. I don't want to start a pattern where I have to use physical force to get him to cooperate. I can't start putting my hands on him because I'm afraid it will only make the problem escalate. You heard what happened when I brought him to the breakfast table and he pulled away. I have too much to lose by physically dominating Tyler."

"If he were my child, I would be putting my hands all over him."

Of course, if I had not been struggling with Tyler for the past few years as I had been I would probably have said the same thing. I wouldn't have understood why an adult could not control a small boy.

"Tyler enjoys negative attention and there would be nothing more negative than for me to physically dominate him," I said. "I think I would be the loser if I physically forced him to get dressed. I have used force on him before and it was never successful in teaching him anything."

She wasn't interested. Her only concern was getting control of her classroom and stopping Tyler's disruptive behavior. I understood her frustration. I was Tyler's mom. It is the job of the mother to see to it that the child arrived at school prepared to work. She didn't understand that I had never really been Tyler's mother. A mother should be able to nurture her child and to teach him to find his way in the world. The relationship I had with Tyler was not that of a mother and son. He wouldn't permit that relationship to develop. From the beginning, he resisted forming a bond with me or with the family. Rather, he played the role of the antagonist, ever fighting to reject his role in the family. In Mrs. Ross's eyes, he should have come to school prepared every day and I was the one failing to make that happen.

"Perhaps, Tyler should lose points for not coming to school prepared," I said, knowing it was a ridiculous suggestion.

"He's so far off today," she said, "he doesn't really have any points to lose."

"I think when you have Mrs. Meyers walk him to the nurse's office to get dressed you're rewarding his failure to come to school ready to work. What if you ignore his pajamas?"

"That would be unacceptable. I can't have a child in my class wearing pajamas."

"Well, I'll do my best to have him dressed for school," I said, knowing we were at a stalemate. "But I can't promise it will happen."

We were not going to come to an agreement on this issue. We had different goals. Mrs. Ross wanted her classroom to run smoothly and I wanted to avoid physical confrontations with Tyler.

"What have you heard about having him placed in a residential facility?" she asked.

"We're still waiting to hear," I said. "The paperwork is moving slowly. I'll let you know if we hear anything."

When Roger woke up, he went to the school district office to see what was happening with our paperwork.

"You're not going to believe this," he said as he came back into the house. "Our paperwork is still sitting in the district office."

"But it's been a month since the *'emeregency* CSE'," I said feeling outraged. "How did they explain that?"

"They didn't explain it. They just promised it would be in Albany by the end of the week."

"I can't believe it's still sitting there. I really thought we had demonstrated how desperate the situation was."

"So did I, but it doesn't seem to be urgent to anyone else because they're not living it."

At 4:00 p.m. Tyler came home. "How was school today?" I asked.

"I had a good day," he said. His measure of a good day was always different from everyone else's. He went upstairs and started bugging Jonathan, slamming his body into Jon's bedroom door.

"I'm going to kill you, Jonathan!" he shouted. "I'm going to get a gun. I'm going to get Daddy's police gun." As I ran upstairs with Roger on my heels, Tyler turned to me and shouted, "I'm going to kill you too!"

Roger picked him up and brought him back downstairs. Trevor stood in the doorway.

"I don't want Tyler to hurt any of us," he said. "I'm afraid."

"It's okay, buddy," I said. "Dad and I are both here and we won't let him hurt you."

I opened my arms and he fell into me. I closed my arms around him and said, "Tyler will be removed from the house soon and things will get better. We just have to be strong for a while longer, okay? Perhaps Jonathan, you and I can have dinner in your room tonight. It'll be like a little picnic and dad can stay with Tyler. How about if I order a couple of Pizzas?

"Yeah, let's do that," said Trevor putting on a brave face.

It was the closest thing to a normal evening I could offer him.

CHAPTER 36
JANUARY 16, 1997

I went to Tyler's room early this morning to wake him up and found blood smeared on his pillowcase and sheets.

"Tyler, what happened here?" I asked shaking him from his sleep. "Tyler, there's blood all over your bed. What happened? Wake up Tyler."

He sat up in bed and looked around. "My nose and toenails were bleeding last night," he said.

"How could that be?" I asked as I pulled the blankets back. His toes were crusted in blood. I looked closer and noticed that two of his toenails were missing. There was also dried blood caked around his nose and mouth.

"Tyler," I said as my stomach lurched. "I don't understand. What happened?"

"My toenails hurt," he said. "So I picked at them until they stopped."

"Tyler, you pulled off two of your toenails," I said in disbelief. "Didn't that hurt?"

"No, it felt good. I pulled out two of my teeth too. See?" He held out two little teeth he had been clutching in his hand.

"Why would you do that?" I asked in horror.

"It was fun. I'm going to pull out all of my teeth." He pointed at two more of his teeth and said, "These two are loose and I'm going to pull them out later today."

"I can't believe you did this. You must not do this again. You need your teeth to chew and your toenails to protect your feet. You could get a serious infection from this."

"Good, then I could go to the hospital, right?"

"Get up," I said, ignoring the last statement. "The bus will be here soon."

I didn't know what else to say. He dragged himself from the bed and headed to the bathroom. I picked out his clothes and went downstairs to wait for him.

In a few minutes, he appeared in the kitchen still wearing his Winnie-the Pooh pajamas, looking sleepy and clutching a brown teddy bear. He looked so cute and innocent standing there that I wanted to take him in my arms and find a way to start over. I wanted to reach deep inside his little soul and find out what made him tick. It was painful to look at this little boy who insisted on fighting the world and making his life so difficult.

He talked to the little bear in a voice almost too soft to hear. He sat down next to the day's clothing and chatted with the bear, acting as if the scene of blood in the bedroom had never happened. I looked at his little red toes and wondered how he was going to get his shoes on.

"Do you want me to put some medicine and band-aids on your toes?" I asked.

"No, they don't hurt. They're fine." He continued to play with the little bear and ignore the task of getting dressed.

"Tyler, put the bear down and get dressed. You have to go

to school."

"We don't want to get dressed, do we?" he said to the little bear.

This was going no where, so I walked over and took the bear away from him. He jumped up and looked at me with ferocity in his eyes. "You never let me play with any toys!" he shouted.

"There's a time to play with toys and a time to get dressed," I said. "Get dressed and then you can have the bear back."

"You never let me play with any toys," he repeated.

I took his chin in my hands. "Look at me," I said. "You could play with your toys if you didn't waste so much time doing the wrong thing."

He crossed his eyes to avoid making eye contact. I was exasperated. Now he was angry and I knew he would not eat or get dressed or do anything I asked him to do. When the bus arrived, he trotted down the driveway in his pajamas.

He returned home that afternoon in a cheerful mood and announced as he frequently did, "I had a great day!" I reached for his backpack to see if Mrs. Ross's evaluation of the day in any way resembled Tyler's. There was a note in the bag.

Dear Mrs. Havlicek,

Tyler says you are taking away the toys he earns in school. I don't think that is productive. He says he is not going to bring any of his reward toys home anymore.

He came to school today with a twenty dollar bill. He said his dad gave it to him. Is Mr. Havlicek missing any money?

Sincerely, Mrs. Ross

The intonation of this note left me furious. I knew she was trying to be helpful, but did she really think I took his toys away because it was fun for me? Why wasn't it clear to her that he lost his toys because he did something inappropriate with them and that he left me no choice. It probably would be for the best if he left his earned toys at school.

I called Roger at work to see if he was missing any money.

"Hi, it's me. Tyler had $20.00 with him at school today and he told Mrs. Ross that you gave it to him. Are you missing any money?"

"Hold on, I'll check. No, it didn't come from my wallet."

"I wonder where he got it. I checked my wallet and he didn't get it from me."

"Have you checked Jonathan's wallet? He had his birthday money in his wallet on his desk."

"I bet that's it. I'll go check. Sorry to bother you at work."

"Don't worry about it. I just wish I could be home more in the evenings to help."

"It's okay. I'll check Jonathan's wallet and see you later."

I went to Jonathan's room and found that he was indeed missing $20.00. Tyler stood in the doorway watching me with a big smile.

"Tyler," I said. "You took this money from Jonathan's wallet. It isn't yours."

"I know," he said. "Jonathan gets everything and I have nothing."

I noticed he was wearing a pair of pants I had never seen before.

"Tyler, where did you get those pants?"

"I pooped my pants today."

"Why did you do that?"

"I didn't want to leave the playground and go to the bathroom."

"But Tyler…"

"I got another pair of pants at the nurse's office."

"Tyler, you haven't had an accident like that in years."

"I didn't care. It was funny."

How could I argue with that? At his age, he should have been embarrassed by his actions. How many more outrageous behaviors could he come up with?

"Can I go play outside?" he asked.

"Okay," I said with resignation. At least if Tyler was

outside, he wouldn't be bugging his brothers. "You can play outside, but it's very cold outside and you must dress warmly."

"I know. It was very cold on the bus."

Tyler allowed me to bundle him up with a hat, scarf, mittens and a heavy winter coat before he went outside. It was too cold for either Jonathan or Trevor to even think about going outside, but Tyler was content to wander around the yard by himself. I checked on him from the kitchen window every few minutes and he seemed to be happily lost in his own world. He talked to himself or an imaginary friend. I couldn't tell which. His hands gestured in motions seemingly trying to support what he was saying. His head moved back and forth with animation as if the conversation was very important. I made another check on him a little while later and found him walking by the chain link fence surrounding our pool and crying. I went to the back door and called out to him, "Tyler, what's wrong?"

"I lost one of my gloves."

"Did you look for it?"

"Yes and I can't find it."

"Tyler, it's getting colder and dark. You should come in now and we'll find the glove tomorrow."

"No, I want to find it now!"

"It's too dark. You must come in."

"No! I need my glove!"

I went out and picked him up because I knew from experience he would stay stuck on the idea of finding the glove unless I physically moved him on to something else. He kicked me and flailed his arms. Although I hated to physically overpower him, I had to get him out of the wet clothes. When he was in dry clothes, I sat him at the table for dinner.

"I'm not hungry," he said as he pushed his chair away from the table. His emotions were running out of control and intensifying by the minute. He ran into the den and pinched at the loose skin around Tootsie's neck. She pulled away from him baring her teeth. He grinned and reached for her again, but she was too fast and darted away from him. He laughed and clapped his hands. He looked at me and barked at the top of his lungs. I knew such sounds could be a symptom of TS, but he often made sounds for the fun of it. Suddenly he stopped and ran up the stairs. I was close on his heels, knowing Trevor and Jonathan would be the targets of whatever behavior he was planning. He stopped at Jonathan's doorway.

"I want my toy school bus back," he demanded.

"No," said Jonathan. "You traded the bus for the Power Ranger."

"Mom took the Power Ranger away from me, so I want my bus back," Tyler shouted.

"It's not my fault you don't have the Power Ranger," said Jonathan.

Tyler hissed at him.

"Tyler, you traded the bus for the Power Ranger," I said. "You can't change you mind."

Trevor had to go to hockey practice that evening, so I

decided we should leave early and stop at the mall on the way. Trevor needed to purchase a book for a book report in school, but in order get to the book store, we had to walk through other stores. As we walked through Sears, Tyler grabbed things—a dress, a book on doing taxes and an electrical socket.

"I need this and I never get anything!" he shouted. We got Trevor's book, but every step was a struggle. I took each item away from him and put it back.

Next we went to 7-Eleven to buy a Gatorade for Trevor. Tyler tried on several pairs of sunglasses. He liked the way he looked in the mirror above the stand as he smiled and posed. He turned to me and repeated his new mantra. "I never get anything!"

"Tyler, put the sunglasses back," I said.

We left the 7-Eleven and moved on to hockey practice. Jonathan, Tyler and I found seats in the bleachers to watch Trevor skate. As I watched the game, I glanced at Tyler and saw him sitting there with a pair of sunglasses on.

"Tyler, did you take those from the 7-Eleven?" I asked.

"No, I found them," he replied although I could see the price tag hanging from the side of them.

Roger and I had often discussed how Tyler was able to look us in the eye and lie so convincingly that it made us wonder, if what we knew to be true really was. He never blinked or flinched, he just lied. I reached over to take the glasses away from him, but he jumped backwards and fell down on the bleachers.

"Oh, I'm hurt!" he shouted. "My mom hurt me. She's always hurting me." Other parents stared at me. I didn't know what to do. We couldn't leave. Trevor's practice had just started.

Without a prompt from me, Jonathan moved down the stairs and stood in front of Tyler with his hands on his hips. "Get up," he shouted with an air of authority.

"Okay," said Tyler shocked by Jonathan's tone. He got up from the floor and followed Jonathan to the box of toys I always brought to practice. Jonathan picked out a matchbox car for himself and one for Tyler. They played together throughout the rest of the practice. On the way home, we stopped at the 7-Eleven and returned the sunglasses.

CHAPTER 37
JANUARY 29, 1997

Dr. Riddick, a psychologist for the school district, called today. "Mrs. Havlicek," he said. "I have some good news for you. We received approval from the New York State Department of Education for Tyler's placement in a residential facility."

"That's good news!" I said. "Everyday things grow more urgent here at home."

"Albany has sent the names of nine schools that might be appropriate for Tyler," said Dr. Riddick. "I really don't know anything about these schools. I think the best approach would be to apply to all nine schools to find out which ones have openings. Then you will have to visit each of those schools to see which one you think might best meet Tyler's needs."

"How long will that take?" I asked. "My family is at an ever increasing risk of harm with each day that Tyler resides at home."

"I don't know," he said, "but we'll move things along as fast as we can from our office."

"I hope so," I said. "Please let me know as soon as you have any further information."

"I will," he said. "I'll call as soon as I hear anything."

I hung up the phone feeling exasperated. We were moving closer to finding a solution for the tense situation, but it could still take months to have Tyler placed. I needed relief now! Two weeks passed without any further word about Tyler's residential placement. Day after day, we struggled with his behavior. Then on February 18, we received a phone call that would make things happen faster than I could ever have imagined.

"Mrs. Havlicek," the caller began. "My name is Robert Gladstone. I'm the New York State Coordinator for Residential Placements. I received a letter from your congressman saying you need help with your son, Tyler. I understand he's been approved for a residential placement."

"Yes, he has," I said.

"I looked over the file on your case," said Mr. Gladstone. "I understand you received a list of schools as possible placements for Tyler."

"Yes, we have," I said. "Our school district is supposed to contact all the schools on the list to see which ones might have openings."

"Well," he said, "I reviewed the list of recommended schools and unfortunately I don't think any of them are appropriate for your son because he's too high functioning and his behaviors are too extreme for placement in any of those schools."

Disappointment washed over me.

"You don't understand," I said anxiously. "We really can't manage Tyler at home any more."

"Oh, I understand that," said Mr. Gladstone, "Tyler definitely needs a residential placement. I just don't think New

York State has a school that will meet his needs. However, there are a couple of schools located out of state that may be appropriate. How would you feel about placing Tyler out of state?"

"I think Tyler needs to be removed from the home before something serious happens," I said. "If he resides out of state, it will be difficult to visit him but, I'm okay with that."

"Good," he said. "The school district has 60 days from the time of the CSE to the time of placement. If they're not moving in a timely fashion, you can request an impartial hearing. You really need to take a firm stand with your school district."

"I think our school district supports us," I said. "But I don't think they understand the severity of our situation."

"Can I ask you a question?" he asked.

"Sure."

"Why did you send this letter to your congressman?"

"I guess I felt the need to seek additional help where ever I could find it."

"It was a smart thing to do. The letter landed on my desk this morning and I've been told to make it a priority. My first choice for a school for Tyler would be the Raymour School in New Jersey. After that, there is a school in Massachusetts and one in Arizona that we could consider if we had to, but the Raymour School would be my first choice."

"What is it about the Raymour School you like?"

"They specialize in behavior management for difficult

children. They have a clinical setting and could evaluate Tyler psychologically. I think they would offer the kind of structure he needs. If it's okay with you, I'll contact them and see how soon we can get him into their program."

"That would be great."

"I'm going to send Tyler's packet to Raymour immediately. You probably should start preparing him. I'm hoping he'll be placed within two weeks. I'll call as soon as I hear something."

"Thanks so much. I can't tell you how important this is for my family."

Two days later we received a call from Amy Jurgens the head of the admissions office at the Raymour School. She had spoken with Robert Gladstone and had an opening for Tyler. She requested I overnight the videotape that had gotten him admitted to the psychiatric hospital along with other records immediately to speed the process along. I spent the rest of the day gathering paperwork with the hope that we would not run into any snags.

The next day, Amy Jurgens called again. She said she had a bed for Tyler, but she didn't have an opening in a classroom until July. He could receive tutorial services while awaiting an opening in a classroom. His behavioral treatment would begin immediately. She wanted me to bring Tyler to Raymour on Wednesday, February 27th.

Roger worked the night before and when he woke up, I told him the news.

"I can't believe it's finally happening," he said.

"Me neither," I said. "What do you think we should say to him?"

"I can't believe he'll care. He's never bonded to our family and he'll probably enjoy the attention he'll receive initially. There's no way he's really going to understand the seriousness of what is about to happen to him. I wouldn't say anything to him or Trevor or Jonathan until the day before."

"That's probably best. I think Trevor and Jonathan will be relieved. And you're right, Tyler lives in the moment. He won't understand the consequences of what is happening."

I stared out the kitchen window while a wide array of feelings ran through me.

"What are you thinking?" asked Roger.

"We should be happy but..." I said.

"Yeah, I know. It's still hard to admit we can't handle a seven-year old little boy, but we've tried for four years now and haven't been able to connect with him. We have no choice but to do what's best for Trevor and Jonathan. They need both parents, not two people working in shifts to handle Tyler."

"I have no doubt we must do this, but it's impossible not to feel terribly sad," I said as my tears fell.

"I know," he said.

CHAPTER 38
FEBRUARY 27, 1997

Since Robert Gladstone became involved, things were happening quickly. The school district held another CSE to approve the placement at Raymour Residential and the final packet was put together. Now all that was left to do was to tell Tyler about the change. I sat him down at the kitchen table.

"Tyler, I need to talk to you," I began. "Dad and I have been looking for another place for you to live because you seem so very unhappy here. We found a place for you to live in New Jersey."

"Good. I don't want to live here anymore," he replied flatly.

"We'll be taking you to your new home tomorrow," I explained wishing with all my heart that there was still some way out of this. "We must pack your clothes and some toys. You can tell me what you want to take."

"Good, let's go pack," he said looking right at me without a trace of emotion.

I couldn't believe how casual this conversation was as if we were talking about a change in the weather rather than discussing the fact that his family was asking him to leave, to go to live somewhere else, far away. It was impossible for me not to feel a deep sense of sadness and failure.

Roger had to work the night before Tyler's departure, so we decided I would drive Tyler to Raymour. I was glad because I wanted to be the one taking him to his new home. I was still his mother. I felt responsible for ensuring that his new residence would be the best possible placement for him. I owed him that much.

Roger came home early that morning to get Trevor and Jonathan off to school before he went to bed. He would be there for them when they returned home. We wanted their day to proceed as normally as possible.

I woke Tyler up at 5:30 a.m. I wanted to get off Long Island before the rush hour traffic began. Tyler barely said good-bye to Roger. It may have been because he didn't understand that he wasn't coming back, but I think he simply didn't care. I loaded him into the van and I gave him a blanket and pillow and he fell asleep.

It was surreal. I struggled to bury my emotions as I pulled away from the home that Tyler had lived in for the past four years. I knew it was the right thing for my family, but still... Tyler had lived with my family through every activity of the last four years and after today he would be gone. I swallowed hard as I struggled to accept the fact that I had failed.

Tyler slept throughout most of the trip, only waking to have something to drink. We arrived at 10:00 a.m. just in time for our appointment with Amy Jurgens, the director of admissions.

"Wake up, Tyler," I said. "We're here."

He sat up in the back of the van and looked around quickly. "I'm not staying here," he said. It was the first time he expressed any resistance to the change.

"Let's look around before we decide," I said as my voice

cracked.

I wanted to say, "Tyler, let's go home and try again. We can make this work can't we?" But I knew that Roger and I had done our best and nothing had changed Tyler's inability to bond to the family. We entered the admissions office and met Miss Jurgens. While she helped me fill out paperwork, Tyler went to the playground with another member of the Raymour staff. She was a young woman, about twenty-four years old and Miss Jurgens introduced her as Beth. I could see her interacting with Tyler from where I sat in the office. He appeared to be having fun, swinging on the swings, playing catch and going down the slide.

"This paper allows us to take Tyler off the campus for community activities," Miss Jurgens said bringing me back to the task at hand. "This one allows us to treat Tyler in case of an emergency." I signed paper after paper while watching Tyler play. Miss Jurgens led me to a pretty, little, Victorian cottage that would be Tyler's new residence. I entered the door and found myself in a large room.

"This is the living room," Miss Jurgens said. "Tyler will not be able to move from one room to another without supervision because each room has a locked door. Tyler will be kept in the cottage initially so we can evaluate him. He'll receive tutoring here rather than attending classes on the main campus. We should have a spot for him on the main campus by September."

"I understand," I said. We returned to the main office just as Tyler and Beth returned from the playground.

"How did you like the playground?" I asked.

"It's good," he said. "You can go. I love *her* now." He pointed at Beth grinning from ear to ear.

I wasn't surprised. I needed to remember I had never been any more than a caretaker for Tyler. One caretaker was as good as another. At that moment, I was relieved. It would have been impossible to leave Tyler if he had actually cared. His reaction made it easier.

"Okay." I said. "I'll call you soon."

"Okay," he said. Then he turned to Beth. "Do you want to play outside again?"

Beth looked at me and I nodded. Tyler took her hand and walked out the door without looking back.

CHAPTER 39
SPRING 1997

After a few weeks, the family relaxed and felt safe again. We were all conditioned to having Tyler disrupt our every activity. Suddenly we had uninterrupted family interactions and watched TV without disturbance. No one in the house yelled and the boys played with their toys without interference. We went out in public and didn't worry about what might happen. It was wonderful to worry about mundane things like getting to hockey practice on time and doing homework. Everything about life at home had gotten easier. I was feeling euphoric with normalcy. I don't mean to say that everything was perfect. It wasn't. No family is perfect, but I was delighted to see my family at peace.

During those first few days, I carried a fear that the Raymour School would call and say it had all been a mistake, that Tyler was a delight to be with and that with some effort we could make this work. I woke up nightly in a sweat from a nightmare in which I struggled to explain to the staff at Raymour why I felt Tyler needed to live away from the family.

In fact, Raymour did call. They said Tyler spent his first week as a model client. My heart rate quickened until they explained that they understood he was going through a "honeymoon" phase and would be on his best behavior until he became more comfortable with his surroundings.

At home, the kids developed an ongoing joke. We would be engaged in some activity and Trevor would stop and say, "Hey, do you hear that?"

We would all listen carefully and then Jonathan would say, "That's the sound of quiet."

On the first Saturday after Tyler's departure, the family sat down to watch a video together, a luxury we had not enjoyed in a long time.

Time passed and every day got easier as we settled into a new rhythm within the family. We all laughed more easily. Trevor's headaches abated and Jonathan smiled more. I struggled to assure myself that I deserved this peace.

We had minimal contact with Tyler in the weeks after his placement. We talked to him on the phone several times, but he had little interest in speaking to us. The conversations were always short and he never asked about coming home nor did he give any indication that he was homesick or missing us. A couple of times he just hung up during the conversation.

Raymour wanted us to stay connected to him. A main goal of Tyler's rehabilitation plan was to improve the relationships he had with his family. After six weeks, the staff suggested we might want to take him off the campus for a day. Just before Easter, I called Tyler to tell him we wanted to visit him for the holiday. Surprisingly, he answered the phone.

"Hi, Tyler, it's mom," I said. "How are you?"

The next thing I heard was Tyler saying to someone, "There's nobody there," followed by a click as he hung up on me. I called back and spoke with Jennifer, a member of the staff. I told her we planned to arrive on Easter Sunday to take Tyler out. She said she would have him ready, but she made no effort to have him get back on the phone.

Tyler's attitude didn't surprise me. It would be foolish of me to expect him to have changed simply because he no longer lived with us. In fact, it made the separation easier. If Tyler had been a normal child who loved his family, I would not have been able to bear the separation.

On Easter Sunday, we picked Tyler up at Raymour. Trevor and Jonathan dreaded this meeting. Their lives had improved immensely since Tyler's departure and they had no desire to see him now.

"Mom, do we have to pick him up?" asked Trevor. "Can't we just stay at the hotel and have fun?"

"No, we told him we were coming," I said. "We're still his family."

"But we hate him," said Jonathan.

"Don't say that," I said. "Tyler is sick and he really can't help the way he acts. We're going to pick him up and take him to the aquarium. You'll like the aquarium. It's supposed to be one of the best in the country."

"I want to go to the aquarium," said Jonathan. "I just don't want to see Tyler."

"It is only for a few hours," I said. "Please try to be nice to him."

"Okay, I'll try," he said glumly.

We drove to the cottages where Tyler lived. Trevor and Jonathan were curious to see his new home, so we all got out of the car and walked across the yard. As we approached the cottage, I saw Tyler's little face in the window.

"He looks so small," said Roger as Tyler waved to us from the window.

"I know," I said. "It's still so hard to believe it has come to this."

A staff member met us at the door. "Tyler, is this your family?" she asked.

"Yeah, where are we going?" he asked looking past us and out the door.

"We thought we would go out to lunch and then visit the aquarium," Roger said. "How does that sound Tyler?"

"Good," he said not looking at Roger as he answered. "Let's go."

"You can bring him back any time," said the staff worker. "There'll be someone here waiting for him whenever you get back."

Tyler ran past us and out the door. He never said hello to any of us, but rather acted as if he had been with us all along. We had lunch and went to the aquarium. He seemed to have a good time, but as I often felt, it didn't matter that he was with any of us. Anyone could have taken him out for the day and he wouldn't have acted any differently. We brought him back at about 7:00 p.m., said good-bye and he turned and walked away without looking back.

In April, we received a phone call from Mr. Jackson, the director of the residences at Raymour.

"Mrs. Havlicek, I've been working with your son here at Raymour since he arrived," he said. "The staff has been trying to develop a behavior management program for him. We're having difficulty because he doesn't respond to typical reinforcement."

"Yes, I know," I said. We had heard this from every educator and therapist who worked with him. "We've struggled to find things that are rewarding for Tyler too. The only thing that satisfies him is disrupting the environment and people around him."

"That's it exactly," he said. "He does not respond to toys or food when used as rewards. We've decided to try some stimulus avoidance techniques. We need to have your approval."

"What sorts of things do you have in mind?" I asked.

"We want to try 30 second timeouts and holding his hands down for thirty seconds," he said. "If he continues to engage in maladaptive behavior, he will be assigned a specific task or chore. Further inappropriate behavior will result in a facial screen for thirty seconds. We may also spray a mist of water into his face."

I tried to picture strange adults holding little Tyler down. "We've tried very hard to refrain from aversive techniques," I said.

"It's always best to avoid aversive therapy if possible," he said. "I can assure you Tyler will not be physically hurt by these measures. We want to use the facial screen because Tyler thrives on the reactions people around him have to his negative behaviors. If he cannot see anyone's reactions, he'll lose the motivation for his behavior."

"That does seem logical," I said. "I'll approve these procedures as long as you can promise me he will not be hurt."

"I promise he will not be hurt," he said. "I'll send you an outline of this plan to sign. I'd appreciate it if you could send it back as soon as possible. "I'll keep in touch and let you know how these procedures work with Tyler."

I hung up wondering if Tyler would ever understand how difficult he made life. He fought against success at all costs, instead, opting for the negative attention that comes with failure. A few weeks later we received a follow up phone call from Raymour. The facial screen was effective in stopping some of Tyler's behavior.

At the end of the school year, Tyler came home for the first time. Roger drove four hours to pick him up and four more hours to bring him home. Trevor and Jonathan were not looking forward to the visit with anything other than anxiety. In fact, we all worried about his visit, but Roger and I felt we still owed Tyler a chance to be a part of a family even if only once in a while. A tenseness we had not seen for a few months settled over the family. As far as we were concerned, nothing had changed. Tyler still hardly talked with us when we called and the staff said he never asked for us. We feared he would simply pick up where he had left off and make us all crazy. However, there was one big difference this time. He would only be with us for four days. His visit would come to an end.

Roger left for New Jersey at 5:00 a.m. to beat the Long Island traffic. He and Tyler arrived back at the house at about

3:00 p.m. Tyler ran into the house and straight to his room. I turned to Roger.

"How was the trip?"

"Not too bad. He slept most of the way back."

"How does he seem?"

"The same. He said he didn't want to eat and cursed me out when I asked him if he wanted a drink. He relaxed when I put on the radio as he rocked back and forth adjusting the pace to each tune. I asked him how he liked Raymour, but he just gave me one word answers and then tuned me out."

"Well, we didn't really expect a big change. Why don't you rest and I'll go see what he's doing."

I went upstairs and found Tyler in his room rocking on his bed. "How's it going?"

"Good."

"How does it feel to be home?"

"Good. Can I go in the pool?"

"I guess so. Your swimsuit is in the draw. I'll meet you downstairs."

Tyler changed his clothes in a flash and jumped down the stairs heading for the pool. I followed him outside. He knew how to swim well enough, but I always stayed nearby when the kids were in the pool. He swam to the bottom and stayed there for as long as his breath would allow. I wondered how a little boy could live with a family for over four years, be taken away from that family and return again without any sign of emotion. I feared his feelings were buried so deeply they might never surface.

Since it was summer, Trevor and Jonathan played outside, riding bikes, roller skating or swimming if things got too tense with Tyler. I kept Tyler as busy as I could. He had grown a few inches and needed new shoes and summer clothes, so we went shopping together a couple of times. He rode his bike around the cul-de-sac because he said he was never allowed to ride his bike at Raymour. I was sure there was a reason for that. Four days was a reasonable time for a visit because as time went on, he showed more anger and on the last day of his visit, he deliberately broke one of Jonathan's favorite toys.

When Tyler returned to Raymour, he began classes on the main campus instead of at the cottages where he still lived when school was not in session. The staff monitored his medications closely now and necessary adjustments were easier with a psychologist right on the campus. However, Tyler's behavior showed no sign of improvement as he broke all the rules, teased other students, destroyed property and resisted authority.

In November, Raymour called to say Tyler had fallen from a jungle gym and broken his ankle. He came home for Thanksgiving weekend with a cast on which didn't slow him down at all. He spent most of his time going through the drawers in the kitchen and in the bedrooms. He found various items and asked, "Do you need this? I don't have one. Can I have this one?"

The things he wanted were odd. He requested a pair of Trevor's old shoes that wouldn't fit him, a spatula, rubber bands, and a box of nails.

"Tyler, you don't need the things you're taking," said Roger one day. "Why do you want them?"

"I do need them," He said.

"Tyler, you don't need these things and I want you to stop going through the drawers." Roger said.

"I DO need them!" Tyler shouted, flinging himself on the floor.

"Tyler, if you really need something, you can ask mom or me," said Roger. "We bought you new clothes because you need them. We'll give you anything you really need, but you can't just keep taking things just because you want them."

Tyler rolled back and forth on the floor tuning Roger out. Throughout the weekend, he obsessed about what was in the kitchen drawers. When I packed his bag for the return trip, I found a tape measurer, thumbtacks, shoe laces and assorted other goods. I quietly took them out of the bag to avoid a scene and packed what he really needed.

Tyler returned to Raymour and never mentioned the items that I had taken out of his suitcase. A few weeks later, we received a phone call telling us he had gotten his cast wet in the shower and it had to be reset. The reset was not covered by insurance but, I was more concerned about the lack of supervision while he was taking a shower.

CHAPTER 40
1998

On the main campus, the staff strictly monitored Tyler's behavior, but now he moved from room to room with less restrictions. At first, he shared a room with another student, but that was short-lived. He harassed and tormented his roommate and before long, he found himself in a room alone. He continued his self-destructive and negative attention-seeking behaviors with the staff and only the facial screen effected a change in his behavior.

In February, the staff at the residence called because Tyler was angry that another student had a new radio. He complained he did not have any "cool stuff." He went to the other student's room, unplugged the radio and threw it across the room, smashing it into pieces. The staff sent him to his room where he took all his toys and electronics and broke as many of them as he could. Then he piled them up in the center of his room and urinated on them. I listened to the staff's account of the incident and was overcome with a deep sadness. I had put many hours into finding the perfect Christmas and birthday gifts for him last fall and now he had trashed them all in one burst of anger. More importantly, Tyler still lived in the moment and didn't see how his behavior would hurt him down the road. The staff took everything except his bed out of his room. His CD player and CDs, his lava lamp (which had a calming affect on him) his flashlight, his boom box and his handheld video games were among the casualties of his anger. Now he was in a room alone with nothing to do. He had just made life more miserable for himself and I wondered how he had been left alone long enough to cause such destruction.

Without any toys to play with, Tyler stole things from other residents of the house. His justification was that he "needed stuff." When asked about missing items, he lied convincingly, denying he had taken them, but somehow these things always turned up in his possession. This behavior happened both at home and at the residence. His lies haunted me because even when I knew he was lying, he looked me in the eyes and denied it. One day. I found about fifty band-aids in his suitcase.

"Tyler, what are these band-aids doing in here?" I asked.

"Oh, I brought those with me when I came here in case I fell or got hurt," he answered making direct eye contact with me.

"No, you didn't. We emptied your bag when you arrived at home and the band-aids weren't in there."

"Oh, yes, they were. You must have missed them when you unpacked my stuff."

"Tyler, stop lying. Why did you take these from the bathroom?"

"Because we don't have any at Raymour. I need them when I get a cut."

"I can't believe you don't have any band-aids at Raymour. I'm going to take these out of your bag and call the nurse at Raymour to see if they need band-aids."

"Okay. She'll tell you we need them."

He never wavered in his story. It was as if he believed the story he told. We soon realized it was necessary to thoroughly search him and his baggage before he went back. Whenever we found something he should not have, he concocted a story about how the item had gotten there often suggesting that Trevor or Jonathan had put it in his luggage.

In August, Trevor tried out for a travel ice hockey team. He had been skating for six years, since he was six years old. He skated two nights a week, every weekend and with a private coach at 4:30a.m.on Mondays before school started. Trevor enjoyed playing hockey more than anything else. He was an intense player and took his position on the team very seriously. He had been asked to try out for a travel team in the past, but the family had been unable to make the commitment when Tyler lived at home. Now Trevor was ready to move to a higher level and the family was in a position to devote the necessary time to the travel position. Traveling in ice hockey is different than traveling in other sports like baseball or soccer. There are hundreds of soccer and ball fields on Long Island to develop one's skills, but a travel ice hockey player must travel some distance to reach other rinks. Trevor was a goalie and there were only about eight positions open for goalies at the peewee level on Long Island. He was thrilled when he was chosen for a spot on a "B" team with, Darryl Richards, a positive coach who treated even the weakest player with respect and made learning new skills fun. The team traveled across six states to play games and made it to the state finals in March. It was a big commitment for the family, but Roger and I loved watching the team play. Hockey is such a fast paced game and we always wondered how the players could move on a slippery surface and still make plays. It never ceased to amaze us.

Jonathan played hockey, but he was not a morning person and hated to get up at 5:00 a.m. to make the ice times. Instead, he played roller hockey because the games were scheduled in the evenings. He had been skating since he was three and now he flew past other skaters of the same age even though he was the shortest kid on the team. He always had fun whether he played a good game or a bad one. He was a happy, social kid with a constant smile. When we traveled with Trevor, Jonathan hung out with a group of siblings from Trevor's team playing hide-and-seek around the rink or video games in the game room.

Now in his second year at Raymour, Tyler enjoyed shocking the staff by coming out of the bathroom after a shower and running through the residence naked or pulling his pants down in public. He often exposed himself when the members of the residence headed out in the van for a weekend activity. He understood they would not turn around and take him back because they couldn't afford to leave the rest of the group short by having a staff member stay behind with him. While Tyler lied to us and stole from us, he did not take his clothes off in front of us. When I asked him why he would have done that at the residence, he simply said, "They're lying."

Throughout the year, we brought Tyler home for Easter, two summer breaks, Thanksgiving and Christmas. The visits were always short, lasting about four days because his behavior deteriorated with each passing day, but Roger and I still felt we owed it to Tyler to make the effort to offer him something resembling a normal family life.

CHAPTER 41
1999

The winter months forced Tyler indoors leaving him with too much excess energy. He needed to be outside or else he found negative ways to burn energy indoors. In February, Tyler was practicing for a school recital when a staff member found him behind a curtain engaging in inappropriate touching with another boy.

"He's getting older, but he's not getting any better," said Roger as he hung up the phone. "I had hoped after being at Raymour for two years he might improve, but he just finds new ways to get into trouble."

"I wonder where the supervision was when this happened" I said feeling frustrated. "I thought he wasn't supposed to be out of the sight of staff for more than five minutes."

"I don't know. Raymour says they'll conduct an investigation into this incident."

"Isn't Raymour required to report such incidences to the Department of Social Services? Perhaps he should be under constant supervision."

"It won't matter. He always finds a way to get around restrictions."

In April, Tyler came home for Easter, a six day visit book ended with two days of travel. He arrived home and acted like he had never left. He never came in and hugged anyone. He barely said hello. He just slipped back into our lives as we all braced for the rough ride.

We maintained Tyler's room for him so he always had a place to play and sleep, but minutes after he arrived home, he trashed his room emptying his suitcase all over the floor.

Invariably, I asked, "Tyler, what happened here? Why is your room such a mess?"

His answer was always the same. "I dunno."

During Tyler's Easter home visit, I asked him, "What do you do at the residence? Is your room always a mess? Don't you have to clean up after yourself when you leave the table at Raymour?"

"No. My staff does that."

I tried not to laugh. "What do you mean 'your staff' does that?"

"You know, my staff at Raymour."

I told Roger that Tyler now had a "staff" to take care of him. From then on, whenever Tyler had difficulty with neatness or organization we looked at each other, smiled and said, "I guess his 'staff' handles that." However, I reminded Tyler that he did not have a "staff" at home and needed to keep his room clean and wipe down the table when he finished eating.

The big difference between his living at home and coming home for visits was that it was easier to overlook things like a messy room because if he didn't clean up it didn't matter. He was only going to be home for a few days and it was easier to ignore the mess than to get in a power struggle over it. I felt the same way about his eating. It was okay if he chose not to eat because he would be back at Raymour before he starved to death.

Tyler's visits usually spanned a weekend filled with Jonathan and Trevor's activities. Trevor's success with his "B" level travel hockey team enabled him to try out for the "A" team and he made it easily. The "A" team required a bigger commitment to time, but Roger and I took turns getting him to the games and practices. Jonathan continued to love roller hockey and played at least three times a week.

When Tyler visited in the summer, the ability to play outside made the visits easier. He rode his bike and rollerbladed in front of the house. He swam in our pool which gave him the deep pressure that helped him organize his movements. We have a large yard and often he walked around talking to himself and gesturing his arms as if in an animated conversation with an imaginary friend. He isolated himself from the family and though we tried to pull him into our activities, sometimes it was just easier to "let the sleeping dragon lie." He rarely tried to play with Jonathan or Trevor and they both avoided him. He only interacted negatively with them, teasing and harassing them.

Throughout the year, Tyler's psychiatric clinician at Raymour initiated weekly phone conversations between Tyler, Roger and me. At Tyler's CSE, the staff established a long list of goals, including improving his relationship with the family. Unfortunately, the clinician rarely offered more than a laundry list of Tyler's inappropriate behaviors after which she put him on the phone so Roger and I could tell him what he already knew--that he needed to improve his behavior. We lived four hours away and he really didn't care what we said.

Tyler came home for a week in November for Thanksgiving

and a week in December for Christmas. Bringing Tyler home was always an option. No one ever forced us to take him. However, many of the kids went home for the holidays and it always seemed like a Dickensian cruelty to leave him at Raymour for a holiday. Whatever problems he had, he was still our little boy.

CHAPTER 42
2000

Tyler came home in April for Easter. One evening I found him seated at the kitchen table with a pile of cookies, a soda and some candy bars.

"Who said you could have that?" I asked.

"Nobody," he said. "I'm just hungry."

"Tyler, you didn't eat dinner tonight. You need to ask before you take food from the snack cabinet."

"I didn't want dinner. I wanted cookies and candy."

"It doesn't work that way. If you don't eat dinner, you can't have junk food." I put the cookies and candy away.

"But I'm hungry.

"Then, I'll make you a sandwich. We have rules in this house which must be followed. I'm sure you can't just help yourself to whatever you want at Raymour. It's the same here."

"Never mind. I wasn't really hungry." he pushed his chair away from the table and went to his room. Later that evening, I told Roger what had happened.

"I think we need to set some basic house rules," I said. "I know we want peace for Trevor and Jonathan, but Tyler can't come here and do anything he wants just because we're afraid of getting into it with him."

"I know," he said. "Yesterday, I couldn't find him in the house. He was outside on his bike. He never asked if he could go outside."

"And his room. He's eleven years old and he doesn't even try to clean up after himself."

"Okay, those are a couple of rules we should establish for his behavior, but how are we going to get him to follow the rules when he never has in the past?"

"Jen at Raymour says Tyler looks forward to his home visits. He enjoys the change of pace. What if we tell him he won't be able to come home if he can't follow the rules?"

"You know, Jen also says that if Tyler is too much to handle when he's here, we can always bring him back early. Perhaps we could take him back to Raymour if he refuses to follow simple rules."

"It sounds like a good plan. Let's give it a try."

We sat Tyler down and told him what we expected. If he didn't behave, we would bring him back to Raymour or refuse to bring him home for the next school vacation. We kept it simple with three rules. He was not to leave the house without permission, take food or drink from the kitchen without asking and he was to try to keep his room neater. We didn't expect him to suddenly become organized, but we did expect him to try. Tyler presented an argument we had heard before.

"I have Tourette Syndrome," he said. "I'm handicapped. I can't remember to do stuff."

"I know some things are harder for you," I said. "But if you can't follow the house rules, you won't be able to visit us."

"I like to come home," he said. "I get tired of being at Raymour. I'll try."

We hoped we had taken a step in the right direction. If he really enjoyed the visits as much as the staff at Raymour believed he did, then maybe for the first time we had a behavioral reinforcement that would work.

Tyler came home in August for four days. When he returned to Raymour, the staff called to say they found sixty dollars, a video game and a set of car keys stashed in a hole in the lining of his suitcase. He told the staff we had given him these things. We had not. Once again, Roger looked at me and said, "He's not getting any better, he's just getting bigger."

Before Tyler came home for Thanksgiving, Trevor and Jonathan found me in the kitchen.

"Can we talk to you?" Trevor asked.

"Sure," I said leaning against the kitchen counter.

"Mom, does Tyler have to come home for every holiday?' asked Jonathan folding his arms across his chest.

"What do you mean?" I asked although I understood perfectly well where this conversation was headed.

Trevor shuffled his feet and looked down. "Well, every time we get some time off from school, Tyler comes home," he said. "We want to have a holiday without Tyler annoying us."

"Yeah, mom," said Jonathan. "Just the four of us."

I took a deep breath. "I know it isn't easy," I said. "But you need to think about how you would feel if you had to spend

Thanksgiving or Christmas without your family."

"That's different," said Trevor finally making eye contact with me. "We love our family. Tyler doesn't care about us."

"I know it probably seems that way," I said, "but he cares in a different way."

"I don't think he cares at all," said nine-year old Jonathan confident he was in the right. "Can't we please have Thanksgiving without him?"

"I don't think that's possible," I said. "Everyone at Raymour, including the staff, spends Thanksgiving with their families and there would be no one at Raymour to take care of Tyler."

Of course that wasn't true, but I just couldn't leave Tyler alone for Thanksgiving. We had adopted him and we still owed him a chance to fit into our family. Jon and Trevor wouldn't understand that. It was easier to tell them there was no one to care for Tyler.

Tyler came home about six days before Thanksgiving. He spent the week with us and then on Thanksgiving Day we went to Lois's house for dinner with all of Roger's family.

Roger's brothers had helped their father add a dining room off the kitchen back in the sixties. Knotty pine covered the walls and the wooden floors creaked every time anyone stepped on them. An opening in one wall gave a view into the living room and a door on the opposite wall led to the small overgrown backyard. A table large enough to seat twelve took up the entire room. Tyler followed Lois around helping her prepare dinner.

272

"Can I help you set the table, Grandma?" he asked.

"That would be wonderful!" exclaimed Lois as she squeezed her bulky body between the table and a wall. "You're always such a big help, Tyler."

"I know," he said as he stiffened his arms and twisted his wrists back and forth. We had been seeing this latest tic all week. "I want to help you because I love you so much."

"I love you too," she said. "And so does Jesus. When you have trouble you just have to ask Jesus to help you."

"I know," he said. "That's why I don't have bad behaviors anymore."

"Oh, I'm so glad to hear that," she said turning around and encircling his skinny body in her plump bosom.

Roger and I sat on a couch in the living room watching this kabuki dance. By this time, we had become inured to the strange relationship between Lois and Tyler. He manipulated her to control her attention and she believed she made a difference by fawning over him whenever she saw him.

"Did you forget to tell me that Tyler no longer had bad behaviors?" Roger whispered into my ear. I covered my mouth with my hand to avoid laughing out loud.

"No," I said. "It's the first I've heard about this."

After dinner, we left Long Island because Trevor had a hockey tournament in Massachusetts the next day. We drove to northern New Jersey where Trevor, Jonathan and I checked into a motel. Roger continued down the Jersey Turnpike in the other direction to drop Tyler off at Raymour. Then he drove back to the hotel where the family spent the night. The next morning we got up at 5:00 a.m. and headed north.

Trevor played well and frustrated the other teams as they tried to put the puck into his net. Between games, he played with his teammates in the hotel game room. We went to the mall and ate our meals at different fast food restaurants. We had a great time and at the end of the weekend, Trevor was awarded a trophy for MVP of the tournament.

In December, the family traveled to Pennsylvania with Trevor's team for a couple of games. On December 9th, the team played against a large aggressive team. At ages thirteen and fourteen, discrepancies between size and muscle development often made the matches between teams lopsided. The opposing team in this game was far stronger and bigger than Trevor's team. The opponents went back and forth with goals in a tight game. During the third period, a play occurred that would change life for Trevor and our family forever.

Trevor stood solidly in his goalie stance as two players sped down the ice towards him, battling for control of the puck. Their sticks locked one over the other as they raced towards the net, fighting to gain control. Neither one wanted to give up. Roger and I watched from the stands. Trevor's eyes stayed focused on preventing the puck from entering the net. The boys never slowed down. They crashed into the net throwing Trevor backwards, slamming the back of his head into the metal crossbar. As the boys slid into Trevor, they swept his feet out from under him. His head bounced off the crossbar and ricocheted off the side post. He fell to the ice and banged his head once more. Roger and I had seen players crash the net before and goalies are often knocked down, but they wear so much equipment that they are rarely seriously hurt. At first, we weren't too concerned, but as we watched, we realized Trevor couldn't get up.

"Oh, no," said Roger as he left me and ran down to the ice. I watched as Roger, the coaches and the refs talked to Trevor who was now on all fours. Suddenly they picked him up and carried him off the ice heading towards the first aid station. I raced down to meet them along with most of the team parents.

"His vision is bouncing, his ears are ringing and he can't support his weight with his legs," Roger told me. "He really slammed his head."

I walked over to Trevor. "How you doing, buddy?" I asked.

"I'm fine," said Trevor. "Are we winning?"

"Don't worry about the game. The other goalie stepped in," I said. "I'm sure the team will win."

"We've called an ambulance," said Roger.

"NO!" said Trevor. "If I just rest a little, I'll be able to play."

"I don't think so, Trev," said Roger. "We need to get you checked out."

An ambulance took Trevor to the nearest hospital where a neurologist determined he had suffered a concussion. He recommended we make him rest for the next week without any physical activity.

The next day, Trevor seemed okay except for a headache that passed within twenty four hours. He returned to school on

Monday with a note prohibiting him from physical activity and he was okay for a few days, but then an inescapable headache stopped him in his tracks. His balance faltered and when he stood up he had the sensation of falling forward. His hands trembled, he was depressed and he had trouble focusing.

We went to a neurologist who did an EEG and an MRI. He said Trevor's symptoms were consistent with post concussion syndrome. The tests showed some bleeding and swelling of the brain, but we were assured his symptoms would improve with time and rest. That was not to be. The headache never went away as we visited one neurologist after another.

The school district provided tutors to teach Trevor his ninth grade classes at home. My heart broke watching my usually vibrant, happy son in so much pain and feeling so sad. All he wanted to do was skate again and be with his hockey friends while I worried whether or not he would ever fully recover.

Meanwhile Tyler developed an interest in how all things mechanical worked. At the residence, he took apart the washing machine trying to understand what powered it. He pulled clocks apart, stripped radios of their wires, dismantled electronic toys and removed battery boxes. He needed to be watched constantly, but he destroyed many things when the staff should have been watching him.

Tyler came home for a week at Christmas. Trevor passed each day in bed because any movement aggravated his pain and made him nauseous. One day, I found Tyler standing in the doorway of Trevor's room.

"What are you doing?" I asked.

"I feel bad for Trevor," he said.

Tyler had never shown empathy for anyone before.

"Yes," I said. "His head hurts a lot."

"Can I get you anything?" he asked Trevor.

"No, I'm okay." said Trevor. Tyler turned and went to his room.

I followed him. "It's nice of you to worry about Trevor," I said. "It makes me happy to see you ask him if he needs anything."

"Thanks," said Tyler.

That was the only bright spot in the Christmas visit. As usual, Tyler remained defiant and oppositional. He tested me to the limit and laughed when I caught him breaking the house rules. We decided to follow through on our threat to take him back to Raymour if he didn't behave. Roger drove him back the day after Christmas, four days earlier than planned.

CHAPTER 43
2001

Raymour moved Tyler from the dorm style housing he lived in on campus to a residence in Cherry Hill, a beautiful community in New Jersey. The large five bedroom colonial house sat on a tree and ivy lined street. Five boys he already knew lived in the house and the staff said it provided a setting more resembling an actual home than the cottages. He still attended the same school, but now, instead of a short walk across the campus to his classroom, a mini-bus drove him to school.

In April, he came home for a week for Easter. I had bought him a new winter coat for Christmas, but now he wore a ratty, gray coat with a torn sleeve.

"What happened to your new coat?" I asked him.

"I don't know. I lost it," he said looking down at the shabby coat and shrugging his shoulders.

"Where did you lose it?"

"We went out to eat and I left it in the restaurant."

"When you left the restaurant and got into the van to go back to the house, didn't anyone notice you weren't wearing a coat?"

"No."

"So where did you get this coat?"

"It belonged to another kid, but he got too big for it."

"Tyler, that's the second coat you lost this year. You need to be more careful."

"Can I go outside?"

"Did you hear what I said?"

"Yeah, can I go outside?"

"Yeah, go ahead."

I couldn't understand how the staff had left the restaurant without noticing Tyler had no coat. I wondered if anyone had gone back to look for it or if they simply handed him another coat. How was he supposed to learn to take care of his things if the staff was so careless? I was angry thinking about how carefully I had picked out that coat and wrapped it up for Christmas only for it to be left behind in a fast food place.

Every week Tyler called the house, a phone call initiated by his clinician, who told us about his every misstep.

"Tyler, tell your mother what happened in the classroom on Monday?" She began.

Invariably, he answered, "I don't remember."

It seemed pointless to me. I was four hours away. What was I supposed to say? "Tyler, you did something wrong a couple of days ago and now you don't remember it, but if I tell you not to do it again I'm sure you won't."

I tried to connect him to the family in these conversations, saying, "That's not language we use in our family," or "no one in our family engages in that behavior," but I never knew what Tyler thought until one day in June.

I answered the phone in the kitchen and Tyler's clinician, Mrs. Dupont, began her weekly rant, "Tyler, tell your mother why you keep teasing the other boys in the house."

"I don't know," he answered.

"Tyler," I said, "Do you want the boys to be angry with you?"

"No."

"Then why do you tease them?"

"I don't know. I want them to like me."

"The boys will not like you if you tease them."

"Oh," he said sniffling into the phone.

"Tyler, perhaps if you try to be nice, the boys will become your friends."

"No, everyone hates me."

"That's not true. Dad, Trevor, Jonathan and I don't hate you. We love you."

"You do?" He asked through gasps of air. "But you don't love me when I do the wrong thing."

"Oh, Tyler, of course we love you no matter what you do. We're sad that you have done the wrong thing, but we still love you.

"When can I come home?"

"You'll be home for summer vacation in about two weeks."

"Okay, good-bye,"

I hung up the phone and turned to Roger at the kitchen table.

"Tyler just told me he wants the boys in his group home to like him," I said.

"Really?" said Roger. "Why, what happened?"

"He's been teasing them and they're mad at him. He was crying because he says they hate him. I've never heard him say he cared whether anyone liked him or not."

"Me neither. He just runs through his day without any thought about how anyone else might be hurt by his actions."

"He also wanted to know if we loved him."

"Really? I find it hard to believe he suddenly cares about what anyone thinks."

"Yeah, I know. Still, that conversation was different from any conversation I've ever had with him."

Tyler came home a few weeks later for his summer break. He had a good visit with no major outbursts. He swam everyday in the pool and we shopped for new school clothes. When the visit ended and Tyler had to leave, he choked up.

"I don't want to go back," he stammered. "I want to stay here."

"Tyler, you have to go back," I said. "Your school is there."

"But I want to stay here," he said trying not to cry. "I'll miss you."

"It'll be okay," said Roger. "Before you know it, you'll be back for Thanksgiving and we'll talk on the phone until then."

"Okay," he said brushing tears from his eyes.

I stood there amazed. I had never seen him react in a sad way when leaving us.

"C'mon Tyler," said Roger grabbing the suitcase. "We'll stop on the Jersey Turnpike and get your favorite ham and cheese sandwich at Roy Rogers. Say good-bye to Mom."

Tyler blinked and stared at me for a few seconds. "Bye Mom," he said.

Under any other circumstances my heart would have broken for him, but I learned long ago how well Tyler manipulated people and lied to them. I had trouble believing he really cared.

Roger returned home eight hours later. The thought of Tyler standing in the doorway had stayed with me all day and now I met Roger as he came into the kitchen.

"What was with Tyler when he was leaving?" I asked. "Did he continue to cry when you left the house?"

"No," said Roger looking exhausted. "As soon as we pulled out of the driveway, he stopped."

"It was strange, wasn't it? Do you think he actually cares about leaving us?"

"No. I think he just likes the less structured atmosphere at home. He can do more of what he wants here and has fewer demands put on him. He can sleep late if he wants to. He doesn't have to go to school. Life is easier here, so he wants to stay here."

"You're probably right."

"When I dropped him at the house, he ran to his room without saying good-bye. I carried his suitcase inside and by the time I got there, he was annoying another boy and had picked up where he left off."

Throughout the year, Trevor continued to suffer from nonstop headaches. We visited several neurologists who always said the same thing, "He has post concussion syndrome. It will improve in time." But I knew something had drastically changed on the day of Trevor's accident. He was a fifteen-year old boy who could no longer go to school and had to sit through tedious tutoring sessions at home while his head pounded in pain, but more importantly, he could no longer do the one thing he loved to do more than anything else and that was to play hockey. I tried to keep him in touch with his hockey friends by bringing him to the practices, but pain always won out and he would have to go home and crawl into bed with pain medication. Just standing erect was enough to exacerbate the pain and sleep was a gift he rarely received for more than a few hours at a time. I checked on him several times each night to offer him company so he would not be sitting alone. Medication after medication was prescribed, but none offered relief. Roger and I could only keep him comfortable and continue to search for an answer to the cause of the pain.

When Tyler came home in November for Thanksgiving, I was curious to see if things would be different. Nothing had changed at the residence where he continued to behave inappropriately, but when we talked on the phone he always asked how long it would be until he could come home. Roger brought him home on the Wednesday before Thanksgiving. As always, Tyler charged into the house, ran to his room and dumped his suitcase. Then he bounced down the stairs two at a time and asked if he could go outside.

He behaved as he always did until later that night. I awoke at about midnight and went to check on Trevor. I met Tyler in the hallway holding a can of diet coke.

"Tyler," I said. "What are you doing? You know you're not allowed to take anything from the kitchen without asking and you're not allowed to bring food to your room."

"This isn't for me," he answered. "I've been watching Trevor play video games in his room because he can't sleep. This soda is for him. I feel bad for him."

"You do?"

"Yeah, his head hurts him all the time."

"I know. It's very sad."

"When will he feel better?"

"Nobody knows. It's very nice of you to keep him company." I walked towards Trevor's room and found him lying in bed with a Nintendo controller in his hand. His eyes had dark circles and I could see that just shifting his gaze towards me hurt. "Tyler is bringing you a soda."

"I know," said Trevor. "He's been watching me play video

games so I won't be alone."

"Tyler, that's very nice of you," I said. "If you want to go to bed now, I'll stay with Trevor."

"No," said Tyler. "I want to stay with him."

"Trevor," I asked. "Is that okay with you?"

"Yeah, I like having him here," he said.

"Ok, I guess I'll go back to bed," I said.

I returned to my room and lay there thinking about what I had just seen. Tyler had expressed empathy for Trevor. I knew this could just be a momentary thing for Tyler, but I couldn't help feeling hopeful that after all this time perhaps he was beginning to realize the world did not revolve solely around his needs. I awoke the next morning to find Trevor asleep in his bed and Tyler asleep on the floor next to him.

Throughout the rest of the visit, we saw two different Tylers. One who wanted to help Trevor and spend time with him and the other one ran through the house breaking the rules and doing whatever pleased him at the moment.

When it came time for Tyler to go home, he went to Trevor's room and said, "I'll miss you."

"I'll miss you too," said Trevor.

I walked Tyler to the car. "When can I come home again?" he asked, choking up.

"You'll be back in three weeks for Christmas," I said. "You know, Tyler, it was very nice of you to help Trevor so much during this visit. I'm very proud of you."

"You are?" he asked.

"Yes," I said. "I'm sure Trevor was very happy to have you here. I'll look forward to your Christmas visit. Try to be good until then, OK?"

"I'll try," he said with a big grin. "I'm proud of me too."

A few days before Christmas, Tyler was back. Once again, we saw two people. One minute he was self absorbed and bull headed and the next, he did whatever he could to keep Trevor comfortable. He sat up with Trevor at night and acted as a gopher fulfilling his every need. Grateful for any moment when Tyler engaged in a positive activity, I always praised his efforts. I hoped his feelings of empathy might someday extend past Trevor's needs.

CHAPTER 44
2002

Tyler's clinician continued her weekly phone calls in the hope of improving his relationship with his family, but now these conversations took a new twist. Tyler showed discomfort when talking about his negative behavior saying, "I don't want to talk about that." He interjected positive things he had done looking for praise from me or Roger. He initiated phone calls to us when he did "the right thing." The staff at Raymour said the conversations with his family had become very important to him.

One day I received a phone call from the residence. Tyler refused to take a shower and they wanted me to talk to him.

"I'm four hours away," I said. "What makes you think I can make him take a shower?"

"He's not listening to us. We have to try something different and he wants to please you," said Dana, the supervisor of the residence. "I'll put him on the phone."

"Hi, mom," said Tyler.

"Hi Tyler, what's going on?" I asked.

"Nothing."

"Dana says you won't take a shower."

"Yeah."

"You need to take a shower every day. You know that. Dad, Trevor, Jonathan and I all take showers every day. It's something our family does. It makes me sad to hear that my son won't take a shower."

"Okay, I'll take a shower now." He passed the phone back to Dana.

"He says he'll take a shower now," I said skeptically. "Good luck."

Thank-you, Mrs. Havlicek," she said.

Tyler did take a shower after he talked with me so it became routine for the staff to call our house whenever he had difficulty with his behavior. He didn't like it when the staff told us he misbehaved. Sometimes he listened to what we told him to do and sometimes he didn't.

Tyler was twelve-years old now and confounding the staff by engaging in sexually inappropriate behavior. For a child who cannot control his impulses, puberty can lead to a multitude of missteps. Tyler ran around the group home naked after his shower and exposed himself to the staff in search of a negative response. He developed a tic which involved rolling his hips as if he were Elvis Presley.

During the home visits we saw the involuntary tic, (which we ignored because calling attention to a tic can make it happen more often) but we did not experience any of the other inappropriate behaviors. Little by little, Tyler was separating how he behaved at home from how he behaved at the group home. Slowly he began to look for positive attention, but that is not to say his behavior completely improved.

Tyler came home for a week at Easter and I was reminded of how well he could lie. Jonathan returned home from playing at a friend's house and went to his room. He found his CD player lying on the floor in the middle of his room. The top had been pulled off and the cord was broken.

"Mom, Tyler broke my CD player!" Jon yelled from upstairs.

I ran upstairs to find Jon standing in the doorway of his room holding the broken player. Tyler rocked on the floor in his room hugging a stuffed rabbit I had given him for Easter.

"What happened here, Tyler?" I asked as Jonathan stood in the doorway.

"I don't know," said Tyler, barely looking up at me.

"Come here, Tyler," I said. "Look at this. What happened?"

He came to where Jonathan and I stood, looked at the CD player and without blinking said, "Maybe Jonathan broke it." There was not a trace of guilt in his eyes or his voice. I turned to Jonathan.

"Tell me again," I said to him. "Where did you find the player?"

"In my room on the floor," he answered becoming more anxious. "He's not supposed to be in my room! You know he broke it!"

I turned again to Tyler. "Were you in Jonathan's room?"

"No, I'm not allowed in there," he answered looking very innocent. I searched his eyes for some change of expression or little hint he was lying. There was none, but I knew he had broken it. Tyler's ability to lie without any remorse or conscience always frightened me.

I turned back to Jonathan. "I'll buy you a new CD player," I said. "From now on, you and Trevor must keep the doors to your rooms locked when you are not in them. Tyler, perhaps we should take you back to the group home now."

"No!" He shouted. "I don't want to go back!"

"Then stay out of your brothers' rooms," I said.

"Okay, I'll be good. I promise," he said as his voice trembled.

Tyler came home at the end of the school year in June. Trevor still lived a life ruled by constant headaches and severe pain behind his left eye. We visited doctor after doctor, but each one said it was either migraines or post concussion syndrome. None of them had any answers for why medication did not work. Tutors came to the house every day for about four hours. Trevor made every effort to stay in touch with his hockey friends, but that got harder with each passing month. When the school year ended and his tutors stopped coming every day, he was lonely, bored, and depressed on top of being in constant pain. Tyler came home at just the right time.

We will never know what pain was inflicted on little Tyler before he came to live with us, but he developed a unique relationship with Trevor after his hockey accident. Tyler stayed up with Trevor late at night to keep him company. He ran up and down stairs to get Trevor whatever he needed. Although Tyler found it difficult to sit through movies or video games, he would do it for Trevor just to be there for him. Roger and I saw this as a great opportunity to encourage Tyler to be thoughtful of others. We never missed a chance to tell him how kind he was being or how happy he was making Trevor. On the fourth day of the visit, we called Tyler into the kitchen.

"You know Tyler," said Roger, "Mom and I are very proud of how kind you are being to Trevor. It means a lot to him."

"Thanks, I like to help him," he said.

"You're supposed to go back to Raymour tomorrow," I said. "But Dad and I think it would be nice to have you stay longer since you have been having such a nice visit."

"Can I?" he asked anxiously.

"If you want," said Roger. "You don't have to be back at school for about five more days and if you can continue to do a good job, you can stay until then."

"I can do a good job," he said grinning.

"Good," I said. "I'll call Raymour and tell them. And Tyler, you're helping Trevor a lot, but that doesn't mean you have to spend your whole vacation with him. While it is a good thing to help him, you should still enjoy your vacation. Ride you bike. Go in the pool."

We wanted Tyler to understand he controlled how long he stayed with us through his behavior. We also wanted to reward him for what he did to help Trevor.

I would love to say that everything got better from this point on, but with Tyler it was always two steps forward and one step back. He went back to the group home after that visit and raised hell. He looked for more positive attention from us at home, but at the residence negative attention was still more rewarding for him. He continued to engage in property destruction, breaking the furniture in his room. He didn't follow rules and pushed all limits. He lunged at the female staff members in a threatening way and even slapped one of them. He never tried this with the male staff. The staff continued to call us to report these transgressions and, as in the past, sometimes he would listen to what we told him to do and sometimes he would not.

Over the summer the staff threatened Tyler with the loss of home visits. They told him if he misbehaved, he would not come home in August. At first, this had little effect on his behavior, but as the time of the vacation drew nearer, his behavior improved so that the week before his scheduled vacation his behavior at the residence was excellent. This was interesting to me because it told me he could control his behavior.

Tyler came home in August and as with the visit in June, he was a pleasure to have at home. We extended his visit again and for the first time since he had left our home, he stayed with us for a full two weeks.

Unfortunately, when he returned to the residence, he behaved worse than ever. He was rude, disrespectful and aggressive towards the staff. One night in October, the supervisor, Dana called to say Tyler was running around the house pulling his pants down and making obscene gestures.

"Mrs. Havlicek," she said. "When I told him I was going to call you, he said he didn't care."

"Put him on the phone. Tyler, what are you doing?"

"Nothing."

"Dana says you're not doing the right thing."

"She's lying."

"I don't think so. Why would she lie?"

"She always lies."

"Put her back on the phone."

Dana came back on the line. "I don't know what to say to you," I said. "He doesn't want to listen to me. I'm four hours away. There isn't much I can do."

"I think we need to threaten him with the loss of his Thanksgiving vacation at home," she said. "That's what's most important to him."

"That seems drastic," I said.

"I know," she said. "But I've talked with the team and everyone agrees it may be the only motivator we have for him. We'd really like to try."

"Well, if everyone on the team thinks it's necessary," I said, "then I'll go along with it, but I'd like to speak to his clinician first. I don't want to ruin the progress we're making at home."

"Okay," she said. "I'll tell her to call you tomorrow."

The next day, I spoke with several members of the team and we agreed to tell Tyler that if he didn't do better he would not come home for Thanksgiving. Dana called me the next night.

"We're having trouble with Tyler again tonight and when we told him he would not be going home for Thanksgiving, he told us your husband would come and get him no matter what. We need you to talk to him." She put him on the phone.

"Tyler. Dana says you're giving her a hard time again."

"I'm not.'

"If you can't behave, you won't be coming home for Thanksgiving."

"I'll be good."

"I hope so, because I want to see you at Thanksgiving."

The next day, Tyler's clinician called me to say he told everyone that it didn't matter what he did, he knew his dad would come and get him for Thanksgiving. Roger and I reiterated to him that if his behavior did not improve we wouldn't be coming to get him, but he challenged everyone to carry through with their promise. He left us no choice. The holiday came and we didn't go to get him. If he was surprised he didn't let on. However, his behavior did improve in the month of December and he came home for Christmas and had a great visit with us.

In December, I took Trevor to yet another neurologist. By this time we had seen six neurologists. The new doctor, Dr. Francois examined Trevor and listened carefully to the description of his accident. He asked Trevor to stand up and get into the goalie stance

"Now," he said, tell me exactly where your head hit the crossbar. Trevor reenacted the accident. Then Dr. Francois reached around to the back of Trevor's head and touched a spot on the lower left side of his skull making Trevor jump in pain. "Well, my young friend," he said, "You've damaged your greater occipital nerve."

"What does that mean?" I asked.

"Well," said Dr. Francois, "Trevor's constant pain is caused by a nerve located in the region of the second and third vertebrae in the neck. The nerve pairings, one on each side, run up the back of the skull. His left occipital has been injured causing the headaches and eye pain. Years ago, doctors would try to remove the nerve, but that always led to increased pain. Trevor is young and in time, the nerve may heal and regenerate to some extent, but it will probably never be the same."

Trevor looked defeated. He sat on the examining table with his shoulders slumped and stared at his feet as if he had heard enough.

"I'd like to try an occipital nerve block," said Dr. Francois, "It involves injecting an anesthetic to 'freeze' the nerve." A few days later, for the first time in over two years, Trevor was pain free.

CHAPTER 45
2003

Trevor returned to school in January. I was relieved to see him moving about without pain, but it didn't last long. By February, the headache returned and Trevor had to get another injection. He was in and out of school as Dr. Francois tried different treatments.

Tyler turned fourteen this year and began to catch up to his peers in size. Although he was now 5'3" inches tall, he continued to be extremely thin weighing only eighty-five lbs. No matter how much he ate, his frame still resembled that of a war prisoner. His ribs stuck out and his stomach looked sunken. He saw several digestive specialists who all said it was just the way his metabolism worked, but I always worried when I saw him without his shirt.

Buying clothes for Tyler was always a challenge. If I bought him a pair of pants that fit his waist, they would be too short. If I bought a pair of pants that fit him in length, he had to wear a belt to gather up the extra inches at his waist.

Throughout this year, Roger and I asked ourselves many times why Tyler wasn't being more closely supervised. One night in February, he was fooling around with another boy at the residence. On a dare, he climbed out the bedroom window onto the catwalk running around the second floor of the house. As he walked around outside, the other boy closed the window locking him out. Snow and ice covered the catwalk and a chilly wind blew through the night air. Tyler left his footprints all around the catwalk as he tested locked windows, trying to find a way back into the house. He went back to his bedroom window and banged on it, hoping the boy who had locked him out would open it for him, but he was no longer in the room. Finally, Tyler raised his foot and kicked at the window until the glass broke, allowing him to crawl back into the house.

The next day, the supervisor of the residences called to tell us about the incident. He had investigated the story and after looking at the tamped down snow and footprints on the roof, he concluded that Tyler had been out on the catwalk for about forty-five minutes.

"I don't understand," I said. "Isn't Tyler supposed to be in sight of the staff at all times? I mean, he was outside for a very long time and nobody checked on him."

"Yes, he's supposed to be in sight at all times," answered the supervisor. "The staff has received a formal reprimand and we'll be making some changes. I'm sorry your son was allowed to be in such a dangerous situation."

"It seems Tyler is often left unsupervised," I said. "Can you assure me that this sort of thing will not happen again?"

"As I said," he answered, "I've made some changes in the staff in his residence and I believe these changes will insure his safety."

"I hope so," I said. "This isn't the first time my husband and I have been concerned about the lack of supervision."

"I know," he said. "I do not anticipate any more problems after the changes we have made to the staff."

But one morning in June, as I lay in bed waiting for Roger to come home from work, the phone rang at 6:00 a.m. I answered it expecting Roger to be on the other end of the line telling me he had a late arrest and wouldn't be home on time, but all I heard was breathing on the other end of the phone. I repeatedly asked, "Who's there?" but received no response.

I hung up as Jonathan came into the room. "The phone woke me up. Is daddy coming home late?" he asked.

"That wasn't daddy," I said. "Go back to bed, buddy."

"Okay," he said.

I went down to the kitchen to make the kids' lunches for school. Fifteen minutes later, the phone rang again. Once more, I answered it and heard breathing at the other end. I hung up, but five minutes later, the phone rang again. I picked it up and said, "Tyler, I know this is you. What do you want?" He didn't answer. "What do you want?" I repeated. Instead of answering, he hung up. I dialed the group home and got Dana, the supervisor at the house.

"Are you aware that Tyler is playing with the phone?" I asked.

"No, he's not," she said. "He's sitting right here having breakfast."

"That may be," I said, "but in the last hour he's called my house three times."

"Oh I don't think so," she said. "I've been in the kitchen the whole time and this is the only room with a phone and it's locked."

"Could he have someone's cell phone?" I asked.

"Oh, I doubt it," she said. "Tyler, did you call home this morning?"

In the background, I heard him reply in a soft voice, "No."

"Hold on for a minute," said Dana. I held on until she returned. "I'm sorry," she said. "He took a cell phone from the handbag of one of the staff. He won't call you again."

That wasn't good enough. I needed to know why he had time to search a handbag and make three long distance phone calls without getting caught. Who was supervising him? Roger and I felt it was time to look for another placement for Tyler. We contacted our school district and asked them to see if they could find a placement with better supervision. They said they would look, but a change would require an opening in an appropriate school, approval from New York State and the always necessary meeting of the Committee on Special Education. It would take some time to get another placement.

Tyler continued to push buttons at the group home. In September, he got angry at Dana, the house supervisor, a young African American woman. She was at odds with Roger and me because now we were always questioning Tyler's supervision. One evening, she and Tyler got into an argument. He turned to her and said, "My mom says all black people are stupid."

She was outraged, appropriately so. The next morning she called me at home.

"We had some difficulty with Tyler last night," she said. "When I tried to talk to him, he said that you told him all black people are stupid."

I was stunned. "You don't believe I said that, do you?"

"I can't imagine why he would make that up," she said smugly.

"You can't be serious," I said. "You know how Tyler likes to shock and push buttons."

"But how would he have come up with that, if he had not heard it from you?" she asked.

"How does Tyler come up with any of the things he says?" I said. "He certainly didn't hear it at home. Have you ever seen a photo of my son, Jonathan?"

"Yes, I was wondering about that," she said.

"You were wondering about that?" I asked, outrage growing in my voice. "Jonathan is a child of color. First of all, I would never say such a racist thing in general and secondly, I could never say such an insensitive and disrespectful thing knowing how much I love Jonathan. How can you give credibility to Tyler's statement by calling me?"

"I just don't know why he would say that," she said. "Perhaps you should ask him." She put Tyler on the phone.

"Tyler, why would you say that?" I asked.

"I thought I heard you say that," he said weakly.

"You know I never said that," I said as my blood pressure rose.

"I must have made a mistake," he said.

"That's a serious mistake," I said.

"Sorry," he said.

"I would never say that," I said.

"Sorry," he said. This was going no where. He put Dana back on the phone. "I don't know why Tyler is saying this, but he's making it up. I'm sorry he's putting you through this, but he's trying to get a rise out of you and he's succeeding. If you think about it, you'll realize that."

We ended the conversation, but there was always tension on the phone whenever we spoke after that. The final straw came at Thanksgiving. After Tyler's visit, Roger drove him back to Cherry Hill. As usual, Roger took him upstairs to get resettled in his room. Another boy living in the group home had lost his temper and gone wild while Tyler was away. He had pulled the door off the frame, leaving it hanging precariously from the jamb with nails exposed. The boy smashed the glass lamp in Tyler's room and it lay crushed on the floor alongside the sharp edges of the light bulb. The staff did not clean the room even though they knew Tyler was due to return. The angry boy had tossed Tyler's bed and the sheets lay on top of the smashed glass. Roger went downstairs, got the vacuum and a hammer and cleaned up the room. Dana made no move to help him. When he returned home we called New Jersey's Department of Social Services. On December 3, 2003, Tyler was moved to Walsh Services in Pennsylvania.

This time, there was no "honeymoon period." From the start, he resisted the rules and engaged in negative behavior. He left supervised areas and locked the doors to the unit without the permission of the staff. He had incidents of property destruction, engaged in inappropriate sexual behavior and had to be restrained as a result of self injurious behaviors and aggression. He tested the staff in every way imaginable, but at Walsh, they stayed on top of him, not allowing him the freedom to do the wrong thing.

Throughout the school year, Trevor was in and out of pain. Dr. Francois gave him acupuncture and botox injections, but these efforts only gave Trevor relief for a few weeks at a time before the pain came rushing back. He went to school when his pain was manageable, and when it was not, the tutors came to the house. I don't know how he found the strength to get up each morning and face another day. Tyler continued to demonstrate empathy for Trevor when he visited, keeping him company and doing whatever he could to make him more comfortable. I hoped that in time his compassion and understanding of Trevor's pain would extend to other areas of his life.

CHAPTER 46
2004

Throughout the year, Tyler behaved erratically. One week he acted out at the residence, while he behaved well at school. The next week he behaved appropriately at the residence while acting out at school. He engaged in negative sexual behavior on a daily basis, making inappropriate gestures and comments. He stole and engaged in property destruction and aggressive behavior, such as hitting, kicking and shoving others. He lost points for threatening staff and his peers when he did not like the consequences he received for his behavior. He had a private bedroom because it was not safe for anyone to share a room with him. The staff installed an alarm on the doorway to his bedroom to alert them if he left his room at night. When in the presence of his peers, he was never allowed more than an arm's length away from a staff member. He wanted his peers to accept him and was easily influenced by them negatively. Receiving attention remained the main motivator for all his behavior. I saw a big improvement in Tyler's supervision at Walsh and the rewards and penalties for his behavior were enforced with consistency.

At school, a strict behavior management program allowed Tyler to shop at the school store if he achieved enough points. However, Tyler dealt more in zeroes than in points. He often racked up as many as twenty zeroes in a single day. But as the year went on, Tyler made an effort to reduce the number of zeroes he accumulated. One day he called me at the end of his school day and announced proudly that he had only gotten four zeroes.

"That's a big improvement, Tyler. I'm proud of you," I told him. "I bet if you work hard you can have a day without any zeroes."

"It's hard for me," he said.

"I know, but you're improving every week. It makes daddy and me very happy to hear that you're doing better. Keep trying and someday you'll make it happen."

"I'm glad when I make you and daddy happy."

"Keep up the good work, Tyler."

At home, Tyler's relationship with the family improved, especially with Roger. Now fifteen years old, he followed Roger where ever he went. Roger joked that if he stopped short, Tyler would end up his butt. Roger was always working on some sort of project around the house and Tyler liked to work alongside him. Roger showed him how to use some simple tools and let him know he valued his assistance. As the year went on, he taught Tyler to drive the tractor around the yard to mow the lawn. Roger and I recognized how important it was for Tyler to feel like a needed and useful member of the family.

Trevor continued to suffer with chronic pain. As a high school senior, he spent more time at home with tutors than in the classroom. He struggled to get through the sessions without pain killers so that his mind would be sharp enough to learn, but immediately after the teachers left, he looked for pain relief. He was accepted to Stony Brook University to attend classes in the fall of 2004, but we had no idea how he was actually going to attend classes. We could only hope to find an answer to his pain by then. He gave up any hopes of ever returning to playing hockey and spent most of his days in his room watching television and playing video games with the shades drawn because the light bothered him.

As the year went on, he received C-2 radio frequency ablations, but the pain relief didn't last long and the treatments, which often required anesthesia, increased his pain before they eased it. Then one day, Dr. Francoise spoke to Trevor and me about an advance in pain management.

"We have new technology used in the relief of back pain and I believe it might offer a more permanent method of pain relief for you," he said. "It's called a neurostimulator."

"How does it work?" asked Trevor.

"The neurostimulator is permanently installed in the body much like a pace maker and interferes with messages of pain to the brain," Dr. Francoise said.

"So I would have to have surgery to implant it," said Trevor.

"Yes," said the doctor. "And it's not a simple surgery. A battery pack would be implanted near your hip. Wires run up the back and come out at the neck to be anchored before continuing up to the occipital nerve"

Trevor looked like he was going to be sick. "I would feel like Frankenstein," he said. "I'm not interested."

"Why don't you think about it and research it online before dismissing it?" I asked.

"I'm not doing it," he said emphatically. "I don't want to be freak for life."

"Of course, it's your body and your decision," said Dr. Francoise. "If you were interested, we would try a temporary implant leaving the wires and battery outside the body to see if the neurostimulator would relieve your pain."

"I'm not interested," said Trevor firmly. There was nothing more to be said. The decision to have surgery was entirely up to him.

Trevor began classes at Stony Brook University in the fall. Roger and I took turns driving him to and from classes. He needed pain medication just to walk across the campus. I knew Trevor really wasn't up to the task, but the alternative was to let him stay in his room and play video games day after day. Roger and I weren't ready to give up hope or to accept that Trevor's life would never be anything more than constant suffering and loneliness. In the classroom he found it difficult to pay attention because the medications fogged his mind. Often, he got nauseous and left the class to throw up. After ten weeks of classes, he was overtired, stressed, depressed, and unable to face finals or do term papers. He took a medical leave while we prayed for a miracle.

As the year progressed, Tyler showed more difficulty separating from the family after a home visit. Initially, we assumed there were less demands put on him at home and that made home a more comfortable place for him, but as time went on we wondered if there wasn't more to Tyler's tears than we thought. His understanding of feelings was increasing and he was beginning to express them. One day as he and I rode together in the car to the doctor, he asked me, "Why do I have behaviors?"

"What do you mean?" I asked.

"Why do I do the things that I do?"

"I don't know, Tyler. I have wondered that for years. Sometimes it's hard for you to do the right thing because you have Tourette Syndrome. That's definitely part of the problem, but many people have Tourette Syndrome and do not have as many difficulties as you do. I think when you were a baby in the orphanage you were not treated well and you became an angry boy who found it hard to trust anyone."

"Trevor and Jonathan don't have behaviors." A look of confusion covered his face.

"No, they don't."

"I wish I didn't have behaviors."

"You know, since Trevor had his accident he has a difficult time getting through a day because of pain. He works very hard at keeping a good attitude. You're both handicapped, but no matter how bad Trevor feels, he would never hurt his family."

Tyler swallowed deeply as his eyes became moist. "Will I always have behaviors?"

"I think it will always be hard for you to control yourself, but I believe you can do much better. Trevor works hard to succeed and you have to work hard too. You can make life so much easier for yourself if you try harder to do the right thing."

"I'm going to try".

The conversation ended because we had arrived at the doctor. I had always wanted to know what Tyler thought about his situation. Now he was talking about it. He was finally beginning to understand he had a problem that he needed to control and that his family was not the enemy.

Tyler felt emotional after our conversation and had difficulty talking without choking up. When the doctor's staff asked him to follow them to the exam room, he asked if I could go with him. Tyler had never sought comfort or assurance from my presence even though it was such a natural thing for a son to ask his mother to come into the doctor's office with him. I was filled with hope that Tyler was actually beginning to regard me as his mom.

As the year passed, I saw another change in Tyler. I knew from books I had read that an adopted child will go through a grieving process as he comes to understand he was born into another family. The adopted child grieves the loss of his biological family.

When Jonathan was about nine years old, he asked many questions about his birth mother and why she had given him up for adoption. With Jonathan, I had quite a bit of information. I knew his birth father had been killed in the civil war that raged for years in El Salvador. His birth mother already had a two - year old and was left to live a life of poverty. She simply was unable to provide for Jon at that time. Statistics showed that one in five children in El Salvador died before the age of five due to malnutrition and disease. After his birth, his mother made the decision to give him up, she moved into the city of San Salvador and took a job as a maid in a motel to be available for the multiple court hearings necessary to place a child for adoption. Most children being adopted from El Salvador came to America at the age of thirteen months because the birth mothers had to be tracked down for three court hearings. Jonathan came home at five months old because his birth mother made the commitment to have him start a better life as soon as possible. I was able to tell Jonathan she gave him up because she cared about him. In Tyler's case I had no information. One day, he approached me with questions about his early childhood.

"Mom, when I was a baby, did I sleep in a crib?" he asked

"I don't know Tyler," I said. "You were already sleeping in a bed by the time you joined our family."

"Did I drink from a bottle?"

"No, you were already drinking from a cup?"

"Did Jonathan sleep in a crib?"

"Jonathan was only five months old when he came home. He slept in a crib because he couldn't walk yet. You were three and a half-years old when we met you."

He acted as if he had not heard what I had said. "Did I wear diapers?"

"No, Tyler, you were finished with diapers before I met you."

"Do you have pictures of me as a baby?"

"No, I'm sorry. I don't, but I do have a lot of pictures of the first few months when you came home. Would you like to look at those?"

"Yeah."

"I'll get the photo album for you."

We sat in the den and looked at the pictures. I told him the story of his adoption. I told him about Russia and his first few months at home. I made everything sound positive. As we looked at the pictures, Tyler did not recall anything about the photos that were taken while we were in Ukraine, but he did remember most of the events of the months following the adoption.

Suddenly, he looked at me, "Can I go outside?"

"Okay," I said. Just like that, the moment was over. It may have been too much information for one day. I decided to spend more time talking with him about what I knew about his early years, but it was going to take time to open all the doors to Tyler's emotions.

CHAPTER 47
2005

From one month to the next, we saw significant changes in Tyler's behavior. One day in January he called to tell us he had a perfect day without any zeroes. Roger and I passed the phone back and forth sharing in his excitement and encouraging him to shoot for more perfect days. By the end of February, he averaged one to two perfect days a week. Little by little, control of his emotions and impulses improved and he took pride in positive achievements.

In February, Tyler came home for a week for the midwinter break. He had an excellent visit and helped Trevor throughout the week. One night before bed he came into my room where I sat reading a book. He stood in the doorway hesitantly.

"What is it Tyler?' I asked.

He held up his arms and said, "Could I have a hug good-night?"

I had waited years for Tyler to allow me to hug him. I jumped up from the bed and walked towards him with my arms out. He met me and we embraced. "I love you, Tyler," I said as tears filled my eyes.

"I love you too," he answered holding on tightly. After that, Tyler came to me every night looking for the hug before bedtime.

At Easter, Tyler came home with a new interest, the weather. He watched weather reports comparing the weather on Long Island with the weather in Pennsylvania. He studied what made weather happen and looked on the internet to learn the meanings of meteorological terms. When he wanted to, Tyler could learn quickly. I was happy to see him develop a healthy interest in something instead of putting all his energy into making everyone around him crazy. He also developed an interest in music of all kinds and like a typical teenager he walked around the house with headphones constantly playing music in his ears.

Tyler came home in June for a two week vacation. He had an excellent visit without any missteps and was in fact a pleasure to have at home. Every night he asked for a good-night hug, but on the last night of his visit he asked, "When can I live at home again?"

This didn't surprise me. The staff at Walsh said Tyler really looked forward to his home visits. I saw him making steady progress and improving his behaviors, but I didn't believe he had truly been rehabilitated. He looked for positive reinforcement from the staff at Walsh and was motivated to do well. In school, he completed his assignments, although he often rushed through them and needed to slow down and take more time to be accurate. The staff said he acted silly in the classroom to get attention and had trouble controlling his laughter. He still made gestures of a sexual nature and behaved inappropriately towards the female staff. Although the staff saw big improvements overall, he still needed to work on controlling his impulses before I could consider taking him back.

"Tyler," I said. "When you lived at home you were mean to the family and you engaged in property destruction. You didn't listen to dad or I and you broke every house rule. I don't think we're ready for you to come back home yet."

"I don't do that stuff anymore at home," he said. "It would be different."

"I'm sorry, Tyler," I said. "You're still giving the staff at Walsh difficulty. How do I know you will continue to behave once you're here everyday?"

"I will. I wouldn't do that stuff at home,' he said sniffling. "You'll see."

"I'm sorry," I said. I had to speak with my head and not my heart. It would be a mistake to allow Tyler to come home before he or the family were ready. "You still need to improve your behavior at Walsh, Tyler, to convince me you can handle being home full time. In the meantime, we'll continue to extend your home visits whenever we can as long as you continue to do the right thing."

Every time I talked with Tyler after that, he campaigned to live at home again. Every phone call ended with, "when can I live at home again?"

Jonathan tried out for a basketball team at the high school. I didn't understand his interest in the sport until I went to his first game. An older boy, Juan, from Central America dominated the team. Jonathan's eyes followed Juan's every move. He had few opportunities to meet other young people of color in our school district. I realized that I needed to do more to help him embrace his heritage.

In September, I took Jon to a Salvadoran Day Parade in Brentwood. After the parade, we walked a few blocks to the street fair. We had a great time and Jon was exposed to the pride of hundreds of beautiful Salvadoran families. We purchased Salvadoran tee shirts and a big flag of El Salvador that he proudly hung in his room.

In June, Trevor became weary of a life in pain. "I think I'm ready to try a neurostimulator. I'm tired of living like this and I trust Dr. Francois. If he thinks it would be a good thing for me, then I should try it."

"I think you're right," I said. "Dr. Francois wouldn't do anything that wasn't in your best interest. If he thinks the neurostimulator will help, it's probably a good idea to try."

Dr. Francois sent Trevor to a pain management surgeon to have a temporary stimulator implanted outside the body to see if it would be effective. Trevor received total relief from the headache. However, because the temporary implant sat outside the body, it was subject to infection and had to be removed after three days. In August, Trevor had surgery to make the neurostimulator permanent. In one afternoon, Trevor went from a teen living in agony to a teen with possibilities. The difference was dramatic.

Tyler came home for a vacation in August when Trevor received his implant. As I helped Trevor into bed after the surgery, Tyler stood in the doorway aghast. Trevor had an incision at the waist to accommodate the battery pack, two incisions on his back where the wires had been pulled through, an incision at the neck where the wires were anchored and an incision at the lower part of the skull where the probe had been placed under the scalp against the occipital nerve to interfere with messages of pain to the brain. Tyler watched with tears streaming down his cheeks.

"Tyler, I need your help," I said. "Don't just stand there crying. Help me get his pillows in place."

Tyler pulled himself together, put the pillows on the bed, and helped me guide Trevor's head onto the pillow.

"Thanks, Tyler," I said. "You can go now."

"I don't want to go," he said. "I'll sleep on the floor in Trevor's room tonight in case he needs anything."

"You don't have to do that," said Trevor. "I'll be okay."

"I want to stay with you," Tyler said.

"If you're sure," said Trevor. "It would be nice to have you here."

"I want to help you," said Tyler.

"I'll come and check on you, Trevor," I said. "Tyler, I'm sure I won't sleep well tonight, so if Trevor needs anything just call me."

"Okay" said Tyler.

I was so proud of both of them. Trevor made the decision to move ahead with his life and Tyler was there to help him.

In September, just a few weeks after his surgery, Trevor stood in the doorway to the kitchen with tears running down his face.

"What is it?" I asked.

"The headache is back. I pushed off the bed with my left arm when I got up. There was a shock and now the pain is back," he sobbed.

"Oh Trevor," I said. "Don't despair. I'll call the doctor right away. Perhaps it can be reprogrammed."

I called the doctor's office and he told me to bring him right in. X-rays of his skull showed the stimulator had shifted and was no longer sitting in the right place. The technology used to make the stimulator work was new and had rarely been used for headache control. New technology to anchor the stimulator and a smaller battery would eventually be designed, but for now, Trevor had to deal with some inadequacies in the technology. To put the stimulator back into place, Trevor needed another surgery.. The following week he had the surgery but his anxiety over whether the stimulator was a permanent fix or not grew.

A few days after the surgery Roger came downstairs after spending some time in Trevor's room and said, "We need to add on to the house."

"What?' I asked.

"I've been thinking about it for some time. Trevor needs more space. I don't think the stimulator is going to be the total answer for his headaches. He needs a larger space to spread out and maybe have some friends over."

"That's a good idea. What do you have in mind?"

"I thought we could add on over the garage, and give him his own bathroom and a private entrance."

"I like the idea."

"I'm going to call my brother and see if he's interested in working with me." His brother was a skilled carpenter. When Roger called him he was eager to help. Within a week the two of them were tearing the roof off and buying lumber.

Tyler heard about the construction and couldn't wait to get home to help so we let him come home for an extended weekend on Columbus Day. Roger strapped a tool belt on him, put a carpenter's pencil behind his ear and used him to fetch tools and supply nails. Roger and I never stopped praising Tyler for his efforts.

Before the end of the year, Trevor needed two more surgeries to secure the placement of the implant. In November as he recovered from one of those surgeries he moved into his new space, a 20 x 24 foot room with a large walk-in closet and a big bathroom. The staircase was off the bedroom and led down to an area off the kitchen where he had a private entrance. Trevor ended the year pain free and with a space of his own.

CHAPTER 48
2006

Tyler showed improvement quickly now. In May, after he had been home for a week, his latest clinician, Mrs. Frost, made the weekly conference call with Tyler to tell me about his progress.

"Mrs. Havlicek," she began, "Tyler says he had a good visit at your house last week."

"Yes, he did," I said. "He helped his brother, Trevor, who recently had to go in for surgery again, this time because one of the neurostimulator wires that runs up his back broke through the skin and was visible. The unit had to be removed and put back in again. It's very hard because the stimulator is the only thing that gives Trevor complete relief."

"Tyler told me about that," she said. "He was proud of himself for helping."

"He should be," I said. "He's been great."

"Tell Mrs. Frost how I helped dad," said Tyler.

"Well, as you know, Roger added on to the house," I said. "There's still a lot of finishing work to be done on the addition and Tyler helped Roger with that. He's been learning a lot about carpentry."

"Yeah," said Tyler. "Whenever dad needs a tool now, I can find it in the garage for him."

"That's great, Tyler," said Mrs. Frost. "Tyler's teachers report that he's doing well in school now."

"I almost never get zeroes now," he said.

"His teachers say he shows interest in all of his subjects and makes great effort to do his best," Mrs. Frost said. "They say when he has free time he asks for extra work to do."

"Wow, Tyler," I said. "I'm so proud of you."

"Thank-you," he said. "I still get silly in class sometimes, but I'm working on that too."

"Good for you," I said.

"He's improved greatly at the residence too," Mrs. Frost said. "The staff here says he's now easily redirected when he gets frustrated. His social skills have improved and he is usually the first to wake up and be ready in the morning. He keeps his room neat and completes his chores as well as extras."

"Sounds like you're really doing well, Tyler," I said.

"I am," he said. "When can I live at home again?'

Tyler had been asking this question for months. I knew he had improved greatly, but neither Roger nor I could be sure that his problems were over.

"Tyler," I said. "Dad and I are not sure that you're ready to come home."

"Oh, I am," said Tyler.

"I don't think that behaving well for a few months is

enough to wipe out years of misbehaving," I said. "Dad and I need to see you behave for a long time to be sure you will succeed at home."

"I can," he said quietly. "How long is a long time?"

"A year," I said. I needed at least that long to convince Trevor and Jonathan to give him another chance. They never wanted him to live at home again. I couldn't blame them. Tyler had robbed them of years of their childhood.

"I can be good for a year," he said. "I've changed. You'll see."

"Until then we'll continue to extend your vacations and breaks and see how you do," I said.

"That sounds like a good plan," said Mrs. Frost.

That evening when Roger came home from work I told him about the phone call.

"Well, you've certainly laid down a challenge for him,' he said. "Are you sure you aren't making the goal impossible because you're frightened, as am I, about the thought of having him live at home again?"

"Maybe," I said. "I'm afraid of disrupting the whole household again. Things are going so well now. Running around to doctor's and pain management specialists with Trevor is all I can handle now. I think by challenging him to behave for a year I may have been putting off the whole idea."

"Well, it should be interesting to see what Tyler does with it," he said. "He's been pretty consistently achieving his goals for a while now."

"It's not that I don't want him to succeed," I said. "I just need to be certain that his good behavior is sustainable."

"I agree," he said. "Now it's all up to Tyler. We've done everything we can to give him the tools to succeed. He just really needs to use them. In the meantime, as you said, we can encourage him and reward him with extended visits that will help him to transition if he succeeds."

"Don't tell Trevor or Jonathan we're even considering the possibility that Tyler may come back some day," I said. "It's still too remote a possibility to make them worry about it."

Jonathan was fifteen now and he had a job as a busboy at a restaurant in nearby Port Jefferson. Most people he served assumed he didn't speak English because most of the other bus boy came from Central America and did not speak English. He made me laugh with stories of people going through odd pantomimes to ask for things like forks or napkins. One man requested a drink for his wife in Spanish. Jon had heard the woman ask her husband for the drink in English, so he knew what to get for her. He never let on to these customers that he spoke English. Jon was comfortable with who he was and found it easy to laugh at himself. He was a very confident young man. He wanted to follow in Roger's footsteps and become a police officer. He was accepted into the junior police academy of Suffolk County over the summer where he trained like a real police officer. He made it his goal to study criminal justice in college.

Throughout 2006, Trevor continued to have difficulties with the neurostimulator. Each of these problems required another surgery. The least bit of movement on the left side displaced it. In June, Medtronics, the manufacturer of the system, referred us to a neurosurgeon with more experience in this type of surgery. He used a new type of anchor to hold the stimulator in place and felt quite confident he could get the stimulator to work permanently, but it involved taking the whole unit out and starting over again. In August, he did the surgery successfully. Trevor returned to Stony Brook in September and finally succeeded in his studies. He was able to drive his car again and get out on his own.

Tyler came home for fifteen days in June, nine days in August and seventeen days in December. A pleasure to have at home, he had excellent visits. In school and at the residence, he continued to act as a model student and resident. He impressed the staff with his ability to follow the rules and to not be led astray by the actions of other students. He called home every day now to tell us how well he was doing. I knew he was going to meet my challenge. I just hoped we were all ready to accept him back into our home.

CHAPTER 49
2007

Tyler came home for Presidents Week in February. He stood taller and smiled more than ever. He now received praise for his success at home, at school and the residence and his self-esteem grew with each passing week. Roger and I were so proud of him. On the last day of his vacation, as he prepared to leave, he said, "Maybe soon I won't have to leave. Maybe soon I will live at home again."

"Keep up the good work and we'll see what happens," said Roger as he picked up Tyler's suitcase."

"If you continue to meet your goals, anything is possible, Tyler," I said as I kissed him good-bye. "We'll see you in a few weeks." I closed the door behind Roger and Tyler and turned to find Trevor standing on the stairs glaring at me.

"You aren't really thinking about bringing him back here to live, are you?" He asked.

"He's improved so much. We're considering the possibility."

"No! Don't you remember what he did to us? Don't you remember what it was like? Don't you remember how he hurt us?"

323

"Yes, I do, but he isn't the same boy."

"I know he's been good on visits, but I don't think that would last if he lived here every day!"

"He's been very good for a long time. He's been especially helpful to you.

"I know and I really do appreciate that. It's just that I don't believe he'll be as well behaved if he lives here again. Do you?"

"I don't know. That's why Dad and I are only considering moving him back home. We haven't made any decisions yet. We're looking very carefully at the situation. We won't rush into this. Just relax. Nothing is going to happen right now."

"Good. I do love him. I just still don't trust him." He turned and left the room.

We had always assured Jonathan and Trevor that we would never take Tyler back. I had no way to know if Tyler's behavior was the result of rehabilitation or a giant manipulative lie. Could he really have overcome such major psychological problems?

Tyler's annual review was scheduled in May. In the weeks before that, Roger and I had many conversations about whether or not to take Tyler back home permanently. No one at the residence suggested we change his placement. I'm sure some of the staff around him wondered why we didn't make a move to bring him back home, but no one ever said anything and I didn't want them to. Roger and I had to make this very personal decision. No one else would suffer the consequences if he failed at home.

As the time drew closer for the meeting, so did the date that would mark the year since I had challenged Tyler and he had by all measures succeeded. A few days before the meeting, Roger and I were still trying to decide what to do. We visited the pupil personnel services office to speak with Charlotte King, the coordinator for students who were educated outside the district.

"Tyler has been doing so well at Walsh that Patty and I have been thinking about bringing him back home to live," said Roger.

"That's a big decision," said Charlotte. "I think it would be very difficult to get him back into the program once he leaves it."

"I know," I said. "Even though he's doing well, we're still scared to bring him home. We're wondering if we could take him home for the whole summer and see how it works out. Would he lose the spot if he were only home for the summer?"

"That's an interesting question," said Charlotte. "I'll call and ask them."

We sat and watched as she called, but the answer was what we had expected. He would lose the spot. It was an all or nothing situation.

The day of the meeting came and we sat at a table with Charlotte King, Anne Xander, the Special Education Advocate and Mr. Mann, a special education teacher from the high school. Tyler, his school principal, his teachers and a representative from the residence were on the phone for the meeting via conference call at the other end.

Mrs. King began the meeting, "Good morning everyone. Tyler, how are you today?"

"I'm good," he said.

Each teacher at Tyler's end reviewed his progress. One by one, they raved about his progress. He no longer had the negative attention seeking behaviors that had so dominated his every move in the past. Now he was a pleasure to have in the classroom and a good role model to other students still dealing with behavior issues. After each teacher spoke, Tyler quietly said, "Thank-you." Roger and I repeatedly interjected how proud we were of him. The residence staff continued the praise. Tyler was the shining star at the residence, always doing his chores, following the rules and helping others. He had earned fifteen minutes everyday to walk around the campus unsupervised and was managing that time well. When everyone finished speaking I turned and looked at Roger. He nodded at me with a smile.

"Tyler," I said, "Last year we talked about when you could live at home again. I challenged you to be good for a year, didn't I?"

"Yeah," he said.

"I think everyone agrees you have earned the right to come home again," I said.

"For good?" he asked. I looked at Roger.

"For good, buddy," said Roger. "You should be very proud of yourself.

Tears welled in my eyes and as I looked around I realized

that everyone in the room was crying, but all was quiet at the other end of the line.

"Hello?" asked Mrs. King. "Did we lose the connection?"

"No, no. We're here," stammered the principal. "Tyler started crying and then we all broke down. He's so happy he can't talk."

"Tyler, you have come so far. You deserve this. You made this happen," I said.

"When will I come home?" Tyler asked.

"We'll have to talk about that," said the principal. "I would guess it will probably happen in July when you finish the summer session. How does that sound?"

"That sounds great!" said Tyler. "I'm so excited! Can I go tell my friends?"

"I'll take him back to the classroom," said his teacher. "He can tell everyone the news."

"We'll talk to you later," said Roger.

As we left the meeting, Roger and I couldn't stop smiling.

"It's time," he said. "He'll be fine."

"I know," I said. "He's improved so much that when I tell people who have only met him recently how bad things were they think I'm exaggerating."

"Now we just have to convince Jonathan and Trevor," he said.

"That may not be possible," I said. "Their memories of life with him are so dark, they can't see past them. Those wounds may take some time to heal."

"Jonathan is so busy with sports, school, and his friends, I don't think the move will have much impact on his life," said Roger. "Remember, Tyler will still be going to school and will develop his own local relationships. As for Trevor, he'll come around. Tyler has been very kind to Trevor over the past few years and I believe those memories will win out over the earlier ones."

"I think so too," I said. "If I believed otherwise, I wouldn't consider taking Tyler back."

Over the weeks that followed, Tyler called every day bursting with excitement. The staff at Walsh planned many activities to help Tyler say good-bye to everyone who had touched his life there. When he came home in June, Roger picked up his winter clothes, his bike, skateboard and rollerblades. Ty picked out a shade of blue for the walls in his room and Roger painted it. Since he enjoyed studying the weather we took sky blue tie dyed fabric and stapled it to the ceiling to look like fluffy clouds floating overhead. Then I tacked glow in the dark stars on the fabric to create the perfect evening sky. Everything was falling into place. The only problem we had was finding a school in our county that would accept him.

Tyler's behavior had improved dramatically, but it was hard to convince any school that reviewed his records to take him. No one wanted to take a chance on him. School after school rejected his application. In July when Tyler transitioned home, he still did not have a placement. Mrs. King had to go to bat for him and finally convinced a school just east of us to take him.

The school was behavior management based and handled students with all types of special needs. We didn't believe Tyler needed a serious behavior management program anymore, but he was still severely delayed academically. As it turned out, it was the perfect school for him. He was in a classroom with five other students and a classroom aide. His teacher, Mr. Charles, was a strong male role model. Throughout the year, Tyler received counseling and the school provided a place where he felt safe to discuss the myriad of feelings that went with returning home and leaving his old life behind.

Tyler came home in June and July for extended visits and by the time he transitioned home, Trevor and Jonathan were accustomed to his presence. In the end, we didn't meet resistance from either of them. They both knew he deserved a second chance.

During his first few weeks at home, Tyler had wide swings of emotion. He was elated to be home. He missed his old friends. He loved his new school. He missed the staff at Walsh. However, his strongest feelings surrounded his early years in our home. When we discussed how his behavior had improved, he sobbed struggling to breathe.

"Tyler, what's wrong?" I asked every time this happened. "You really should be so proud of yourself. You've overcome so much."

"I know. I just....." He was too upset to finish the sentence.

"Calm down and try to explain what you're feeling," I said. "Take a few deep breaths. Slow down and breathe."

"It's just....I'm so sad when I think about what I did to my family," he said. The words were so mixed with tears that I had difficulty understanding him.

"Tyler," I said. "You must concentrate on how well you're doing now. What happened in the past was not your fault. You were just an angry little boy. You couldn't help yourself. I don't know anyone else who could have overcome such a difficult beginning and turn into such a fine and responsible young man. Be proud of yourself."

"I'll try," he said.

We would have many, many conversations regarding Tyler's regrets over the past, but it would be a long time before he forgave himself and truly understood all that he had overcome.

CHAPTER 50
2008

In June, Roger and I drove down a long lane flanked by wooded areas to arrive at Tyler's high school early for the graduation ceremony. We walked into the reception area at the front of the building and signed in.

"Oh, you're Tyler's parents!" said the receptionist. "I'm Mrs. Clark! I love Tyler! He's such a delight!"

"Thank-you," said Roger. "He wasn't always."

"I've heard that," she said, "but it's hard to imagine. He's so kind and polite."

"He's come a long way," I said.

"You must be so proud of what you've done for him," she said.

"We didn't do anything but provide an environment in which he could succeed," said Roger. "Tyler had to make the changes himself, but we're very proud of him."

"Well, I hope you enjoy this very special day," she said. "You can walk down to his classroom, if you like."

"Thank-you," I said. "I think we'll do that."

Tyler was finishing up at this school and moving on to a vocational training school next year. Roger and I never thought we would see the day that Tyler would be regarded as a model student, but now he was a favorite of the staff. I grabbed Roger's hand with a grin that I knew spread all over my face as we headed down the hall. Near the classroom, someone tapped me on the shoulder. I turned around to see a woman whom I had never met.

"I'm Mrs. Channing," she said. "Are you Tyler's parents?"

"Yes, we are," I said.

"I'm the music teacher," she said. "What a great kid he is!"

"Thank-you," I said. "He *is* great, isn't he?"

"You know," she said, "so many of the children here come from sad backgrounds. It's been a pleasure to see Tyler come to school happy every day with such a great attitude."

"Thank-you," I said again.

She smiled and walked away. I turned to Roger. "Can you believe this?"

"I'll never get tired of hearing positive comments about Tyler," he said.

We reached Tyler's classroom and peeked in. He was removing his suit jacket and putting on his graduation gown.

Mr. Charles opened the door. "The class is very excited and it's pretty noisy, but you're welcome to come in," he said.

"That's okay," said Roger. "We're going over to the chapel now."

"Okay," said Mr. Charles. "After the ceremony, refreshments will be served in the cafeteria. I'll see you there."

Roger took my hand and we headed across the campus to the chapel. As we walked along, I said, "If you had told me years ago that Tyler would one day be a happy young man who was kind and thoughtful of others, I would not have believed it"

"Me neither," said Roger. "It all seemed so impossible and overwhelming when he was little."

We arrived at the chapel as the other classes from the school filed in. Pomp and Circumstance played. My throat tightened as the emotion of the day washed over me. I turned to the back of the chapel and saw Tyler marching down the aisle in his burgundy cap and gown with a stride of confidence and pride. I glanced at Roger and saw his eyes welling up as were mine. Tyler took his place at the head of the chapel with his six classmates and looked out across the chapel. He had experienced so much loss and separation in his life every time he moved to a new residence or campus and here he was saying good-bye to friends and staff again. He had had the best year of his life and it was hard to move on.

The ceremony began and Mr. Charles introduced each student. He spoke about what it had been like to teach each of them and then gave the student a chance to speak. Tyler was the third student called up.

"When Tyler Havlicek came to us on the first day of school this year, no one knew what to expect," said Mr. Charles. "Here was this new kid from Mount Sinai who apparently had some serious behavioral problems in the past. Tyler came into our room the first day with a big smile on his face. There has not been a day since then that Tyler hasn't been smiling. Tyler is one of the hardest working kids we have ever had in our school. He is the perfect example of someone who has grown up from misbehavior and disrespect, and turned into a man. Tyler never gives up, no matter how difficult things get. He is the ideal student in his manners, positive attitude, and he is as genuine and real as people come. This year, Tyler has never had to go to the crisis room and I can honestly say he has never been disrespectful to Mrs. Powers, me or anyone else in the school. Tyler loves to sing, especially on school trips and on the bus and always makes other people smile when he's around. He is a true gentleman and a pleasure to teach. Tyler is also an expert in computers, meteorology, flying cars and earning bonus bucks. He will truly be missed by all."

Tears flowed down Tyler's cheeks as he stepped up to speak. "I have enjoyed being here," he said sniffling through the words. "I have made many friends and I want to thank all of the staff here for all they have done for me."

At that moment, he glanced over at Roger and me and began to cry uncontrollably. He couldn't continue. Mr. Charles stepped up. "We are all so proud of you," he said. The chapel exploded in applause as Tyler looked around trying to hold it together. He looked at Roger and me and smiled.

"I love you," I mouthed and his smile grew bigger. Tyler's struggle with his past had ended and he had a bright future. It was everything I had ever have hoped for.

When the new school year started in the fall, Tyler attended classes at a vocational school with other learning disabled students. Although relatively high functioning, his behavior throughout his many school years kept him from advancing his education. He had particular difficulties with basic mathematical ideas. The part of his brain responsible for those concepts had not developed when he was in the orphanage. The vocational school helped him with some of those deficits while exposing him to various work settings that had been created on the campus.

The curriculum was split into two half year sessions. During the first half of the year, Tyler worked in an office setting, learning to file, work a computer, use a copier and improve his math skills with the help of a calculator. The office skills were taught in the morning and in the afternoon, he went down the hall to work in a little store in the building. He stocked shelves, made coffee and learned to make change while using a cash register.

During the second half of the year, he spent the mornings working in the campus floral shop, making bouquets and arrangements. This was my favorite part of the curriculum because Tyler often brought home the arrangements he made. In the afternoon, he moved on to hospitality training where he learned to work in a hotel setting. He made beds, set tables and did housekeeping. Overall, he loved the program and quickly became a favorite of the staff who described him as cheerful, polite and always smiling. Within a few months, he was conducting tours of the program for students who were considering attending this school.

CHAPTER 51
2009

At the end of the year, the vocational school and its many students put on a talent show in the format of the TV show, American Idol. Tyler, wearing a black suit, played the part of Ryan Seacrest.

"Hey!" he shouted to the audience. "Are you ready to have some fun?"

The crowd cheered in response.

"Welcome to our school's American Idol," he said with all the confidence of a professional emcee. "Today some very talented young people will show off their skills."

The crowd applauded as the music began. A class of twelve students climbed the wooden stage with a New York City skyline at night as the backdrop. The Mylie Cyrus song, "The Climb" played. The class sang along with the hit recording, "ain't about how I get there--it's the climb." The students swayed back and forth rhythmically while Tyler lip synced from the far right side of the stage. He pretended to play a guitar and bounced up and down with each beat. When the record produced a cascade of drum beats, Tyler became a drum player with imaginary drumsticks in each hand. He stole the show. Roger and I heard people in the audience commenting on Tyler's performance.

"This kid is amazing," one said. "He has the whole show memorized. He's just having so much fun."

As the song ended, the class stepped to the side revealing a panel of judges behind them.

"Judges, wasn't that a great performance?" Tyler asked enthusiastically.

"It was phenomenal," said the student playing Paula.

"I loved it. This group was great!" exclaimed the judge playing Randy.

"What do you think, Simon?" asked Tyler.

"I think they need to go back to the recording studio and work harder," said the young man playing the overly frank Simon Cowell. A rumble of laughter rolled through the audience.

Tyler directed the class off the stage and led the next group to come up and take its place. Once again, he danced and lip synced as the group performed. Throughout the show, he never missed a word as his skinny body moved to each note of the songs. When the show ended, staff and parents told us how much they enjoyed his performance. We never tired of hearing people praise Tyler. We knew what they didn't. Tyler had grown up disrupting activities not making them successful.

At home the boys were becoming young men. Trevor was a junior at Stony Brook University and getting close to his goal of graduation Numerous surgeries and pain management treatments caused him to drop out several times, but the neurostimulator had given him back his life and he planned to make the most of it. Most people would have given up, but Trevor persevered with a strength and determination that few people possess. He kept his great sense of humor and just as I started to feel weary, he lightened my mood and made me laugh.

"How are you doing?" I asked him one day as he came into the kitchen with dark circles around his eyes. "You look like you have a headache?" Although the stimulator controlled most headaches, he still had occasional breakthrough headaches.

"I'm okay," he said.

"Are you going to school?" I asked.

"I have to," he said. "I can't miss a class."

"I don't know how you do it," I said. "A lesser person would crawl into bed and feel sorry for himself."

"That wouldn't help," he said. "I'd still have the headache. I don't feel sorry for myself. I'm still lucky. I have you and dad and a nice home and my brain still functions well although it causes me pain from time to time. It could be so much worse."

"Always the optimist, aren't you?" I said.

"No, it's just that despite everything," he said. "I'm happy."

The next day I hung a sign at the bottom of the stairs in his apartment. The sign had words that Winnie-the Pooh had said to Christopher Robin. "Promise me that you'll always remember that you're braver than you believe, stronger than you seem and smarter than you know." It summed up perfectly how I felt about Trevor.

One day, a classmate fixed Trevor up with a blind date. Kate lived around the corner from us, but he had never met her before because for Trevor, most of high school took place in our kitchen. They went out to dinner and have been together ever since. Kate is a delightful, intelligent, young lady with a fun loving spirit. Roger and I immediately fell in love with Kate and feel fortunate that Trevor found her.

Jonathan graduated from high school and enrolled at the local community college to study criminal justice making the dean's list each semester. He wanted to follow in Roger's footsteps and become a police officer. He had a very active social life and in addition to working at the restaurant in Port Jefferson, he had a job as a promoter at the dance clubs.

When Jonathan was younger, he sometimes asked about his birth mother. I always told him that she had sent him to America to have a healthy and happy childhood and that when he turned eighteen, if he wanted to meet her, I would help him find her. As he got older, he stopped asking about her. Jonathan loved our family and wanted to put a tattoo on his upper arm that said," family forever" but I didn't want him to have a tattoo. I often referred to him as my "solid citizen" because he always worked hard and did the right thing. One night, he came home soaked from head to toe.

"What happened to you?" I asked.

"I'm the most responsible kid ever," he said.

"What does that mean?" I asked.

"A kid brought some alcohol in his car and drank it before he came into the club tonight. He was really drunk," he said. "I took his keys and brought him home. His father told me to dump him in the shower as he turned on the cold water. He was so sick I couldn't do that to him. I held him up in the shower and that's how I got all wet. After I dried him up and helped him get into dry clothes, his father told me that I was the most responsible kid he had ever met."

"Wow! That was really nice of you," I said. "You're a young man of good character. Character matters in life. I'm very proud of you."

In the fall, Tyler transitioned to adult services which offered him a choice of several programs. He chose to work on a thirteen acre ranch a few miles from our house. He took horseback riding lessons, mucked stalls and cared for the horses along with other farm animals. At the entrance to the ranch sat a large pond with a pretty fountain. The main building located on a hill overlooked the rest of the ranch. Beyond that building, was a huge, rustic barn where horses stood in the paddocks and training areas. In large corralled spaces, other horses ate grass and roamed lazily. When the weather warmed, Tyler worked in the big hot house behind the barn growing flowers. At the far end of the ranch was a large vegetable garden. The flowers and vegetables were sold to the public to earn money for the ranch. Tyler loved everything about this program especially the opportunity to spend so much time outdoors. Every afternoon, he came home exhausted, but happy.

CHAPTER 52
2010

Every year the ranch put on a show demonstrating the skills of the young people in the program. On a hot August day, Roger and I walked on the sandy paths past the paddocks out to the large arena at the far end of the ranch. Excitement was in the air as the families gathered. Large tables displayed the vegetables and flowers produced in the gardens and greenhouses. One by one, riders took their horses around the ring as the families applauded. Tyler demonstrated barrel racing, but before he started, he searched the crowd of spectators around the corral to find Roger and me. He grinned and gave us a thumbs up sign. He sat straight up in the saddle exuding confidence as he took his horse around the ring demonstrating various gaits. At the end of the show, he led a drill team of eight riders into the ring. He called out a command and each rider moved precisely into formation awaiting Tyler's next order. The team performed flawlessly and the crowd cheered loudly.

Trevor graduated from Stony Brook University with a double major in history and linguistics. It had taken six years but, he never gave up. Kate moved into the apartment and she and Trevor got engaged, although she had to finish college and he wanted to have a career and some money in the bank before they married.

At nineteen, Jonathan still worked at the restaurant as a waiter. He had been there for over three years. He was a funny kid who didn't mind showing how much he loved his family even if it didn't always seem cool. I remember one day in particular. Jonathan had to go to the restaurant where he worked to pick up his paycheck. He insisted I come along and meet some of his coworkers. We ordered lunch and sat at a table as his coworkers came in and out, stopping to sit and chat with us. He was happy to include me in the conversation. "You're such a momma's boy," I teased him after lunch.

"That's right," he responded with a big smile, but then Jonathan always seemed to be smiling.

One day, as I gardened in front of the house, a carload of young men came to pick Jon up for a trip to the mall. He jumped in the car and as it circled the court and came around past me, he rolled down his window and yelled, "I love you mom!" I grinned and waved to the car.

That night when he came home I asked, "Is it really cool to be yelling 'I love you mom,' when you're out with your friends?'

"I don't care what they think." he said.

Jonathan and I were very close. He went food shopping with me because he said, "I didn't buy enough "Jonny foods." But the truth was, we enjoyed each other's company.

At nineteen, Jonathan went to dance clubs designed for young teens. He loved music and had a natural rhythm. A year earlier, Jonathan and Tyler had stolen the show at my niece's wedding in Florida with their dancing. For months after the wedding, guests continued to comment on what a hit "the boys from New York" had been.

My three sons had all faced challenges and overcame them.

"This is the best my life has ever been," I told my best friend, Lori. "The boys are all healthy and doing well. Roger and I are happy and I love my home. What more could I ask for?"

CHAPTER 53
DECEMBER 19, 2010

I woke at 4:30 a.m. to the sound of the doorbell. The dogs heard it at the same time and scrambled down the stairs with me following closely behind. I opened the front door as they barked wildly. Two gold shields clanked against the glass of the storm door. Suffolk County Police Detectives. I held up an index finger asking them to wait a minute while I hustled the dogs out the back door onto the frosty deck in the frigid morning air. I glanced up. There were no stars in the black December sky. I returned to the front door. A male and female detective stood on my front porch. I looked past them to see if Jon's car was in the driveway. He was the only one who had gone out last night. I breathed a sigh of relief, seeing the car sitting there. Surely, Jon was asleep upstairs.

"Mrs. Havlicek? Is your husband at home?" Asked the male detective, a man with gray hair who appeared to be about forty- five and wore a dark suit.

"Yes, come in. He's still sleeping. He could sleep through a tornado," I answered. "What's up?"

"Please go get your husband," he said sternly. The blond female detective in a skirt and black topcoat just stood there.

"Has something happened to Jon?" I asked.

"Please get your husband," he repeated.

"Is Jon okay?" I asked, not really believing that anything could have happened to him.

"Please get your husband," he repeated. I glanced at the

female detective who met my eyes for a second and then looked down.

"I'll go get him," I said.

I ran upstairs to Jon's room and threw the door open. He wasn't there. My heart dropped like a stone. I went down the hall and woke Roger up. "There are two detectives downstairs and Jon's not home," I told him.

He threw the blankets back, looking annoyed, as if he thought that Jon might have been arrested for something. "Tell them that I'll be right there," he said.

Tyler stood in the hallway upstairs. The dogs had awakened him.

Stay in your room," I told him.

I went back downstairs. "Jon isn't home," I said to the detectives. "Are you here about him? Has something happened to him?"

"Let's wait for your husband," the male detective said. The female detective stared silently at the floor.

I stood in the dining room. They were in the center hall. Roger came downstairs.

"Why don't you sit down," the male detective said to me. I sat on a stiff backed dining room chair just off the foyer.

"What's going on?" Roger, always the cop, asked as he pulled out his police ID to let them know he was retired from the job.

"There was an accident tonight in Smithtown," said the male detective grimly. "Unfortunately Jon didn't make it."

"No," I said. "Not Jon."

Roger sank down on the stairs in disbelief.

Jon didn't make it, I thought. It sounded as if he had failed in a tryout for a team.

"It doesn't appear that alcohol or drugs played any part in the accident," said the male detective. The driver and the other two passengers made it out with minor injuries."

"NOT JON!" I screamed as what I was being told sank into reality. "NOT JON!" NOT JON!" Jon didn't take risks. Jon was reliable. This had to be a mistake. My hands flew to my head and grabbed a hunk of hair on each side of my head as if that action could somehow help my brain absorb the shock.

"The car hit black ice and spun out hitting a tree," the male detective continued. "Jon was in the backseat where the tree hit the car."

"NOT JON!" It couldn't be. "NOT JON!" I got up and walked around the kitchen in confusion. I had to tell Trevor. I slammed my fist on the door to his apartment off the kitchen, calling his name. "Trevor! Jon's been killed in a car accident!" I cried.

"What are you talking about?" asked Trevor, stumbling down the stairs.

"Jon's been killed in a car accident!" I repeated. He threw his arms around me as we both sobbed.

"Tell me what happened," he said.

"I don't know" I said. "It seems he was in a car that spun out on black ice and hit a tree."

"I have to wake Kate," said Trevor. He went back up to his apartment. I stood stunned in the kitchen not knowing what to do next.

"Someone will have to come to the morgue to identify the body," the male detective said to Roger.

The body. My vibrant, nineteen-year old had left the house last night to break dance at a club. Now he was being referred to as *the body.*

Roger pulled himself up off the stairs and met me in the kitchen. We were holding each other and crying when we realized Tyler had come down stairs and was watching us. He had heard what was said and was crying hysterically.

"Jon's gone, buddy," said Roger as he pulled Tyler into his arms. It was hard to know what to do or say next. The detectives handed Roger a business card and let themselves out.

Robotically, I made a few phone calls. I called my best friend, Lori. She was at church, but she came right over. I called Roger's sister, Rosemary. As I talked with her, my eyes took in all the Christmas decorations and the pile of gifts under the tree. How would we ever get through this? I called my brother in Florida. He and his wife would come to New York the next day.

Rosemary arrived a few minutes later. She and Roger

drove to the morgue to identify *the body.*

I went upstairs to Jon's room. I cleaned his desk and rummaged through his draws. I sat on his bed and looked around. There had to be an explanation for this madness. How could this be? "NOT JON! NOT JON! NOT JON!" I turned his closet inside out. Surely, something here would help me understand this madness. Then I found the composition. Jon had written a college composition I had never seen before. It was about me and titled "The Caring Mom." He talked about my love of animals and my passion for gardening. He talked about how I had been feeding a baby deer that was born in our sump and whose mother had been hit by a car, but what broke my heart and brought the depth of my loss into focus was the last three paragraphs.

Jon wrote, "As admirable as all my mother's interests are, the most important thing about her is that she always cared deeply about her children. She would do anything to support me and my two brothers; in fact that's why she adopted me. I was a Hispanic child born in El Salvador, one of the poorest countries in Central America. My mother saw that I was in need of a mother who would love me, feed me, support me and educate me throughout my whole life. After seeing a picture of me that the adoption agency had sent her, she sent my father to El Salvador to get me. Personally, I think she saved my life when she adopted me. Similarly when my brother, Trevor, had a hockey accident and injured his occipital nerve, my mom did everything she could to get him help. She didn't care how much healthcare cost; it was simply not a factor to her. She would never let money get in the way of caring for her child.

My mother has taken care of me and my brothers our

whole lives. There is nothing I can hide from her, and I trust her one hundred and ten per cent with anything I tell her. I can tell my mom the most personal things that have happened to me and she will always understand; it doesn't matter if it is something that I have done wrong or advice I need.

No matter what, I can always turn to my mom for anything. All my life she has taken care of my whole family, my pets and even hungry wild animals. Being passionate, caring, loveable and trustworthy is what my mom is all about."

"NOT JON!" I screamed through tears. "NOT JON! NOT MY BABY! NOT JON!"

CHAPTER 54
2011

Words cannot describe how difficult it was for the family to go on without Jonathan. We all felt the piercing pain of the gaping hole that Jonathan's absence created in our family. Memories of his vivacious personality inhabited every corner of our minds and our home. Nothing would ever be the same and life would forever be measured as the time before Jon's death and the time after.

During the winter months, I spent many hours sitting in the den staring into the blazing fireplace. I knew I should probably get up and do something, but I was obsessed with remembering everything about Jonathan, imprinting mental snapshots of him on my brain, afraid I might forget some detail about life with him. I pictured his features-his crooked front tooth-his coarse, black hair- the little scar on his cheek. I remembered little details about his physical cadence, his laughter and his expressed love for his family.

Hundreds of people had come to the one-day wake and a second room had to be opened while many stood waiting on line outside for as long as forty five minutes in the frigid December air. I stood in the front of the room near the casket and asked each visitor, "How did you know my son?" I heard many amazing stories. Jon, in his short life, touched so many people and these stories helped to buoy me in the months to come.

In the weeks that followed, if I did nothing else, I gathered up the strength to walk the dogs, which now numbered five. I feel strongly that dogs deserve a daily walk and that a good dog is one that has exercise. As a result of being a regular dog walker, everyone in the neighborhood knew me and people often stopped their yard work to chat as I went by, but now, as I walked, I felt people avoiding me.

"It's odd," I said to my best friend, Lori, "I'm sure it's my imagination, but I feel like people are steering clear of me."

"Well," she said. "They might be. Carol told me she saw you passing and didn't know how to approach the loss of Jonathan with you, so she ducked into her garage until you had gone by."

"I guess it's hard to know what to say to me."

"Sure, no one wants to upset you."

I already felt fragile as if I might snap like a weak tree limb under the strain of a heavy snow. Now I knew that everyone around me saw how vulnerable I was. I had handled the difficulties Tyler had as a young boy with great strength. I had handled Trevor's numerous surgeries without faltering, but now, I wondered how I would get through each passing day knowing that my youngest son would never again tell me the best and worst parts of his days.

March came and the weather warmed. I stepped out onto the deck to clear the flowerbeds for spring. Tears came to my eyes as I worried my memories of Jonathan might fade with each passing season. Trevor appeared behind me.

"Are you okay?" he asked.

"Sure," I said putting on a brave face.

"You know," he said trying to lighten my mood. "Jonathan could be a real pain in the ass sometimes. He was such a tease and a real little bugger. One night a couple of months ago Jon came home late at night with a girl that I had never met. Kate and I were in the kitchen making late night snacks. You and dad were sleeping. Jon introduced the girl to me and she whispered something to him which made him break out in big grin. She asked Jon if I was adopted. He told her that, yes, I was adopted and the family had regretted it for a long time."

"He really was such a tease," I said. "Remember how he liked to hide the remote and change the channels as I tried to figure out why the TV wasn't working. And he was always coming in late at night, waking me and, of course, the dogs, so I would get up and talk to him while he made something to eat."

"But the thing is," he said taking my face in his hands, "he was our little pain in the ass and our memories of him will get us through this together."

For Tyler, the house became quiet. He longed to see Jonathan practicing his dance steps around the house. He missed massaging Jon's feet after work and talking to him into the wee hours of the morning. He yearned to jump in Jon's car and listen to music while Jon drove him to his Friday night activities at Brookhaven Town Recreation Center. Tyler had suffered many losses in his short lifetime, but the death of Jonathan seemed too much to bear. He struggled to suppress tears every time Jon's name was mentioned.

In March, Roger had his left hip replaced. After experiencing severe pain for over a year, his physical activities had become limited. The surgery went well and the doctor, who knew we had recently lost Jonathan, released Roger from the hospital early because he felt that being alone in the hospital for large portions of the day might depress him and slow down his recovery. When Roger came home, he needed help with everything.

"Dad, can I get you anything?" Tyler asked as he got ready to go to the ranch in the morning.

"I could use some help changing my clothes," Roger said.

"Sure, I can help," said Tyler. "When mom lays out your clothes, I can help you get into them. Would you like me to make you some waffles and coffee?"

"That would be very nice."

"Okay. I'll be right back."

"Thanks, buddy."

In the evening, when Tyler came home from the ranch, he and Trevor helped Roger with the exercises the physical therapist had given him. Even though Jon was gone, we stilled pulled together as a family and I greatly appreciated the help of my two fine sons. Within about six weeks, Roger's hip improved and he resumed most of his activities without pain.

In the spring, the staff at the ranch chose Tyler to train as an advocate for the disabled. About once a month, he traveled to Albany, our state capital, with other advocates to meet with representatives of our state legislature. New laws threatened to cut funding for group homes and activities for the disabled. At one meeting, the state representative spoke about these cuts and then asked if anyone had any questions. After a quiet pause, Tyler raised his hand.

"Can you tell me specifically, how these cuts will affect my plan to someday live independently in a group home?" He asked the question with such poise and confidence that he surprised everyone on the room. Tyler continues to be an integral part of the advocacy program.

Throughout the summer, Tyler shadowed Roger. They replaced the deck in the backyard and rebuilt the shed to meet the town's specifications. Tyler had become quite the carpenter's assistant and could easily find any tool or gadget Roger might need from his workshop. The once oppositional Tyler now thrived on the praise he received for a job well done.

At the end of the summer, the director of the agency that sponsors the ranch asked Tyler to assist in preparation for the Annual Celebration of Life Gala Hosted by The Foundation for Human Potential. The staff wanted to feature Tyler's easy going confidence in its video presentation. He spent several weekends in September and October traveling to group homes and dayhab programs interviewing clients. These interviews were put together in a video to be featured on the night of the gala in November.

Early in September, Roger developed problems with his stomach. He lost his appetite and perspired excessively. After watching him for a few days, I feared this might be more than a stomach virus and took him to the local hospital emergency room. When the doctor came in, I described Roger's symptoms and my concerns to him.

"He has a gastro intestinal virus," said the doctor flatly.

"How do you know that without getting blood work or touching him?" I asked.

"Oh, we see this all the time," he said dismissively. "I'll run some blood work and hydrate him, but I'm sure this will get better in a few days, although sometimes this type of virus can hang on for longer"

Five hours later we headed home no better off than when we arrived. Because Roger did not have an elevated white count, the doctor said he had a virus, although I felt more testing should have been done. Roger spent the next few days in bed while we waited to see an improvement in his condition, but his symptoms persisted. He slept most of the day and I changed his sheets every few hours because he dripped with sweat. He had little interest in eating and seemed weaker each day.

A few days later, on September 9th, Trevor came home from dinner at Kate's parents' house complaining about pain in the back of his head at the site of the neurostimulator wires.

"What does it feel like" I asked trying not to reveal my anxiety. "Is the stim working?"

"It seems to be working," he said with trepidation, "but I'm feeling tenderness and severe pain around the site. There's a spot here that feels like a little pimple."

I looked at the sight and saw a small, little bump that oozed puss when I touched it. I felt physically sick. I called the surgeon who said to bring him right into the hospital emergency room. I called Tyler downstairs.

"Ty," I said feeling my chest constrict and my breath

become raspy. "I need you to take care of dad. Trevor is having some problem with his stim. Kate and I need to rush him to the emergency room in Nassau County. Here's Aunt Rosemary's phone number. Call her if you need help. I'll keep in touch with you throughout the night. Make sure dad continues to drink plenty of fluids because we don't want him to become dehydrated. There are clean sheets in the linen closet if his get too wet from perspiration. Can you handle this?"

"Sure, mom," he said.

I didn't doubt for a second that he would stay up all night and watch over his dad.

Trevor, Kate and I arrived at the hospital at 1:30 a.m. The doctor examined Trevor and said, "The stimulator is infected. Since there is no blood flow to the stimulator to deliver antibiotics to kill the infection, it must be removed immediately before the infection spreads throughout his body. This could be life threatening if it's not taken care of immediately. I'm so sorry."

"When will you be able to put it back in?" I asked wanting to look past the agony that Trevor now faced.

"Not for a while," said the doctor. "We'll have to make sure all signs of infection are gone before we can put another stimulator back in."

The surgery threw Trevor back into excruciating pain. Removing the unit meant opening the old scars again, but worse than the incisions was the nonstop headache that pounded in his head as soon as the unit came out. Unfortunately, the lab determined that Trevor had a drug resistant infection. Before he received a new stim, all signs of the infection had to be gone and that would take months. The surgery took place at 4:00 a.m. while Kate and I waited in Trevor's hospital room, falling in and out of sleep in oversized chairs that the staff brought in for us. The surgeon wanted Trevor to have intravenous antibiotics for at least twenty four hours before releasing him so we spent two nights at the hospital. When the nursing staff wheeled Trevor back into the room, he was on strong pain killers and feeling sleepy. Kate, unwavering in her need to be there for Trevor, stayed with him while I went down to the cafeteria to get some sandwiches for both of us. As I walked the hospital halls, I felt weak and dizzy. I imagined Jon coming down the hall and assuring me that everything would be okay. I missed his positive spirit and strength. I phoned home and Tyler told me that Roger was still showing no signs of improvement. Tyler changed the sheets twice during the night and kept him hydrated. Rosemary was on her way over to check on him and make them something to eat. I needed to be home and at the hospital. I felt myself slipping into a state of numbness as I found myself exhausted and unable to process the wide range of emotions. I didn't have the luxury of time to process what was happening to my family. The next morning the doctor released Trevor and I drove slowly home because every bump in the road or turn of the car caused Trevor pain.

While I was in the hospital with Trevor, Roger developed a pain in his artificial hip, so as soon as I returned home, I took him to see the hip surgeon.

"It would be very unusual to develop an infection in the hip six months after surgery," the surgeon said. "But I'm going to run some tests to be sure."

As we left the surgeon's office, I said to Roger, "I think we need to go to University Hospital for another opinion. We can't wait for the lab to complete the blood work."

"I agree," he said. "I'm feeling worse with each passing hour."

At University Hospital a team of doctors did extensive testing and diagnosed Roger with a ruptured gall bladder. The doctor said that if we had waited a few more hours, we would have lost him. Emergency surgery was performed on September 14th, but by this time, a raging staff infection had spread throughout his body and infected his artificial hip. As with Trevor's infection, the artificial hip did not receive blood flow, allowing the infection to grow unchecked on the surface of the implant, so the hip would have to come out after he healed from the gall bladder surgery and would not be replaced until all signs of the infection in his system were gone. He would be laid up for several months. The doctors said Trevor's infection and Roger's infection were not related and just happened to coincide but, could have been the result of weakened immune systems following a stressful time.

When I told Tyler the news about Roger, he cried. "Are you sure dad will be okay?" he asked with panic in his voice. "I don't want him to die."

"Oh, Tyler," I said as I pulled him close to me. "I think he got to the hospital just in time."

"Trevor just got out of the hospital and now Dad is in the hospital and I miss Jonathan," he sobbed. "This isn't fair."

"I know, but we need to pull ourselves together to help

Trevor and Dad."

"I understand. My family helped me get through the tough times when I was younger. Now it's my turn to help."

Tyler idolized Roger and hated to think of him in pain. Still dealing with the loss of Jonathan, two members of our family underwent serious surgeries in two different hospitals within days of each other. I had lost twenty-two pounds following Jon's death from stress and anxiety and now I needed to reach deep within and find the strength to nurse Roger and Trevor back to health while assuring Tyler that everything would be okay. I couldn't allow myself to be pulled under by the quicksand of emotions raging inside me. One minute I was sad and broken hearted, the next angry and feeling the unfairness of life, the next defeated and lost.

Tyler helped me immensely, but I was the only driver in the house now and that meant he had to scale back on his social activities because I didn't want to leave the house in case Roger needed me. Kate became the primary care giver for Trevor, spending the many days of his recovery in the apartment. She changed his dressings and administered antibiotics and pain medications. She made sure he ate and watched movies with him. I felt an incomparable gratitude for Kate. I could never have done this without her. I didn't feel much like eating during those autumn days as the weather chilled and the leaves fell, so Tyler often found himself eating dinner alone in a house filled with grief and medical struggles.

"How are you doing buddy?" I asked him one day. "I know we've been asking a lot of you lately and you haven't been having much fun."

"I'm okay," he said. "I still see some of my friends at the ranch."

"I know," I said, "but Dad and Trevor are stuck in bed while they recover and there's nothing for you to do on the weekends, since I don't want to leave the house."

"I've been thinking," he said. "I might be able to be more independent if I went into a group home"

"That's a decision only you can make," I said. "We can certainly start looking into the possibility."

The next morning, I called Tyler's social worker, Jane Metzger. Tyler was already on a waiting list to get into a group home, but when Ms. Metzger heard about what the family was going through, she arranged to have Tyler moved to the top of the waiting list based on family need.

Early in November, Mrs. Metzger came for a home visit. Roger was slowly recovering from his infection and gaining strength every day, but he still faced two more surgeries—one to remove the infected hip and one to put a new one back in. Tyler, Roger and I sat down at the kitchen table with Mrs. Metzger.

"Tyler, we've been talking about finding a group home for you and now there's an opening out east," Mrs. Metzger said. "The residents are high functioning and do not have negative behaviors."

"Really?" asked Tyler. "How far away from my home is it?"

"It's about forty minutes away, but since the ranch is only a few miles from here, you could come home to visit your family after a day at the ranch. You'd still be just a few minutes away from your family during most of the week."

"How often could I come home?" he asked.

"Every weekend, if you wanted to," Mrs. Metzger said.

"Perhaps you should go to look at the house," Roger suggested.

"That would be the first step," said Mrs. Metzger. I've told everyone at the house about you and they're anxious to meet you. If it's okay with you, they would like you to come to the house with your mom and dad tomorrow night for dinner. How does that sound?"

"Sounds good," Tyler said grinning.

"Great," Mrs. Metzger said. "I'll call the house and get back to you."

Mrs. Metzger left and Tyler turned to me. "This is exciting, but I'm nervous."

"That's understandable," I said. "You don't have to say yes. If you're not comfortable at this group home, you don't have to accept the opening."

"Okay," he said. "I know I won't live with Dad and you forever. I know what it's like to live in a group home and I think I can become more independent and not rely on you and dad for rides, but who will help you and dad?"

"Don't worry about us," I said. "You won't be that far away in case of an emergency. Just keep an open mind and if it's not right for you, we can continue to look at other homes."

The next night Roger and I drove Tyler to the group home for dinner. Although Roger still was experiencing pain in his hip and recovering from the gall bladder surgery, he forced himself to go with us. The ranch style house sat on a lazy street. Corral fencing surrounded the property and we parked in the circular driveway in front of the house. A resident of the house held the front door and welcomed us inside where we saw a cozy living room to the left. Several residents watching television said hello and a few of them got up to shake our hands. Tyler smiled confidently. A fireplace sat on the far wall of the living room and a big window gave a sunny view to the front of the house. The dining room was straight ahead and the smell of home cooking wafted from the kitchen behind the living room. A long table with enough chairs for twelve people was set in the dining room.

The house mother came out of the kitchen to greet us. "I'm Sandy. You're right on time. Dinner is just about ready."

The residents took their places at the table and invited Tyler to sit at an empty chair halfway down the table. The cook emerged from the kitchen with a large plate of pork chops. Fresh rolls, mashed potatoes, salad and string beans were served by the residents. I knew Tyler had not had such a well balanced meal at our house in weeks. As Tyler took his seat at the table, I fought back tears. My emotions were everywhere. I didn't want Tyler to leave our home, but he had become a sociable young man and he needed to be around people other than Roger and me. It wasn't fair to ask him to stay in our quiet house. I also was bursting with pride knowing how much he had overcome and I felt very excited for him.

"Tyler, this is Robbie," said Sandy. "If you decide to come

here to live, he will be your room mate.

A twenty-eight year old man with Down's Syndrome and a cherubic smile said, "Hello."

"Robbie, show Tyler your room," said Sandy. We walked down the hall off the dining room. Tyler's room was the first room on the right. Painted a warm yellow, the room had twin beds and two night stands. Each resident had his own closet and the two men would share the bathroom near the back of the room. A window between the two beds offered a view of the expansive backyard.

If Tyler decided to choose this house, his evenings and weekends would be fuller and he could still see us frequently. Selfishly, I didn't want Tyler to leave home. I wanted to hang on to the son he had become, but I couldn't hold him back from a good opportunity.

The feedback from the initial visit was positive. The residents of the home, all adults without aggressive behaviors, wanted Tyler to come to live with them. The staff invited Tyler to take the next step and spend a weekend at the group home. The social worker moved quickly because in the up coming weeks both Roger and Trevor would be going in for surgery again-Roger to have his hip removed and Trevor to have the stimulator implanted again.

Tyler called the house several times over the weekend. "I'm not sure if this is the right placement for me," he said.

"What's wrong, Tyler," asked Roger.

"I don't know," he said. "Maybe I'm just not ready to move from home yet"

"One step at a time, Ty," said Roger. "Finish out the weekend and then we'll talk about how you're feeling."

Tyler came home on Sunday with mixed feelings. "I don't think I want to move," he said.

"Did something happen at the group home?" I asked.

"No, everyone was very nice, but I missed my family."

"Change is always difficult, Tyler. But this isn't like the last time you went into a group home. We're going to be very close and you can come home on the weekends. If you need to see us during the week, we can always run over to the ranch and be there within ten minutes. I think you should take some time and think about this. It seems like a good opportunity. Don't forget Dad is going to be in bed for the next few months when his hip is removed and there's really nothing to do at home. Trevor is still recovering and he can't drive you anywhere yet. In the end, it's your decision. We certainly don't want you to go. You've become such a pleasure and a big help to have at home, but I often feel we're not being fair to you. We've been asking too much of you."

"I don't mind. I like to help you and dad."

"I know, but what about having fun? What about going out to the movies or bowling or eating dinner with friends? You deserve that."

"My roommate seems like a nice guy. I'm just afraid to make the move."

"Why don't you give it a try? If you aren't happy, you can always come back to live here."

"Would that really be okay?"

"Sure. I wouldn't want you to live in a place where you weren't happy. Just remember, you'll always be a part of our family."

"As long as I can come back if it doesn't work out, then I want to go."

I called Mrs. Metzger and told her to go ahead with the arrangements.

The day of The Celebration of Life Gala arrived on November 4th. Roger and I attended the event excited to see Tyler's video presentation, a highlight of the evening. The Gala took place in a well known catering hall in Nassau County and began with a cocktail hour unlike anything I had ever seen. Tables of appetizers, meat cut from the bone, grilled fish and fresh fruit seemed endless. By the time we moved to the large dining hall for the formal dinner, I didn't think I would be able to eat another bite. As we found our seats, a group of disabled individuals sang a medley to rival any chorus. Tyler wore a tuxedo that the staff had purchased for him and his video followed the chorus. In the presentation, he walked around the ranch talking about living with a disability and how important it was for the disabled to maintain their independence. Then he interviewed other disabled people asking about their dreams and aspirations. Finally Tyler was called to the front of the room and given a plaque that read;

A Special Thank-You to

Tyler Havlicek

For Your Charm and Inspiration

Roger and I beamed with pride. After the presentation, a deejay took over and filled the room with dance music. Tyler bounced around the floor in his tuxedo, looking joyful. As dinner was served, person after person approached us at our table. "Are you Tyler's parents?" they asked, followed by, "I love him." I watched as Tyler air-guitarred and lip synced a song he had requested the deejay play. When he was a little boy, I prayed every night, "God, please help Tyler find some peace and joy in life." Never could I have imagined that the little boy who had struggled so much, would be a source of such great pride, but he had made it happen. The evening proved to be a great escape from the troubles of the past year. I danced with Tyler when I could get him away from the other guests and found myself laughing for the first time in a long while. Unfortunately, Roger still had difficulty moving around, but he had a nonstop grin as he watched from the dinner table.

On November 22nd, Roger's hip was removed. After three months on antibiotics, his infection was finally under control. Thanksgiving was November 24th and we spent it with Roger at University Hospital. The next day, Roger came home from the hospital just in time to wish Tyler luck as he moved to the group home.

Tyler and I had spent the week deciding what to pack. I reminded him that he didn't need to take everything, because he would be coming home regularly and if he needed something we could always bring it to him. I ordered a bedspread with horses galloping across it and purchased two large pictures of horses to hang on the walls.

The following weekend, Tyler was ready to move out.

"Mom is going to drive me now," he said to Roger who was

stuck in bed unable to walk without a left hip which would not be replaced for months.

"Good luck, buddy," Roger said. "I'm not going to say good-bye because I know I'll see you here for a visit soon, so I'll just wish you luck with the transition. Remember, if it doesn't work out, you always have a home and a room here and I love you very much."

They hugged and Tyler cried. Roger held Tyler at arm's length and said, "It's going to be okay, Tyler. You'll be seeing us all the time."

"I know," said Tyler. "I'm just going to miss you so much."

"You won't have time to miss me," Roger said. "You'll be too busy and we'll see you on weekends. Take care of yourself and call me tonight."

"Okay," said Tyler. "I love you."

"I love you too, buddy," said Roger. "Call me tonight."

Tyler and I dragged his suitcases out to the car.

"When can I come home to visit?" Tyler asked obviously nervous and very emotional.

"How about next weekend?" I said. "And until then, you can call us every night."

"Okay," he said. "I'm going to miss you."

"I hope you won't have time to miss me," I said. "I hope you'll be busy making new friends."

Before we went to the house, we needed to stop at the office of the agency that sponsored the group home to sign paperwork. The agency admissions director, a social worker and a psychologist attended the meeting.

"This paper gives us permission to treat Tyler in case of a medical emergency," said the admissions director as Tyler reached across the table to sign it. "This paper allows us to administer any medications that are prescribed for you to take."

"We need to explain your rights as a person with a disability," said the social worker. "If you feel uncomfortable about anything at the group home, you must tell someone. No one is allowed to hurt you or to make you do anything that you do not want to do."

"Who do I tell if I have a problem?" Tyler asked.

"Well, first you would tell Sandy at the house," said the social worker. "Then if you weren't happy, you could talk to me or someone at the main office here."

"Can I have a piece of paper?" asked Tyler. "I want to write down the chain of command. I need phone numbers."

Everyone at the table smiled. Tyler would never be a victim. His advocate training had made him a young man who knew how to protect his rights and himself.

We left the administration building and drove to the house. I helped Tyler bring in his luggage. We spread the galloping horses across his bed and hung the pictures. He put his alarm clock on the nightstand along with a picture of Roger and me.

"That looks very nice," said Robbie.

Dinner was almost ready and the other residents were finding their places at the table. Tyler walked to the door with me.

"Good-bye, Mom," he said as his eyes filled with tears.

"I'm not going to say good-bye," I said. "I'm going to say-see you next week. We'll talk to you on the phone every night. You are my *FOREVER* son and that means we'll always keep in touch and see each other regularly. No more long good-byes. I'm so proud of you and I love you."

"I love you too," said Tyler smiling weakly. The following weekend Tyler came home and his worries about the move had been allayed.

On December 3rd, Trevor went into the hospital to have his neurostimulator put back in. Technology had improved greatly since his last surgery. The surgery only required two incisions now because the battery was placed on his chest where one might find the battery for a pacemaker. The new position of the battery gave Trevor more freedom of movement because the old placement was easily disrupted when Trevor used any muscles in his back, neck or sides. The new stimulator also offered more options for coverage of the nerve than the old stim had. We brought Trevor home the next day and by Christmas, he had his life back.

Tyler adjusted well to the group home and was very happy living there. He came home on holidays and many weekends. Every night he called to tell us about his day. He went to the ranch during the week and had employment there. We saw an increase in his maturity that came from his increased independence and responsibility.

CHAPTER 55
2012

Once Tyler's initial nervousness about leaving our home passed, he settled easily into the rhythm of life in the group home with its new responsibilities. Tyler had always relied on the family for transportations, but now he made weekly reservations for special   public buses known as SCAT or Suffolk County Accessible Transportation.   The buses provided curb to curb service to individuals with disabilities. If Tyler didn't make the reservations or made them incorrectly, he remained at the group home unable to go to the ranch.

Tyler was also responsible for his laundry. No longer could he expect someone else to know what happened to his blue shirt or why he didn't have clean socks. The clients of the house took turns with chores like setting the table, helping to prepare dinner and taking the garbage out. Every weekend he went food shopping with the house cook and a couple of other residents. He enjoyed filling up five shopping carts and pushing the massive purchase to the register. He was always treated as an adult and was proud to be more independent.

Although much younger than most of the clients, Tyler got along well with them. I hoped that new clients coming to the group home would be closer in age to him, but for now, he was glad that the other residents did not have aggressive or destructive behaviors. Tyler was now wary of behaviors that he displayed as a little boy. When conflicts arose between the clients, Tyler did not fear losing his possessions or being physically hurt as he had when he was younger. Of course, Sandy, the house parent, set the tenor of the house. An energetic individual, her positive attitude assured the residents that she was always in charge. She had a talent for not letting things get to her. She respected each resident as an individual capable of contributing to the household in his own way.

When Tyler moved out, he was worried he might miss his family too much, but he talked to us on the phone every night and visited frequently. The proximity of the ranch to our house allowed him to visit often.

On February 21st, after three months with only a cement spacer for a hip, Roger finally received his new hip. He worked hard at extensive physical therapy sessions to regain as much of the strength and mobility that he had before the infection as possible, but second hips are never as good as the first.

In March, my friend Lori and I went to Suffolk Community College to see Tyler tell his life story. Now twenty-two years old, he enjoyed dressing up on special occasions. He wore khaki pants, a crisp gray plaid shirt and a charcoal sweater that zipped up the front. He had cast off his ranch work boots and wore a pair of brown leather laced shoes. His blond hair had the tousled look so fashionable at the time. He stood 5'9", but weighed only 120 pounds. No matter what he ate, he never gained weight, but at least now he had the defined muscles of an active young man. He was one of a group of eight young adults with stories about difficult beginnings. Each story was fascinating. One young man talked about being raised by his grandfather who passed away when he was fifteen, leaving him homeless. A young woman talked about being sexually abused by a family member as a young girl. The audience was spellbound.

Tyler was one of the last to speak. I wondered if he would

feel more emotional knowing that I was in the audience, but he told his story without faltering until the end. When he began to talk about the loss of Jonathan, he broke down crying and had to leave the stage. Lori and I found ourselves sobbing along with him.

In the fall, Roger and I attended the annual meeting at the ranch to discuss Tyler's progress. Mrs. Metzger (the service coordinator), Jane Fletcher (the ranch director) Sandy (the house mother) and Roger and I met at the ranch.

"Tyler has had a very good year at the ranch," Jane began. "We're so pleased to have him here. Sophie, his riding instructor, says that his riding skills are improving and he will soon be riding independently."

"Wow," I said looking at Tyler. "That takes a focus and concentration that you didn't always have. I'm impressed."

"Thank-you," he said smiling with pride.

"His responsibilities at the ranch continue to increase," continued Jane, "He uses a weed whacker, works in the green house and muck stalls for the animals. His boss tells me that he works well independently and does not require the supervision of a work coach as most of the clients here do."

"I'm proud of you, Tyler," said Roger. "Remember how nervous I used to be when you were around my power tools? Now you are trusted to use a weed whacker by yourself."

"Thank-you," said Tyler. "I know. I was so impulsive, but now I try to think before I act." I laughed to myself. Words from years of psychological counseling sessions often slid into his conversational language.

"Tyler has learned about growing plants in the greenhouse," said Jane. "As you know, we sell those plants to raise money for the ranch."

"It's all about the secret ingredient that we mix in the soil," said Tyler.

"Oh, really," said Roger. "What's that?"

"Horse manure, of course," said Tyler laughing. "When we muck those stalls, we have to do something with it."

"Sounds like you've been very successful here," said Mrs. Metzger. "Are you happy with this program?"

"Oh yeah," he said. "I love coming here. I have friends and the staff is great. It's fun being around the horses and other animals"

"Good," said Mrs. Metzger. "Sandy, how are things going at the group home?"

"We love having Tyler at the group home," Sandy responded. "He's such a polite and responsible young man. He always obeys the rules and is doing very well. In fact, I have been talking with the staff about giving him a little more freedom and allowing him to walk to the local 7-Eleven by himself." She looked at Roger and me. "Would you be comfortable with that idea?"

"Could he carry a cell phone when he goes on the walk?" asked Roger. "You know, he can be very trusting and naïve. I wouldn't want Tyler to run into any difficult situations if he were out on his own."

"Yes," said Mrs. Metzger. "I agree that he should have a phone to call the house if he feels uncomfortable."

"We can certainly handle that," said Sandy.

Tyler grinned as a shuddering tic ran through his body.

"Well, Tyler," said Mrs. Metzger. "You seem to be succeeding well in both the group home and at the ranch. Is there anything you need from us?"

"No," said Tyler. "I'm happy and I'm glad that I can see my family regularly."

"Mr. and Mrs. Havlicek," said Mrs. Metzger, "do you have any questions?"

"Not at this time," I said. "Tyler's progress has made us very happy. You really can't imagine how difficult Tyler was as a child. It still amazes me to see how far he has come." I looked at Tyler and smiled, but he wasn't smiling back at me. His face became red and his eyes filled with tears. Within a matter of seconds, he was sobbing softly. Everyone at the table looked at me.

"What's wrong, Tyler?" I asked.

"It's just...." he stammered.

"Tell me, Tyler," I said.

"It just...it just makes me so sad to think about what I put you and dad through."

"Oh, Tyler," I said, "That was a long time ago and the only reason I mentioned your past difficulties was because I want everyone to know how much you've accomplished and how hard you've had to work to become the young man everyone so admires and loves now. I'm so sorry I upset you."

Tyler smiled through his tears and pulled himself together. This wasn't the first time Tyler had struggled with feelings about his childhood. In fact, it happened rather frequently. The following weekend he came home for a visit and I made a point of starting a conversation about the emotions he had experienced at the meeting. I found him sitting on his bed listening to music and I sat down next to him.

"Ty, I want to talk to you about what happened at the meeting last week," I began. "Talking about the past really upset you."

"I know," he said. "It's so sad for me to think about the things I did."

"You shouldn't feel sad. It wasn't your fault. You were mistreated in your early years and you were afraid to love or trust anyone."

"I know."

"You need to concentrate on your achievements. Most people with your background would have given up. You could have stayed angry at the world, but you worked hard to overcome your problems and you need to give yourself credit for that."

"It's just hard to think about it all." He sniffled and choked on the words.

"It will take time, but you have nothing to feel bad about. I hope some day you will be able to put everything into perspective and be as proud of yourself as *I* am of you."

Tyler and I continue to have these conversations. His past still haunts him and although we talk about his accomplishments, he is still saddened by his memories of his early years.

CHAPTER 56
2013-2014

On an unusually cool and windy August morning, Roger, Tyler and I headed east to Bridgehampton for the Hampton Classic Horse Show. Throughout the spring and summer, Tyler had competed in horse shows for the disabled to qualify for the Hampton Classic as a special needs rider. We pulled into the long driveway and headed towards the show area passing hundreds of horse trailers with owners standing nearby prepping their horses for competition. Tyler was competing on Guardian, a horse he frequently rode at the ranch. His riding instructor, Sophie, was bringing the horse to Bridgehampton in her trailer. Tyler was beyond excited and his tics sparked every few seconds, especially the tic that caused him to shake like a wet dog. Looking very professional, he wore a navy blue blazer, a tie, riding pants, chaps and riding boots and carried his helmet. We arrived early, so we had time to walk around the grounds. Hundreds of vendors sold horse related items. We joined the other riders in Tyler's category for a breakfast overlooking the main competition area where championship riders tested their skills jumping over ponds, hedges and fences.

"Tyler, I hope you know how proud I am of you," I said as I buttered a bagel. "When you were younger, I could never have imagined that you would have enough focus and concentration to ride a horse in competition. Even if you don't win any ribbons today, it is an achievement just to qualify to be here."

"Thank-you," he said. "I am proud of myself, but I'm very nervous."

"Stop worrying and just have fun with it," I said.

"Okay," he said as a tic shivered through his spine and up to the top of his head.

After breakfast, we found Sophie and Guardian and proceeded to the ring where Tyler would compete. We found seats in the steel grandstands in front of a group of staff and clients from the ranch who had come to cheer for Tyler and another boy from the ranch. Sophie led Tyler and Guardian to a warm up area while we waited for the competition to start. I looked to the west and noticed dark, ominous clouds off in the distance. I hoped this special day wouldn't be ruined by bad weather.

Finally, the time came for the competition and Tyler led his horse to the ring along with the other riders. He sat straight up in the saddle as he moved around the ring. The judge called for the riders to line up. When Tyler's turn came, he performed flawlessly doing a series of figure eights and putting Guardian through his paces at different gaits. When all the riders had completed their performances, the spectators from the ranch cheered loudly as Tyler was awarded three ribbons!

"Wow," I said to Roger as I felt a surge of pure happiness.. "Did you ever think...?"

"Never," he said. "Remember when it was an accomplishment to just have him sit at a table and eat a meal?"

"Yeah, and now he amazes us every day." I knew I would never tire of reveling in Tyler's successes.

The wind picked up and the clouds grew darker as Roger and I found Tyler. We hugged him and congratulated him on a job well done as we followed Sophie and Guardian back to the trailer. Just as we said good-bye, the skies opened up and raindrops as large as grapes fell on us and splattered on the dusty soil while thunder boomed overhead. We raced back to the car laughing all the way. No storm could ruin the joy that Roger, Tyler and I felt on this memorable day.

In the spring of 2014, Tyler was offered an opportunity for a less restrictive living environment. He joined three other men living in a small house a few miles from our home. In this new house, he has his own room and the men share a living room and kitchen. There is no supervision overnight at this "training house." Tyler was eligible for this last step before moving into an apartment of his own because he had demonstrated the ability to administer his medications independently and to be left without supervision for long periods of time.

As time goes on, I know that Tyler will continue to succeed. From the beginning, he has astounded everyone conquering hurdles beyond expectation. I know there were many people throughout his life who helped him to come as far as he has, but I truly believe that his own determination brought him to where he is today and that same determination will serve him well for the rest of his life. Above all, I know that now, at twenty-four years old, he is a happy, successful young man who is very attached to his family.

I can't wait to see what the future holds for Tyler!

Made in the USA
Charleston, SC
16 January 2015